THE JEWISH WARS

Reflections by One of the Belligerents

EDWARD ALEXANDER

SOUTHERN ILLINOIS UNIVERSITY PRESS
Carbondale and Edwardsville

99 98 97 96   4 3 2 1

Library of Congress Cataloging-in-Publication Data

Alexander, Edward, 1936–
   The Jewish wars : reflections by one of the belligerents / Edward
Alexander.
      p.   cm.
   Includes bibliographical references and index.
   1. Israel—Foreign public opinion, American.   2. Public
opinion—United States.   3. Jews—United States—Attitudes
toward Israel.   4. Antisemitism—United States.   5. Holocaust,
Jewish (1939–1945)—Influence.   I. Title.
DS102.95.A43   1996
956.9405′4—dc20   95-21533
ISBN 0-8093-2011-8 (cloth : alk. paper)   CIP

356354

I will state the facts accurately and impartially. At the same time the language in which I record the events will reflect my own feelings and emotions; for I must permit myself to bewail my country's tragedy. She was destroyed by internal dissensions, and the Romans who . . . set fire to the Temple were brought in by the Jews' self-appointed rulers, as Titus Caesar, the Temple's destroyer, has testified.
—*Josephus,* The Jewish War

In one year they sent a million fighters forth
   South and North,
And they built their gods a brazen pillar high
   As the sky,
Yet reserved a thousand chariots in full force—
   Gold, of course.
Oh heart! oh blood that freezes, blood that burns!
   Earth's returns
For whole centuries of folly, noise and sin!
   Shut them in,
With their triumphs and their glories and the rest!
   Love is best.
   —*Robert Browning,* "Love Among the Ruins"

CONTENTS

viii   Contents

INTRODUCTION

Hannah Arendt once observed that twentieth-century political developments "have driven the Jewish people into the storm center of events."[1] Except perhaps for a brief period following the Second World War, when even some of their traditional enemies felt that the Holocaust had given antisemitism a bad name, the Jews, despite being an absurdly small minority (as noted in one of the essays in this book, 997 out of every 1000 people in the world are *not* Jews), have been unable to extricate themselves from this storm center or, if I may change my metaphor, to evade or prevail over the forces arrayed against them in a war that seems to have no respite although it assumes different forms and names.

The essays in this collection deal with a brief recent phase of this war, from the *intifada* that began at the end of 1987 in the disputed territories administered by Israel through the autumn of 1994, when the process of Israeli withdrawal from those territories and the inexorable march of the Palestinian Arabs toward an independent state were well under way. Although the *intifada* was even less effective, from a military standpoint, as an instrument of Arab warfare against Israel than Arab tanks and planes had been in previous wars, it was tremendously effective as a propaganda weapon. The spectacle of young Palestinian Arabs (at least in the early stages of the uprising, before the violence became highly organized) facing Israeli soldiers won for the Arabs precisely the victory they had sought: it swung liberal, including (if not especially) Jewish liberal, sympathy decisively to the side of the Arabs and against Israel. The strategy of inversion by which the Arab nations had sought, in the years following their defeat in the Yom Kippur War, to project their own imperialism, racism, destructive intentions, and obsession with territory upon their Jewish target now won its greatest success.

Of course, this success could not have been achieved solely by the young Arabs flinging stones and Molotov cocktails; it had to be prosecuted by Arabs, still more by their sympathizers, in the realm of ideas and ideologies, the one realm of battle where, as Norman Podhoretz and Ruth Wisse have pointed out, Jews had long been supposed to be superior. In his essay of 1838 on Jeremy Bentham, John Stuart Mill wrote that "speculative philosophy, which to the superficial appears a thing so remote from the business of life and the outward interests of men, is in reality the thing on earth which most influences them, and in the long run overbears every other influence save those which it must itself obey."[2] The concluding essay of this book, dealing with the implications of Israel's embrace of the PLO, is a kind of concession speech on my part. That is to say, it acknowledges that the ideas of Israel's traditional antagonists—the subject of unfavorable attention in most of this book's essays—have achieved their ultimate triumph: they have been adopted not only by the Israeli intellectuals I have criticized but also by the leaders of the current Israeli government. Indeed, an observant reader of my discussion of "Antisemitism, Israeli-Style" will be struck by the fact that three of the Israelis singled out in that essay of 1988 for their rhetorical licentiousness and venomousness toward Judaism—Shulamit Aloni, Dedi Zucker, and Yossi Sarid— are now cabinet ministers or prominent spokesmen of the government of Yitzhak Rabin.

Perhaps the presumption of Jewish skill in the realm of ideological combat was a grave error in the first place. What the anti-Zionist (yet often very shrewd) writer Christopher Sykes[3] used to refer to, and with considerable respect, as the Zionist propaganda machine has been in a very creaky state since 1967. Since then, the campaign to undermine the moral image of the people Israel and the land of Israel has flourished mightily. Even the most brazen calumniators have, with relative impunity and with a pugnacious energy and inventiveness little short of demonic, disseminated a shared body of clichés, myths, and outright lies. In these circumstances, I felt an obligation to do my part to combat this campaign, even though keenly aware that I was bringing to the struggle only the meager faculties and bounded knowledge of a literary scribbler. Still, as Rabbi Hillel used to say, in a place where there are no men (or, at any rate, not very many), try to be a man yourself.

The recurrent topics of this book are the war of ideas against Zionism, the relations between the Jews of America and those of Israel, the incorporation of anti-Zionism into the ideology of "multiculturalism" and the conventions of literary discussion, the politically motivated distortion and exploitation of the Holocaust, the strategies of moral and political discrimination employed against the State of Israel, the strategies employed by some prominent American and Israeli Jews to evade the implications of this discrimination, and the growing impunity with which antisemitism can be preached, at both ends of the political spectrum. Special attention has been given to some of the more brazen and flamboyant combatants in what I have called "the Jewish wars"—Edward Said, Patrick Buchanan, the late George Ball, Alexander Cockburn, Michael Lerner, Noam Chomsky—and still more to certain omnipresent personality types: the timorous Jew cloaking his timidity in the robes of the biblical prophet; the treacherous Jew presenting betrayal of his own people as ethical idealism; the ferocious antisemite parading as a dispassionate "critic of Israeli policies"; the journalist and publicist exploiting to the full the public-address and public-relations systems afforded by his profession while complaining that his voice is being "stifled" by "the Jewish establishment."

During the years when I was shuttling back and forth between teaching assignments in Seattle and Tel Aviv, one of my Israeli students, on the first day of my return for the spring semester, said (facetiously): "What do you want to come back *here* for?" "Well," I replied (not quite as facetiously), "I want to lead a quiet life for a while." For me—though not of course for the Israeli who must pay the world's highest taxes, endure countless strikes, serve in the army through age 54, live with a constant burden of peril and threat of war—there was actually some truth in this wisecrack. Being constantly available, in America, for service in the war of ideas being waged over the Jewish land and the Jewish national ethos is hardly to be compared with being constantly available, as the Israeli is, for the summons to military service, but it can be trying nevertheless.

The essays and other writings in this book have been arranged in chronological order except where, as in the sections on Patrick Buchanan and Alexander Cockburn, pieces originally published a year or more apart were so closely linked in subject that it seemed foolish to separate them. For the most part, I have resisted the temptation to update the essays, and have allowed them to retain the marks (if any) of their particular occasion. The one major exception to this rule is the essay on Michael Lerner. Since Lerner was elevated—and this with an avalanche of publicity—to the status of an unofficial White House advisor in the spring of 1993, I decided to expand and update the essay I had written about him in the spring of 1989. In most other instances, changes in the original essays have been made only to eliminate repetition. The book's concluding essay, which is also its lengthiest, has not been published previously.

Some of the essays in this book elicited a lively correspondence in the journals where they were originally published. In an least one instance, the essay on Edward Said, a letter-writing campaign organized by the American-Arab Anti-Discrimination Committee produced such a flood of (vituperative) complaint that my response to "critics" outgrew not only in length but also in import the original piece. Ideally, I would have liked to print in full the objections of my critics as well as my replies to those objections, but this—for reasons the reader may readily surmise—proved impossible. In the instances where I have included my rebuttals to critics—the essays on Leonard Fein and David Novak, Said, Cockburn, and Chomsky—I have tried to quote enough from critics' letters to convey the essence of their protestations. Readers wishing to read these letters in their entirety will usually (and always where *Commentary* is concerned) find them in the same issue that contains my rebuttal.

The majority of the essays in the book originally appeared in *Commentary* and *Congress Monthly*, and I am grateful to the editors of those journals, Neal Kozodoy and Maier Deshell, for help and suggestions of various kinds as I was writing.

Seattle, Washington
January 1995

THE
JEWISH
WARS

CHAPTER 1

Making Arabs into Jews: *David Grossman's* The Yellow Wind*

The Yellow Wind is David Grossman's account, written for the Israeli weekly *Koteret Rashit*, of his "seven-week journey through the West Bank" in 1987. It was undertaken in order to understand "how an entire nation like mine, an enlightened nation by all accounts, is able to train itself to live as a conqueror without making its own life wretched."[1] Among the eighteen chapters, unequal in length and not logically parallel, are accounts of the Deheisha refugee camp, of a professional study of the dreams of Arab and Jewish children, of the Jewish settlement at Ofra, of Bethlehem University, of a village to which refugees were allowed to return in 1972, of proceedings in the Nablus military court, of a village divided in 1949 by the newly drawn Israel-Jordan border, of travelers crossing the Allenby Bridge, of illegally employed Arab laborers in Holon (near Tel Aviv), and of settlers' reactions (and Arab lack of them) to the burning of the Moses family of Alfei Menashe. There are also interviews with a nonreligious leader of the Jewish settlement movement, Moni Ben-Ari, with Raj'a Shehade, Arab lawyer and author, and with the father of an Arab who took part in the murder of two Jewish couples. One chapter is a fictional inside view of an Israeli intelligence officer in the

---

*Reprinted from Commentary, June 1988, by permission; all rights reserved.

civil administration; it serves as a reminder (just in case the rest of the book should fail to do so) that Grossman is not merely a journalist but a novelist of solid achievement and high reputation.

The great English novelist George Eliot once said that, since opinions were a poor cement between human souls, the novelist's task should be the creation and diffusion of imaginative sympathy among those who differed from each other in everything except their shared suffering and their human status. Grossman too eschews opinions and aspires "to display wide-hearted humanism," but he does so by means of an inversion that directs all sympathy to one party while turning the other into a metaphor. Grossman leaps across the divide between Jews and Arabs by making his Arabs into Jews. In Deheisha, impressed by the insistence of Arab children that their homes are in Jaffa, Lod, and other Israeli towns that neither they nor their parents have ever seen, Grossman thinks of the lyrically expressed longings of Yehuda Halevy for the sweetest land he had never seen. He listens to an Arab grandmother singing the praises of her original village, and "discovers that she reminds me of my grandmother, and her stories about Poland" (6). He sees a boy on the roof of a Deheisha house playing on a comb wrapped in paper as "fiddler on the roof" (20). He tells of an Israeli friend who has devoted himself to studying the material culture of the Arabs in the area because "they remind him entirely of his forefathers" (111). What may at first appear to be an act of imaginative identification soon becomes cloying and eventually, especially when Grossman's fictional Israeli, Gidi, sees in an Arab notable "something which reminded him of his father" (142), reveals itself, after all, as ideology, in all its formulaic staleness, triteness, and falsehood.

Grossman maintains that the Palestinians "are making use of the ancient Jewish strategy of exile, and have removed themselves from history. They close their eyes against harsh reality, and . . . fabricate their Promised Land." Like the Jews in exile, they are "not willing to compromise" or to "try to improve [their] lives" (7–9). Where, in this licentious equation between Palestinian Arabs and Diaspora Jews (by no means original with Grossman), is the Jews' belief that they were exiled because of their *own* sins? Where, in this desperate attempt to decorate the Arabs with the tattered coattails of Jewish suffering, is the equivalent of the Jews' enrichment of their life in exile by the elaborate pretense that they were already living in the Holy Land? Where, among the Arabs of Deheisha and Balata, is the equivalent of the Torah that sustained the Jews in Exile—unless it be what Grossman refers to as "the oral law" (26) of Jew-hatred now passed from Arab mouth to Arab ear in the absence of antisemitic textbooks confiscated by Israeli soldiers? When Grossman—who was born in 1954—claims that Arab children who chant, "By throwing stones and burning tires we will free the motherland" remind him of Jewish children "who sang patriotic songs when British soldiers passed by" (26–27), he does not merely mock memory and history, he comes perilously close to those Israelis—like the fifteen who signed up for passage on the PLO ship intended "to echo the voyage of the *Exodus*"—who can discover their Jewish identity only by pretending to be Arabs who are themselves pretending to be Jews. When Grossman walks down the Ben-Yehuda mall in Jerusalem he succumbs to the illusion that he sees behind every Jew "a sort of double peeking out . . . his double from Nablus" (28).

Thomas Macaulay, that lover of paradox, insisted that if James Boswell had not been such a toady and sycophant, he could not have written so great a book as *The Life of Johnson*. To Dr. Johnson, famously contemptuous of Scotsmen, Boswell pleaded that he could not *help* being a Scotsman. To which Johnson replied: "That, sir, is what a great many of your countrymen cannot help." In reading this eloquent, and (compared, say, with such productions as David Shipler's *Arab and Jew*) relatively honest book, one thinks too often of this famous exchange. Grossman is a model of self-effacement as he listens submissively to Arabs who tell him that "the Jordanians took only our national identity from us, and you took everything" (12), or expound on "Israeli rudeness, cynicism, idiocy, and arrogance," or regale him with the tale of the yellow wind that comes hot from hell to seek out "those who have performed cruel and unjust deeds"—by which they mean his Israeli countrymen—and "*exterminate* them, one by one" [italics mine] (76). Raj'a Shehade tells Grossman that although the Arab world is one of oppression, he is confident that the emergent Palestinian nation can be entirely free of the faults of Israel because he has seen that such great nations as England, America, and France are proud and nationalistic without oppressing their minorities. To such arrant nonsense, the author—who must somewhere in the course of his Hebrew University education have heard about the internment of innocent Japanese citizens in America and German Jews in England during World War II—cannot find the means to reply.

Susceptibility to balderdash disappears, however, and self-effacement turns to strident self-assertion when Grossman finds himself among the Jews. Among the Arabs, even when he sees children receiving "education in blind hatred," he tries "to be neutral. To understand. Not to judge" (25). He entered Deheisha as if returning to the land of his ancestors. But he comes to the Jewish settlement of Ofra fully armed with suspicion, hostility, and partisanship, a "wary stranger" among people who remind him neither of his grandmother nor of anything human, especially when they are "in the season of their messianic heat" (52). (Later in the book, Grossman makes much ado about an Israeli child's reference to an Arab cleaning woman bent over a pail as "a little bit a person, a little bit a dog" [214].) In Ofra, Grossman does not want "to let down his guard" and be "seduced" by the Sabbath "warmth" and "festivity" of these wily Jews. (34) Although most of his remarks to Arabs in conversations recounted in the book are the perfunctory gestures of a straight man to whom his interlocutors pay no serious attention, he angrily complains that the Jewish settlers don't listen to or "display a real interest" in him. He asks them to "imagine themselves in their Arab neighbors' places" (37), and is very much the angry schoolmaster when they don't dance to his tune or accept his pretense that this act of sympathetic imagination is devoid of political meaning. Neither are the settlers, despite their experience in creating a "well oiled publicity machine" (a rich joke, this) nimble enough to make the appropriate reply: "My dear fellow, we will imagine ourselves as Arabs if you will imagine yourself as a Jew." But Grossman has no intention of suspending his own rhythms of existence long enough to penetrate the inner life of these alien people. "What have I to do with them?" (48).

Grossman's American promoters who have likened him to Agnon—an extravagance that may have just a little to do with their sympathy for his politics—would do better to compare this chapter with its analogue called "Judea" in Philip Roth's *Counterlife* to see the real meaning of imaginative sympathy in a novelist.

Grossman's resentment of the Jewish settlers is at least as much "cultural" as it is political. In Deheisha he had been much taken with the elderly Arab woman who told him: "We are people of culture! . . . You can't understand this culture. It's not a culture of television!" (15). But in Ofra he complains that the settlers have "little use for culture," speak bad Hebrew, indulge in "Old Diaspora type" humor, and own no books, "with the exception of religious texts" (46). And these, far from mitigating the barbarity of their owners, aggravate it. The final image of the Jews in this long chapter is of "potential terrorists now rocking over their books" (51).

The succeeding chapter also treats of culture and books, including religious ones. Grossman has come to Bethlehem University, one of several universities in the territories that have been punningly described as branches of PLO State. Here Grossman, though he acknowledges the school to be "a stronghold of the Democratic Front for the Liberation of Palestine," sees no terrorists rocking over books, but rather idyllic scenes that remind him of "the pictures of Plato's school in Athens" (57). Bubbling with affection, eager to ascribe only the highest motives, Grossman is now willing to forgive even readers of religious books. He has not so much as a snort or a sneer for the Bethlehem English professor who ascribes Arabs' supreme sensitivity to lyric rhythm in English poetry to the "rhythm of the Koran flow[ing] through their blood" (59). The author's ability to spot racism at a distance of twenty miles when he is among Jews slackens when timeless racial categories are invoked in Bethlehem.

Yellow Wind is, however, by no means lacking in harsh criticism of Arabs; but these are almost always made by other Arabs. A schoolteacher is "against Arafat, because Arafat wants peace" (22). A mukhtar from the Israeli side of the divided village of Barta'a recalls the self-abasement required of Palestinian Arabs by Jordanian soldiers. A resident of the Jordanian side of the same village excoriates Israeli Arabs for lack of honor, taking everything from their country and giving nothing in return: "While you do reserve duty forty-five days a year," he tells Grossman, "they go to the beach" (123). One Arab moderate, a businessman educated at Hebrew University, seconds the view of another Arab that if the Israelis were to leave the territories there would be a "second Beirut." Unlike the author, who believes in truth even though the heavens fall, this man speculates on the likely consequences of Israeli withdrawal: "There will be a great slaughter. . . . First they will kill whoever had any connection with Israel, and those who did business with Israel. . . . And after they kill half of the population here, they will begin killing each other in a struggle for power" (91).

Grossman himself remains aloof from such vulgar imaginings about the years to follow the realization of "peace now," though it seems clear that a "second Beirut" in the immediate vicinity of Jerusalem and Tel Aviv would be a catastrophe for Israel infinitely greater than the original, Lebanese version, a very hot yellow wind indeed. Despite the obvious political implications of what he writes about the Israelis and those Arabs who make themselves "a partner in my crime" (94–95), Grossman does not wish to appear to assign his own, explicitly political meaning to the people and events he describes. Therefore he talks with no politicians, Jewish or Arab, and claims that "it is not a question of who is right," but strictly of "facts and numbers" (215). It is true that for many of the "facts" that he does not get from personal observation he relies on sources that are profoundly entangled in politics. On three separate occasions he reports that he "checked the facts with Dr. Meron Benvenisti" (12), confidently withdrawing from the latter's "data bank" some of the most debased currency in Israel. Yet there is also much evidence that Grossman really is as innocent of politics as he claims to be.

It is characteristic of *Yellow Wind* to remove facts from their history in such a way as to suggest the author is either massively ignorant of politics or fiendishly mischievous. After describing the terrible conditions of the Deheisha camp he casually remarks that "It doesn't matter at all who is really guilty of the refugee camps . . . " (26). For Grossman to have explained how and why the Arab nations are guilty of the camps might have been boring work for a novelist, and might have made the book less palatable to the *New Yorker*, which published excerpts from it after the *intifada* began in December 1987; but it would have been appropriate for someone who professes to believe that "to become human" is to pass "from speech to moral action." Grossman is guilty of similar irresponsibility when he declares that "the hard kernel of the entire conflict" is "two nations which still don't recognize each other's legitimacy" (110). But the UN plan of 1947 envisaged a Jewish state and an Arab state in western Palestine; the Jews recognized the Arab state, but the Arabs did not recognize the Jewish state—or, for that matter, the Arab state (any more than they had done in 1937, when the Peel Plan would have given the Arabs nearly all of Palestine except for the coastal plain between Tel Aviv and Haifa). For whatever reasons the Arabs started the war on November 30, 1947, Israel's refusal of recognition of Palestinian Arab sovereignty was not one of them. Granted, it is a tedious business to keep repeating these things, almost as pedestrian a task, especially for a novelist, as locating the Jordan River in the same place every time you draw a map.

The Yellow Wind concludes with two chapters ostensibly about the murders of Jews, members of the Moses family whose car was fire-bombed near Alfei Menashe and two couples killed by a gang of Arab terrorists. These terrible stories afford Grossman an opportunity to display his wide-ranging "humanism" and generous inability to curb his benevolence. But the benevolence is directed toward the father of the captured terrorist because his house had been destroyed, and the anger reserved for Gush Emunim activists accused of exploiting the sorrow of the Moses family and friends. And what of the families of the victims? Grossman says that he cannot begin to measure their sorrow. Yet he also cannot resist the itch to speculate darkly about these people whom he has not bothered to meet: "I do not know if the families of the victims find any comfort in fostering hatred of the murderer, his family, his nation. How can we judge them if that is how they feel?" (195–96). How generous of Grossman to forgive these people for sins they have yet to commit! There is such a thing as a heart too full for weeping, a silence more eloquent than speech; but David Grossman cannot, in *The Yellow Wind*, demonstrate these qualities of the sympathetic imagination when he is dealing with Jews.

CHAPTER 2

To Mend the Universe or Mind the Vineyard?

PART ONE: *Leonard Fein, David Novak, and American Jewry**

American Jews have been conspicuously absent from Israel during the six months since the Arab uprising (*intifada*) began in December 1987. Virtually every tourist one sees here in Jerusalem is a Christian; and some hotels report cancellation rates by American Jewish groups approaching 100 percent. One touching item in the press reported that numerous Conservative rabbis, planning to attend the Rabbinical Assembly here in July, will be forced to cancel their visits because "many rabbis were planning to come with tour groups from their congregations to help cover expenses. But . . . many of these tours are not coming." The few prominent Jewish intellectuals who do keep their commitments to participate in conferences or performances are received with a beggar-like gratitude in no way diminished by their compulsive desire to bite the hand that feeds them (very lavishly) by publicly "testifying" against Israeli policies.

The *intifada* in its various forms—they include fire-bombings in Judea, Samaria, Gaza, and even Tel Aviv, stabbings and fatal shootings of yeshiva students in east and west Jerusalem, a pogrom against a group of high school students on a hike,

---

*Originally published as "Where Is Zion?" reprinted from Commentary, September 1988, by permission; all rights reserved.

and the destruction by arson of over 100,000 dunams of land and all its wildlife—has kept most Israelis too busy to worry about the mysterious absence of their American cousins. But awareness of it grows apace. One young acquaintance of mine, just back from three weeks of reserve duty (now increased to sixty days a year) in Nablus, asked me sharply: "What are your American Jews, who are always declaring 'We Are One,' doing while we are dodging bricks and petrol bombs?"

Some of them, I answered, are dutifully reciting, for the benefit of the great American public, what might be called the Anthony Lewis conjugation, in serialized weekly numbers: Israel will lose its soul; Israel is losing its soul; Israel has lost its soul. Others, including editors of Jewish magazines and heads of large Jewish organizations, are queuing up in the television studios to explain why their Jewish ethical idealism—which has already earned them the plaudits of Edward Said and the Arab League—requires that they condemn all Israeli use of force against Arab rioters in the most forceful language they can marshal. Still a third group—so I told the astonished young soldier—was deeply immersed in considering the special Jewish mission to gentile America, a mission it defined as nothing less than *tikkun olam*, repairing the universe. The concerns of the earthly Jerusalem, pressing though they may seem to its inhabitants, can hardly be expected to distract those who are building the heavenly Jerusalem in America.

Now, the idea of America as a new Zion was a prominent theme of the Puritans who built the country, and even the enlightened Thomas Jefferson wanted "Israel" on the seal of the United States. But recently the idea has been infused with a specifically Jewish (and also anti-Zionist) energy, and it has found articulate spokesmen in more than one sector of the ideological spectrum of American Jewry.

Thus, in March 1987, a few days after Jonathan Pollard had been sentenced to life imprisonment for spying for Israel, the eminent scholar Jacob Neusner, a political conservative, published in the *Washington Post* an article designed to show the absurdity of American Jews' attaching themselves to Israel when they were already walking the streets of El Dorado: "If ever there was a Promised Land, Jewish Americans are living in it." As it happens, this is the same Neusner who in a 1981 book (*Stranger at Home*) had written that "American Jewry simply does not add up to much. Its inner life is empty, its public life decadent." Yet here he was, at a particularly delicate moment in relations between Israel and the United States, praising the cohesiveness, security, prosperity, philoprogenitiveness, and "authentically Jewish voice" of the American Jewish community.

A much more ambitious attempt to relocate Jerusalem in a greener, more pleasant, and more peaceful place than the state of Israel is that of the leftist Leonard Fein, the founder and first editor of *Moment* magazine and a veteran fomenter-from-within of American Jewish agitation against Israel's government, especially when that government has been dominated by the Likud coalition. "Where is Jerusalem?" is the crucial chapter in Leonard Fein's *Where Are We?*, a book whose title conveys the sense of befuddlement of someone lost in a troubled universe, a sense not belied by the text, despite the author's air of confident, easy familiarity with Sinai, the prophets, and God. Although Fein's stated subject is "the inner life of America's Jews," he can only approach that subject by elaborately disentangling himself from the claims of Zionism or, as he puts it, by constructing a "theory of American Jewish life" that can match that of Zionism, a "coherent ideological view with which to counter the ideological argument for *aliyah.*"[1]

But, like many others who reject Zionist claims, he has no qualms about appropriating the language and accomplishments of the Zionists. He refers, for example, to Jewish immigrants to America as coming to the land "to build it and be rebuilt by it" (6), thereby transferring the language of Zionist pioneers to the mixed multitudes of Ellis Island. He readily admits that in 1967 Israel became the "faith" of the American Jew, and just in time too, because starting in about 1963 (the year of the Kennedy assassination) many Jews were losing their faith in what leftists took to calling Amerika. He grants as well that without Israel American Jews, in the aftermath of the Holocaust, would not have been able to reject despair. Why, then, does Fein feel compelled to guide the American Jewish community into spiritual, psychological, and political competition with the Jewish state?

The answer is implicit in the anecdote with which the book begins. It is a tale of nineteenth-century East European Jews who believe in their moral superiority to the goyim and in their ability to sustain that superiority in Jerusalem, where they would "prove that even with guns we will not become hunters." Since that time, according to Fein, and especially "in our generation, the Jews have come to power, in Israel and in America." Fein does not believe in the virtue of powerlessness and is indeed so certain that Jews are now "an empowered people," an "empowered community," that he confidently declares: "Today it is no longer our physical safety that is the principal item on the Jewish agenda." Having generously offered his Israeli cousins the protective covering of that possessive pronoun, Fein reveals that the principal item is "whether, now that we have guns, we are on the way to becoming hunters" (xv).

Between formulating this supreme question in his introduction and handing down the verdict, eighty pages later, that it is "now plain" that the Israelis "have come to hunt, have even perhaps become hunters" (80), Fein sets forth his view of "Jews, God, and Judaisms," and of the special relationship between Sinai and Leonard Fein. "The question of whether or not there was a Revelation at Sinai seems to me considerably less important than the question of whether or not I was there" (26). Fein presents himself as (by traditional standards) a "non-believing Jew" who takes what he likes from tradition; who does not admit the Jews to be a chosen people; who prefers anarchy to authority; who is eager to "reassure" the reader that his "references to God neither presume nor recommend belief"; and who rejects the characteristically Jewish idea of distinction that separates Jew from non-Jew, clean from unclean, man from woman. To the Christian reader this last item will have a familiar ring, since it was Paul who thanked Christ for freedom from the law's confinements and for a new covenant recognizing "neither Jew nor gentile, neither free man nor slave, neither male nor female."[2]

Fein does allow that Judaism is "a religious way," but repudiates the notion that there can be "a 'Jewish view' of this or that." His oceanic receptivity to all forms of Jewish experience, "from studying Talmud to marching with the lettuce workers" (19), calls to mind Joseph Epstein's severe judgment that "in our age vulgarity does not consist in failing to recognize the fish knife or to know the wine list but in the inability to make distinctions." Yet even Fein must draw the line somewhere, must show that he can say no to something, and he does. "I have," he writes, "set 'us' against the Orthodox. . . . " Because they have failed to see that "relativism" is the "necessary consequence" of the Enlightenment, the Orthodox force him to speak of "Judaisms, not a single Judaism" (46–47). What Fein, for his part, has failed to see, despite his exhortations to "talk Jewish" and his invocations of Sinai, "whether or not it happened," is that for a person who believes in God a thousand difficulties about doctrine do not add up to a single doubt, any more than the great difficulties we may encounter in solving a mathematical problem lead us to doubt that it has a correct solution.

The real question about "Sinai" is not whether Leonard Fein was there, but whether he can get his case of I-strain into remission long enough to see that, in morals as in physics, the stream cannot rise higher than its source. Therefore the worship of your own mind, however intense it may be, will never raise you one single inch above the earthly level from which you began.

Despite his uncertainty about whether or not Sinai "happened," Fein is sure that American Jewry's double obsession, with the Holocaust and with Israel, threatens to usurp Sinai's place as the starting point for Jewish life. This jealous resentment of Holocaust Judaism, a perfectly ordinary sentiment in the Jewish Studies establishment, is expressed with more than ordinary nastiness by Fein: "If Sinai is too remote or too mysterious, look to Auschwitz. . . . Look to the one thing that absolutely sets the Jews apart. . . . Look to the chimneys, o the chimneys" (65). He acknowledges the "shameful silence" of American Jews during the Holocaust, but only to allege that guilt over that silence is what now binds American Jews so powerfully and uncritically to an Israel that remains for most of them more an "imagined" than an "earthly" Jerusalem, a place whose "ordinariness" they cannot accept. In fact, it is Fein who, despite having (as publicity for the book blares) "visited Israel, for periods ranging from nine months to three

days, forty times," does not understand that, as people here
sourly remark, Israel consistently does the extraordinary and
the impossible; it's the possible she can't do.

Although Israel is, for valid historical reasons, "the binding
element of the contemporary Jewish understanding, the raison
d'être of many Jews," it is also, for Fein, the major impediment
to American Jewry's reascent to Sinai, which it obscures by
involving American Jews in the politics of its defense, thereby
reducing "a religious civilization . . . to a political action committee" (134). American Jews do not, to be sure, go on aliyah,
for they don't feel themselves to be in exile, yet they are in-
timidated and made to feel inadequate, Fein complains, by the
Zionist argument for Israel's centrality in Jewish life as the
one place where a coherent Jewish culture can survive. He
therefore undertakes to reassure his countrymen by enlisting a
distinction advanced by the Zionist thinker Ben Halpern: the
distinction between merely geographical exile, or dispersion,
and Exile as the symbol of a disordered condition of the universe. The Jews' physical exile and its theological meaning are
by this means psychologized and universalized into a condition
that can never be cured by return to Zion, but only by *tikkun
olam*, the repair of the whole universe. "A Jew is also in Exile
whether he lives in Boston or in Jerusalem." Here, then, is the
real reason why American Jews are not to be seen in Jerusalem:
not that they are hesitant about serving in the army for thirty-
seven years, or about paying the highest taxes in the world,
or about living permanently in the midst of pitiless enemies
bent on Israel's destruction. No: "They stay where they are,
reject the return, because they await the larger Redemption."
They reject the earthly Jerusalem for the heavenly one, the
"Jerusalem that remains a yearning, answer to Exile, home."
Israel can hardly be "home" for American Jews since "no place
can be in a world of pain" (119).

The Israelis who stubbornly refuse to concede that the
Jews who stay away from the earthly Jerusalem may do so for
"high-minded purpose in the name of a universal messianism"
are viewed by Fein in very much the way that Augustine
viewed stubborn, unspiritual Jews of an earlier era. "The
Church," said Augustine, "admits and avows the Jewish people
to be cursed, because . . . they continue to till the ground of

an earthly circumcision, an earthly Sabbath, an earthly Passover." Unspiritual beasts that they are, Israelis such as A. B. Yehoshua accuse American Jews of having fallen in love with the flesh-pots of Diaspora. But Fein retorts that their love affair with Exile is less an attraction to its comforts than a Jewish thriving on "marginality" and "limited liability," symbolized for him by no less a spiritual striver than Woody Allen (122, 126).

Given Mr. Allen's squalid display of cravenness mixed with Narcissism in his statement of dissociation from Israel in the *New York Times* last January, Fein could hardly have chosen a more fitting emblem of his own deep-seated desire for "limited liability," that is, for power without responsibility, the charac-teristic desire of ethically incomplete and infantile people. Al-ready well known for his efforts to make and break Israeli governments "from the banks of the Charles," as Ruth Wisse wrote in 1982, Fein now claims the same irresponsible power for himself in American politics. "Here, it is easy enough to dismiss the rednecks with contempt; they are not, after all, *our* rednecks. But in Israel, they *are* our rednecks" (126). But if, as Fein repeats *ad nauseam*, American Jews are an "empow-ered community," surely they must take responsibility for *some-thing*. The "rednecks" may not be ours, but the reds certainly are, especially if we take seriously Fein's boasting that "more than half the delegates to the 1965 national convention of SDS . . . were Jews," and so was Mark Rudd, "and so were Abbie Hoffman and Jerry Rubin, and so were I. F. Stone and Noam Chomsky and Herbert Marcuse, . . . and so were William Kunstler and Leonard Boudin" 226–27). Any nurse who ever lifted a bedpan has done more for *tikkun olam* than all these world-betterers listed by Fein. If he really believes that such people—whose "contributions" to American society include irreparable damage to its universities (Rudd, et al.), acting as paid agents (I. F. Stone) of the KGB, undermin-ing free speech (a bourgeois ruse, according to Marcuse), sus-tained apologetics for Pol Pot and collusion with neo-Nazi "re-visionism" (Chomsky), agitation for the "dismantling" of Israel (Kunstler)—were imbued by "Jewish" ideals of universal social justice, he can hardly claim "limited liability." This whole sorry discussion should put us in mind of the young idealist who asked Thomas Carlyle how best to go about the task of reforming the world, and was told by the Scottish sage: "Make an honest man of yourself, and then there will be one rascal less in Scotland."

Contemptuous of American Jewry's "obsession with survival" (145), insistent on a specifically American Judaism based on "values" that converge with those of American culture, Fein resurrects for the 1980s (more specifically for the election year of 1988) the "mission" theology of German Reform Judaism, according to which the Jews have a moral mission to carry the universal ethical content of their religion to a world that has not yet realized the ethical culture of monotheism. Only that mission, argued the Reformers, justified the continued existence of Jews as a religion and a culture. For Fein too, this mission is the *only* acceptable raison d'être of future Jewish existence. What is remarkable here is not merely his adhesion to a bogus theology that has been exploded a thousand times over[3] but his attempt to resurrect it in explicit opposition to Jewish attempts to respond meaningfully to the two most momentous events in the past two thousand years of Jewish history, the Holocaust and the emergence of the sovereign state of Israel. "It is unlikely the Jews can survive, and *it would be unseemly if they did* [emphasis added], except as a community organized around values and committed to *tikkun olam*" (207), Fein writes in the most scandalous formulation in this book. To this does liberalism always come with respect to the Jews. Only they must serve a higher meaning, a "mission," if they are to be permitted to survive. It is not "unseemly" for the nations that gave the world Hitler and Stalin and Mao to carry on without a special mission; they may live without saying why they do. The same writer whose liberalism is so profoundly offended by the Orthodox Jews who say "This is *the* way" declares dogmatically to the Jewish people who may, just may, want to go on living without being able to articulate or "justify" this mysterious urge that there can be only one admissible reason for their survival, namely, "political activism," "lofty utopian ambitions": Liberty, Equality, Fraternity/Sorority—or Death. That is Fein's ultimatum to the American Jewry he has come to rescue from the clutches of Israel.

Ironically, Fein himself supplies the best justification for the Jewish survivalism he contemns when he announces, from under his prophetic mask and long robe, that "The moral life is the good life, the proper life; it is the right way to live whether or not it promotes Jewish continuity . . . " (212). So much for all the maundering about Sinai; for could anybody who really believes the Jews are a covenanted people possibly make such a statement?

Emil Fackenheim wrote recently that he was impressed by the declaration of a Christian that "If it's good for the Jews, it's good for the Christians." But he added that "it is more deeply true to say, especially when I remember all that has happened, 'if it's good for the Jews, it's good for the Christians, and therefore it can't but be good for the world.'" It is, of course, precisely to Fackenheim that one must turn to recover the real meaning of *tikkun olam*, a meaning so grossly distorted by current exploiters that it may already be beyond recovery. *Tikkun*, a notion of some intricacy, refers to a mending of what has been broken, a reunion of ruptured historical and cosmic realities. It is not the crude utopianism of Leonard Fein or Michael Lerner (who use it as a mere cover for a highly specific politics). In *To Mend the World* Fackenheim, while eschewing any attempt to "justify" the Holocaust retrospectively as God's or history's evil means to a greater good, asks what *tikkun* might repair that catastrophic rupture:

> What then is the *Tikkun*? It is Israel itself. It is a state founded, maintained, defended by a people who—so it was once thought—had lost the arts of statecraft and self-defense forever. It is the replanting and reforestation of a land that—so it once seemed—was unredeemable swamps and desert. It is a people gathered from all four corners of the earth on a territory with—so the experts once said—not room enough left to swing a cat. . . . It is a City rebuilt that—so once the consensus of mankind had it—was destined to remain holy ruins. And it is in and through all this, on behalf of the accidental remnant, after unprecedented death, a unique celebration of life.[4]

This *tikkun*, far from being "parochial" or "particular," has within it the potentiality of being a *tikkun olam*, because the Holocaust "called into question not this or that way of being human, but all ways." To mend that rupture would be to offer consolation and hope to the whole world, far more effectively than by turning American Jewry into a little army of soup-kitchen organizers, precinct committeemen, ACLU lawyers, and dancers at charity balls.

The practical consequences of having Jews carry their utopian zeal into what Fein calls "the public square" have already been suggested in a widely reported recent debate between him and Milton Himmelfarb on "The New Jewish Politics." (The debate took place at the 1988 annual meeting in New York of the American Jewish Committee.) Himmelfarb urged that Jewish voters recognize themselves as (among other things) a special-interest group and vote accordingly. Noting that in 1984 and now once again the Democratic party has "conspicuously refused to be anti-anti-Semitic" (since its liberal condescension towards blacks prohibits any utterance that might be construed as critical of Jesse Jackson), he warned that failure by Jews to react strongly to such pusillanimous and hypocritical acquiescence in Jew-hatred would be "pretty near suicidal for the American Jewish community." Fein, for whom Jewish history follows an arrow-straight course from Sinai to the left wing of the Democratic party, pretended that Jackson's offense against Jews had consisted of his "Hymietown" remark, and described Farrakhan's ravings merely as "unmitigated particularism." According to the *Jerusalem Post* (24 May 1988) account, "Fein urged Jews not to vote just on the basis of narrow interests." (It was, of course, precisely their ability to rise above "narrow interests" that once led American Jews into what Fein himself terms their "shameful silence" during the years when their European brothers were being done to death; needless to say, this is a contradiction Fein neglects to explore.)

Himmelfarb's view of the conflict between Jewish liberalism and Jewish pragmatism in America is expressed more fully in a little volume called *Jews in Unsecular America*, which contains the edited proceedings of a conference held in 1987 under the auspices of the Center for Religion and Society on the interaction between religion and politics in America. Of the many shrewd things Himmelfarb had to say both in his formal address and in the ensuing discussions, perhaps the shrewdest is his insight into the apparently incurable tendency of Jewish liberals to allow ideology to drown prudence and common sense, with respect to school prayer, or Israel, or abortion, or welfare. He notes that although three out of four Jews polled in 1984 supported government programs of welfare and food stamps, two out of three believed that these programs have many bad effects on the very people they are supposed to help. Such Jews are what Fein repeatedly calls "caring" people. (This repellent expression—which means exactly nothing, since there is no such thing as people who "care" in the abstract, but only people who care *for* something specified—identifies do-gooders, that is to say, people who think they are doing good when they feel good about what they are doing.)

The conference started from the premise that the Jewish community's assessment of its relation to society at large must begin with recognition that (as editors Richard John Neuhaus and Ronald Sobel claim) America is "incorrigibly and increasingly religious," and that "the religion in question is overwhelmingly Christian."[5] The Christian participants in the conference, including evangelicals, genuinely wished to hear Jews speak to them *as Jews* about their relation to American society. The most striking response to their request for instruction came from David Novak, a spokesman for traditional Judaism but also—probably to the surprise of many—for the idea of the "Mission of Israel" within America. Novak recalls that this idea, at first strengthened in America by its resemblance to the "Social Gospel" of certain Protestant groups, eventually lost favor and was discredited because it always trailed obediently after liberal political programs whose outlook was wholly secular. Felix Adler saw that mission theology as articulated by the Reformers was only a halfway house on the way to Ethical Culture (though he did not see that Ethical Culture was a halfway house on the way to atheism). Neither was mission theology helped by the fact that nearly all its advocates were anti-Zionists.

But now, Novak maintains, something like the Mission of Israel has emerged among the most traditional Jewish thinkers in America, although they avoid using the slogan. Whereas Fein derides halachic Judaism because "it ignores the circumstances, the culture, the consciousness of each generation," Novak insists on its capacity for doctrinal development and on the genuine concern of traditional Jews with the moral and spiritual life of the general society. Although such Jews remember that "the *raison d'être* of Judaism is not to teach the gentiles but to obey God's Torah, whether the gentiles are interested in it or not," they are now (he argues) a sufficiently integral part of America to formulate opinions on issues of public debate and to desire "that America develop along ethical and religious lines that are not antithetical to Judaism's *theocratic* view—namely, that the revealed Law of God is to be the basic norm for every society" (49).

Novak believes that if Jews are true to themselves, which for him means true to the recognition that ethics is law and cannot be removed from theology, they will be taken seriously by American Christians as "Jewish Jews." Awareness that law and not a few "Marxian" sentences of social vision ripped out of context from the prophetic books is at the center of Judaism will also save Jews from the "utopian pseudo-messianism" that has engulfed so many in this century.

Novak sees clearly that what the Enlightened Jew eager to diffuse light among the nations has in the past generally foisted upon these unsuspecting gentiles was not Judaism at all, but the particular mode of egress he had chosen from Judaism: specious theories, seductive utopias, new idols. Fearing that democracy not bolstered by religious values cannot withstand its enemies, who include true believers of a nonreligious kind, Novak wants Judaism to play an active role in American society. He is not, like Fein, impelled to invent a theory of American Jewish life mainly in order to fend off Zionism. Nevertheless, he must understand that the very notion of a special American Jewish mission in America—even if that mission is defined more modestly, honestly, and cogently than liberals past and present have been wont to do—will draw Jews away from Zionism and Israel. If the liberal Jewish missionaries are busy offering America prophetic visions of freeing the oppressed and clothing the naked, the traditional Jewish missionaries, according to Novak, will offer lessons, drawn from experience, about "the danger of depersonalization," "the danger of deculturization," the dialectic between faith and history. Neither the liberal missionaries nor the traditional ones seem much interested in putting on their "new agenda" (a phrase used with alarming frequency by these writers) that form of *tikkun olam* adumbrated by Fackenheim, a mending of the world that begins in the earthly Jerusalem.

Meanwhile, as all this missionary activity is being planned by some American Jews for the benefit of their fellow citizens in the spiritual Jerusalem, the earthly Zion is burning, not metaphorically but literally. Several times in his book Fein subscribes to the metaphor of Jews as "a family," yet when he quotes his favorite passage from Isaiah 58 he emphasizes only the socially visionary lines about clothing the naked and feeding the hungry, but not the line that follows them: "And not to ignore your own kin." If you really believe that American Jews belong to the same family as Israeli Jews, then averting your eyes from, or failing to join in defense against, the unprecedented onslaught today sustained by the Israeli branch of the family, makes you guilty of telescopic philanthropy. The text to be pondered by American Jews today is not Isaiah 42:6: "I have given you as . . . a light to the nations," but Song of Songs 1:6: "They made me a keeper of the vineyards; but my own vineyard I have not kept!"

PART TWO: *Edward Alexander Replies to His Critics**

Since Leonard Fein complains, in his letter, about my objection to his use of the word "caring," let me try to explain it more fully. "Caring people" and "people who care" are meaningless expressions unless they are followed by a phrase beginning with the little word *for*. There are no people who "care" in the abstract. The expression is repellent because, as the critic Robert Heilman has remarked, it is typically used by people who want to give themselves the warm inner glow of civic virtue without saying what they mean. Thus Leonard Fein adduces as an example of "what real caring is about" the declarations by professed lovers of Israel that they "are often trou-

Reprinted from Commentary, *February 1989, by permission; all rights reserved.*

bled by the policies of the current Israeli government." Just what is it, one wants to know, that these people "care" *for*?

I never said that Mr. Fein "omits" Isaiah's injunction against ignoring your own kin when he quotes Isaiah 58. I did say that he "emphasizes only [its] socially visionary lines." The problem is not that he misquotes the passage from Isaiah but that he misreads it. He has two extended references to the passage. On pp. 219–20 he quotes it to buttress his preference for the "political activism" of prophetic Judaism over the quietism of the rabbis, and he singles out from it "the religious injunction to heed the needs of the stranger." In his introduction, Mr. Fein offers an explication of the chapter which stresses loosing the fetters of wickedness, letting the oppressed go free, breaking every yoke, dealing bread to the hungry, bringing the poor into your house—and says not one word about the obligation to attend to your own kin. In other words, Isaiah 58 is for Mr. Fein exclusively an exhortation to the telescopic philanthropy he adores.

The continuing saga of Israel's struggle to live up to Mr. Fein's severe standards for the use of Jewish force does not end with the "hunting" passage he now quotes from his book to indicate that he had not rendered a guilty verdict against the Israelis. In the book's next paragraph he cited Golda Meir's famous remark that she could forgive the Arabs their killing but not their having forced Jews into killing; and he adds that although he had thought her sincere when she said it, and still believed in Israel's moral superiority to the hunting Arabs when he visited the country in 1967, twenty years of "occupation" have changed his mind. "Golda Meir's sentimentalism notwithstanding," he now wonders whether even in 1967 he was justified in seeing the Arabs as the hunters. In his note (303) amplifying this discussion he reports that "a very substantial literature" now questions whether Israel was forced into *any* of its wars. (The only example of this "literature" he mentions is a demented book by Simha Flapan, the "revisionist" writer who transposed the Nazi view of European Jewry—all-powerful, sinister, calculating—to the State of Israel.) Mr. Fein's view of who is responsible for the continuation of the Arab-Israeli conflict may also be found in the summer 1988 issue of *Reform Judaism*, where he states that "very many Israelis," i.e., the majority who oppose abandonment of the territories, "do not want peace."

Mr. Fein complains that I have taken his list of Jewish world-betterers out of context. But the "context" of Mr. Fein's roll call of "Jewish" radicals is his claim that the Jewish people "has for 3,200 years . . . been committed to building the kingdom of heaven here on earth," and that "lofty utopian ambitions" are the quintessential expression of Jewish love of mankind. Since most of the Jewish all-stars on Mr. Fein's roster turned out to be more adept at building hell on earth, and since Mr. Fein considers utopian leftism a genuine expression of Judaism rather than a form of egress from it, he might have indicated how false messianism has often plagued the Jews and how utopianism, in its insistence on perfection, often turns into hatred of mankind.

The objection to Jewish voting "just on the basis of narrow interests" was attributed to Mr. Fein by the *Jerusalem Post* in its 24 March 1988 account of the debate between him and Milton Himmelfarb. He now denies having said any such thing. I hope the *Post* was also wrong in quoting him as deploring the "degree to which the energies and attentions of Jewish agencies and organizations are so invested in matters relating to Israel," a sentiment perfectly consonant with the argument of his book.

One can hardly be unaware that Mr. Fein has visited Israel when the publicity for his book blares that he has done so, "for periods ranging from nine months to three days, forty times." Each time he returns with fresh evidence of what he calls the "ordinariness" of the earthly Jerusalem, fresh fuel for his doctrine that Jerusalem is as much exile as Boston, and obsession with Israel the major impediment to American Jewry's reascent to "Sinai." American Jews, he laments, cannot accept or understand this ordinariness. What Mr. Fein, despite his forty visits, cannot understand is that, as Martin Buber wrote: "Zion is the prophetic image of a promise to mankind; but it would be a poor metaphor if Mount Zion did not actually exist. This land is called 'holy'; but it is not the holiness of an idea, it is the holiness of a piece of earth. That which is merely an idea and nothing more cannot become holy."[6]

Mr. Fein's rhapsodic description of himself and his constituents as involved in a "joint endeavor" with Israelis does nothing to erase the fact that while the characteristic contribution of the "ordinary" Israeli to this joint endeavor is paying the world's highest taxes, serving thirty-seven years in the army, and living in constant expectation of war, the characteristic contribution of Leonard Fein has been organizing newspaper advertisements condemning Israeli policies, advocating (in 1982) a boycott of travel to Judea and Samaria, and writing a book warning American Jews that their defense of Israel has reduced "a religious civilization to a political action committee" (134). A fine, equitable scheme for the division of labor!

It is impossible not to benefit from the measured criticism of so fine a scholar as Jakob J. Petuchowski; and since he does not argue very aggressively for the ancient provenance of Reform Judaism's mission theology, I will reciprocate by not pressing too hard the implications of the fact that the passages he cites from Isaiah assume that it is only *as a nation* that Israelites can be "a light unto the nations." It is true that, as he states, both Zionism and the Mission of Israel theology are products of the nineteenth century. But since Zionism did not, as a rule, claim biblical authorization, it cannot be "exploded" by demonstrating that secular Jewish nationalism finds no basis in Torah. If both are myths, the question becomes not which is demonstrable as fact, but which has created attitudes and engendered actions that have sustained and will perpetuate Jewish life.

I grant that even the best doctrines have little defense against the uses to which they are put. But is there not something about the idea of Israel as "a light unto the nations" that lends itself too readily to the political exploitation of a Leonard Fein or the high-minded blindness of Rabbi David Novak?

I did not, of course, argue (as Rabbi Novak alleges) against "any Jewish moral concern with any society other than the state of Israel." What I did say was that, at the present time, this incessant nattering about Jewish "values" and the Jewish "mission" to the gentiles is faintly suspect because it cannot help drawing Jews away from support of Israel. The present time, in case Rabbi Novak has not noticed, is one in which Israel is besieged by arsonists, religious fanatics, bomb-throwers, and slanderers—all bent on the common aim of annihilation—while American Jews are assailed by artful propagandists who encourage moral discrimination against Israel based precisely on the doctrine that Israel's survival is contingent on its being a light to the nations. Rabbi Novak deplores an immoderate devotion by American Jews to Israel's survival and to its right to be treated as an equal among the nations as idolatrous nationalism. A rabbi who writes thus can hardly have given much thought to what the post-Holocaust religious life of American Jews would be without the state of Israel. Rabbi Novak's zeal to light the way for the gentiles reminds one of the blind man who can direct others on their way, but cannot walk straight himself.

CHAPTER 3

Antisemitism, Israeli-Style*

> Is there another people on earth whose sons are so emotion-
> ally and mentally twisted that they consider everything their
> nation does despicable and hateful, while every murder, rape
> and robbery committed by their enemies fills their hearts
> with admiration and awe? As long as a Jewish child, nurtured
> by generations of pain and hope, can come to the Land of
> Israel, and here catch the virus of self-hate . . . let not our
> conscience be still.
>
> —Berl Katznelson, 1 May 1936

That Jews may themselves be antisemitic long ago ceased to
be an occasion for surprise, except to those completely ignorant
of the history of Jews in Europe. Self-hating Jews have made
such large contributions to the ideology and politics of antisemitism that it may fairly be called a product of the "Judeo-
Christian" tradition. Examples are plentiful. Before Pope Greg-
ory IX ordered the Talmud to be seized, examined, and publicly
burnt in Paris and Rome, he was presented in 1239 with a
detailed analysis of the manifold evils of the Jews' religious
books by the Dominican brother Nicholas Donin, a Jewish
convert. In the sixteenth century Martin Luther's seemingly

---

*Originally published as "The role of the Holocaust in Israeli
Antisemitism," reprinted from Remembering for the Future, Theme
1: Jews and Christians During and After the Holocaust, pp. 989–
1001, copyright © 1988 Pergamon Press plc, with kind permission from
Elsevier Science Ltd, The Boulevard, Langford Lane, Kidlington OX5
1GB, UK.

innovative program of burning synagogues, destroying Jewish homes, confiscating the Talmud and all other Hebrew books, was in fact derived from the proposals of Johannes (formerly Josef) Pfefferkorn, the Jewish convert who had years earlier exhorted his German countrymen to "drive the old Jews out like dirty dogs and baptize the young children" and "take their goods and give them to those to whom they belong." Christians appear to have invented, all by themselves, the belief in Jewish male menstruation, but doubters among them received reassurance from Jewish converts such as Franco da Piacenza, who in 1630 revealed to the world the shameful secret that Jewish males of the lost tribe of Simeon menstruated four days a year.

When we "advance" from the old era of religious Jew-hatred to the modern one of political antisemitism, we still find Jews doing very well in competition with their gentile neighbors in the production of antisemitic fantasies, slanders, and lunacies. Karl Marx, converted to Lutheranism at age six, imputed to Jews other than himself false language, bad manners, sexual aggressiveness. Of the "Jewish nigger" Ferdinand Lassalle (himself a Jewish antisemite of formidable derangement) Marx wrote: "Always this constant babble with the falsely excited voice, the unaesthetic, demonstrative gestures . . . and also the uncultivated eating and the horny lust of this 'idealist.' . . . As his skull shape and hair prove, he is a descendant of those Blacks who accompanied Moses on the exodus from Egypt. . . . Now this combination of Jewishness and Germanness upon the Black basic substance must bring forth a strange product. The pushiness of this fellow is also niggerlike."[1] (Are these, one wonders, the sentiments for which Marx is today revered in the third world and segments of the Israeli Labor party?) Even today, when the whole world has known for almost half a century that antisemitism visited upon the Jews, including antisemitic Jews, evils greater than anyone had imagined possible, the tradition of Jewish antisemitism continues unabated, although it has taken on new, highly imaginative names, if not entirely new forms.

Zionism, in the nineteenth century, proposed to establish for Jews a refuge from antisemitism. In the first instance, this would be a political refuge. Even so surly an anti-Zionist as

Hannah Arendt was forced to admit that the Zionist movement was the only political answer Jews had ever found to antisemitism. But Zionism also aspired to cure the antisemitism of the Jews themselves, sometimes referred to as Jewish self-hatred (an awkward term because it so frequently identifies those very Jews inordinately consumed by self-love). Once liberated from the constant sense of danger that came from living as a feared and despised minority within an alien Christian culture, the more timorous Jews would no longer be driven to desperate stratagems for diverting gentile hatred of Jews in general onto certain segments of Jewry: *ostjuden* or Oriental Jews or Yiddish-speaking Jews, or Jews who were slow to shorten their jackets and beards and memories.

The Zionists also sought to "normalize" Jewish existence. Once Jews had the power and the responsibility of managing their affairs in a state of their own, they would surely repudiate the superstitious belief that suffering and powerlessness confer virtue. The protagonist of Haim Hazaz' famous story "The Sermon," when he is in his Zionist mood, declares that "Everything is rotten around suffering . . . history, life itself, all action, customs, the group, the individual, literature, culture, folk songs . . . everything! . . . Sorrow is prized higher than joy, pain easier to understand than happiness." Gershom Scholem thought that Hermann Cohen's description of them as "those people who want to be happy" was the wisest criticism ever made of Zionists. It was, of course, recognized by Zionists that normalization would bring with it many things less intrinsically desirable than happiness and national independence: Jewish prostitutes, Jewish thieves, Jewish political parties and their attendant insanities. Few Zionist theorists, however, anticipated that the normalization of Jewish existence would bring with it, along with the other vices, crimes, and historic hatreds of European societies, antisemitism.

It might be argued that some element of antisemitic feeling was already latent in Zionist ideology insofar as it repudiated the life of the European shtetl and ghetto as stunted, abnormal, and demeaning to Jews, a travesty of the great nation whose history was recounted in the Bible. Many a Zionist writer reacted as did the English poet Samuel Taylor Coleridge to modern Jewish decadence viewed against the background of a noble past. "The two images farthest removed from each other which can be comprehended under one term, are, I think, Isaiah—'Hear, O heavens, and give ear, O earth!'—and Levi of Holywell Street—'Old Clothes!'—both of them Jews, you'll observe."[2] Hazaz's protagonist gave classic utterance to the Zionist revulsion from Jewish life in the Diaspora: "Jewish history . . . has no glory or action, no heroes and conquerors, no rulers and masters of their fate, just a collection of wounded, hunted, groaning, and wailing wretches, always begging for mercy . . . I would simply forbid teaching our children Jewish history. Why the devil teach them about their ancestors' shame? I would just say to them: 'Boys, from the day we were driven out from our land we've been a people without a history. Class dismissed. Go out and play football.'" Many an Israeli work of fiction turns upon a generational conflict over the choice of names for children. The old folks, still tied to Diaspora memories, favor "Jewish" names like Mendele or Moishele or Zeitl, whereas the young, native Israelis want Hebrew or at least biblical names, such as Osnat and Ehud. Ben-Gurion himself was a prodigious redesigner of immigrant names that had the exilic taint on them.

One group of Israeli thinkers, called the Canaanites, carried these anti-Diaspora tendencies to the point where they sought to sever all connections between the state of Israel and the Jewish people. They believed that a new national identity was being formed in Palestine and later the state of Israel that was not Jewish at all. They argued that it was the anachronistic notion of Israel's Jewish identity that kept any sense of unity and shared history from developing among the various peoples in the Middle East: Maronites, Druze, Alawis, Kurds, Bedouins. For the Canaanites, Israel was rightly a nation of Hebrew-speaking gentiles. The Canaanites may have begun with certain ideas latent within Zionism, but they carried these to such extreme and radical form that they were recognized, and correctly, by the Zionist leadership as anti-Zionist in their aims and outlook, and were repudiated.

One does not require a specially refined taste to recognize the antisemitic flavor of Canaanite ideology. Here is a sample from Yonatan Ratosh's 1944 manifesto called "Discourse": "Here in the Hebrew land the Jew has removed the furry tails (shtreimel) from his head, cut off his side locks, learned to mouth the Hebrew language and to utter slogans about a homeland and nationalism. . . . But let us look with open eyes. He is the same Jew, the eternal Jew of the eternal Diaspora. In France he pretends to be a Frenchman, in Germany a German. Here he plays his game in Hebrew. . . . He is the enemy who eats up all the best parts. He is the one who tramples on the best of our children with his obsequious pleading and fund-raising. . . . ”[3] The Canaanites failed as a movement, but the ideas of some of their leaders still make themselves felt today among certain segments of Israeli society, especially the militantly secularist left, whose influence is likely to increase in the future.

Nevertheless, it would be simplistic to allege that antisemitic feeling in Zion today derives primarily or even substantially (if indirectly) from Zionism itself. If Zionism repudiated the Jewish life that existed in the ghetto and shtetl, it did so in order to perpetuate Jewish life and not extinguish it. The Zionists acted from the conviction that distinctions could be made between those beliefs, customs, and attitudes that were peculiar to Jewish life in exile and those that were permanently, intrinsically, and universally Jewish. Along with other Jewish enlighteners, the Zionists believed that traditional, religious Jewish culture could be secularized in such a way that, as Hillel Halkin has written, it would remain genuinely and identifiably Jewish in all its aspects “while at the same time serving as the basis for a modern society whose members will share a common cultural identity that draws on what each of them has brought to it.”[4]

But perhaps I have put the cart before the horse in speculating about the roots or antecedents of Israeli antisemitism before having given evidence that such a thing even exists. Indeed, I am more than a bit squeamish about providing anti-Zionists (as antisemites now call themselves) with yet another stick with which to beat the Jews, but I am afraid that the secret is already out. Awareness of it crops up in all kinds of places, sometimes in humorous form. The American novelist Philip Roth in *The Counterlife* (1986) introduces a character who explains why she, notoriously stingy, contributes money to Israel. “ ‘You know why I give to Israel?’ . . . ‘Why?’

Grossman said. 'Because in Israel you hear the best anti-semitic jokes.'" The Israeli humorist and cartoonist Dosh, in a column of 22 May 1987 in *Ma'ariv*, drew a picture of a shopper in a supermarket specializing in antisemitic merchandise reaching for the top shelf carrying the most expensive package, which is adorned by a Stuermer-like caricature of a Jew and prominently labeled "Made in Israel." The article that this cartoon illustrated spoke of Israel's need to increase exports by embellishing products available elsewhere in the world with unique local characteristics. Israel had done this with certain fruits and vegetables in the past, and now she was doing it with defamations of Israel, produced in Israel. Market research had shown a strong demand for documentary material to justify hostile attitudes to the Jewish state; but it also showed that customers were becoming more selective, and no longer willing to make do with grade B merchandise produced by British leftists or German neo-Nazis. No, these discriminating buyers wanted authentic material, from local sources; and Israeli artists, playwrights, intellectuals, aware of the tremendous opportunities for exporting antisemitism from Zion itself, were responding with alacrity to the opportunity.

But if Roth and Dosh are joking about antisemitism in Israel, it may well be that, as the French say, they laugh in order not to cry. Contemplate the following incidents and ask whether they would have provoked jokes or outrage if they had occurred in any country except Israel. In 1984 a minor Israeli poet named Yitzhak Laor published a series of seven poems in a literary journal supported by the Arts Council of Israel, that is to say, by government funds. They dealt with the war in Lebanon from a leftist point of view, but with a virulence that went beyond garden-variety leftist effusions toward something distinctly reminiscent of the propaganda of Nazi Germany. General Rafael Eitan was called "a lead nose-ring in the snout of the State," and Menachem Begin was described as a "greedy, grunting blood-sucker," but the most inflammatory epithets were reserved for religious young men in the army who had studied in the *hesder* yeshivot of the Gush Emunim movement. In a poem entitled "A Hymn to the Gush," Laor puts the following speech into the mouths of the Jews: "They scorned us, but we shall celebrate this festival of our freedom, this feast of unleavened bread, with pious shakings, and holiness and with devotion, and in our matzot there will be the blood of Palestinian youth, for just the same it's all a heathen slander." In spring of 1987, a much better-known Israeli figure, the left-wing Member of the Knesset, Dedi Zucker, followed Laor's lead. A few days after a Jewish woman named Ofra Moses was burned to death by a fire-bomb thrown into her car by Arab terrorists and the other passengers were badly burned (the son Moses died of his wounds some weeks later), Zucker, a leader of "Peace Now," and much beloved of Western television reporters seeking Israeli-accented condemnation of Israel, took it upon himself to interpret the religious significance of the event. In a speech to those he called his "Palestinian brothers," delivered on the fourth day of Passover, Zucker said: "The Jewish settlers need Ofra Moses' blood. They are drinking it."[5] Thus did Zucker, whose previous excursions into the realm of theology had generally been on the level of Bob Dylan, his "culture hero,"[6] perform a public service by supplying the one element of a traditional, "normal" European Passover that had been sorely lacking in Israel during the first thirty-nine years of its existence: the blood libel.

Both the poetical and the political blood libeler, it should be noted, defamed the religious Jews of Israel with impunity. A few people had the temerity to ask whether Laor's ejaculations ought to be subsidized by public funds, but they were shouted down with the usual cries of censorship. Zucker was not even criticized publicly, even though it is difficult to think of a democratic parliament anywhere in the world that would not have censured him or expelled him from elected office for thus indulging his baser impulses. [He would go on to become a leading figure in the Rabin government elected in 1992.]

In recent years several grisly incidents redolent of European antisemitism have shocked the Israeli public, or at least some segments of the Israeli public. In June of 1986, following a series of disputes between religious and secular Jews over the opening of movie houses on Friday nights and the destruction of Jerusalem bus kiosks displaying half-nude women in suggestive poses, a synagogue in Tel Aviv was vandalized, swastikas were painted on its walls, and many of its holy books burned. In December of the same year some soldiers, during their swearing-in ceremony at the Western Wall, flung to the ground the copies of the Hebrew Bible with which they had been presented. In August of 1987 an eleven-year-old boy wearing the long curls (payot) of the orthodox, was set upon in a Jerusalem street on the sabbath and shorn of his locks.[7]

But these sporadic outbursts of secularist zealotry are less important in the burgeoning of antisemitic feeling in Israel than a weirdly refracted, nightmarishly distorted memory of the Holocaust. Many desperate Israelis, too lazy to think through the implications of the Holocaust for the Jewish state or too craven to acknowledge them,[8] have decided that in this as in so many other things they will, like the ape in Kafka's story, "Report to an Academy," imitate the average European. We all remember how this clever ape, in order to find a way out of his cage, in which he can neither stand nor lie nor sit, imitates the ways of his captors, however disgusting they may appear to him: if they spit, he will spit, if they smoke foul cigars, so will he, and if they drink schnapps, he will drink schnapps. The half-educated Israeli intellectual or politician, descended from this ape, if he wants to evade the terrifying fact that Israel has for over forty years been a beleaguered nation surrounded by enemies eager to reduce her to sandy wastes, will imitate the half-educated intellectuals and politicians of Europe by identifying some or all of his countrymen with Nazis, who must deserve such relentless enmity.

The equation of Jews with Nazis antedates the Holocaust and the establishment of the State of Israel. It appears to have been a British invention, one Conor Cruise O'Brien has traced back to British official circles, which in 1941 were using the epithet "Jewish Nazi state" to refer to Jewish Palestine.[9] By now it is a mere commonplace in the parlance of Israel-haters. The same Conor O'Brien, fresh from many conversations with Britons in 1982, proposed making this vilification a kind of litmus paper for the detection of antisemitism: "If your interlocutor can't keep Hitler out of the conversation, . . . feverishly turning Jews into Nazis and Arabs into Jews—why then, I think, you may well be talking to an anti-Jewist."[10]

The first step in transforming Jews into Nazis and Arabs into Jews is to "universalize" the Holocaust by concealing the specific identity of both the killers and their victims. Few historical "revisionists" have done this with the gross blatancy of Israel's most aggressively antireligious politician, Shulamit Aloni. Describing the Demjanjuk trial as "more a vendetta than a punishment," she alleged that Holocaust education in Israel had failed because it taught youngsters that "the Nazis did this to the Jews instead of the message that people did this to people."[11] Transform the Holocaust from a crime of clarity committed by Nazis against Jews into an indiscriminate part of man's inhumanity to man, and you have opened the door wide to the people whose political purposes are served by making Arabs into Jews and Jews into Nazis. [Aloni would later serve as minister of education in the Rabin government.]

Israelis of the far left, it goes without saying, have been heavily involved in this sordid enterprise for many years. Such desperadoes as Israel Shahak, Felicia Langer, and Lea Tsemel have for over a decade adorned their statements to the press on the Arab-Israeli "conflict" with references to Israel as a Nazi state, and to Palestinian Arabs as Jews. Shahak, in a book of 1975 called *Le Racisme de l'Etat d'Israel*, went a step beyond his competitors in slanderous bombast by stating that "The Jews of Israel, along with most of the Jews of the world, are at present undergoing a process of nazification."[12] But in recent years figures much closer to the center of Israeli political and intellectual life have also plunged into the mire. In April of 1982 the journalist Amos Elon concocted a story, which turned out to be a tissue of lies, about books allegedly banned by the Israeli military government in Judea and Samaria. When questioned closely by Melvin Lasky of *Encounter* about what appeared to be gross misinterpretation of the facts, Elon replied: "It's all part of the preparations for a fascist regime! Soon we'll have it all, concentration camps as well as the burning of the books."[13]

During the war in Lebanon a host of Israelis, ranging from publishers of pornographic newspapers to university professors, whom nobody outside of Israel had heard of before became instant celebrities in Europe and America by characterizing the Israeli government, in the words of Professor Yeshayahu Leibowitz, as "Judeo-Nazi." Since 1982 Israelis of the most modest intellectual endowments discovered that the

licentious equation of their country with Nazi Germany provided a short, ready, and often lucrative path to radio and
television appearances and to the lecture circuit. They could
also be enshrined as prophets in books about Israel that fall
into the category known as Israel-bashers. David Shipler's best-
selling *Arab and Jew*, for example, relies heavily upon testimony from Israelis that their country is the one true inheri-
tor of the regime that perpetrated the Holocaust. Shipler
showed special diligence in ferreting out Israelis ready to ma-
lign their country according to formula. Dov Yermiya, who
has made a profession of speechifying around the world about
Israel's similarity to Nazi Germany, assured Shipler that he and
his friends had predicted, way back in 1945, that the Holocaust
would "affect . . . Jews in Israel for the bad," that the former
victims would become "more or less similar" to the victimiz-
ers.[14] Another Israeli, a young publisher, told Shipler that
when his army unit told the people of Nabatiyeh to come out
of their houses and separate according to sex, he instantly saw
in his mind's eye "the trains in the '40s in Germany, one side
children and women, one side men." Ran Cohen, the leftist
Knesset member, revealed to Shipler (not very reluctantly, we
may be sure) his feeling that searching the Palestinian population for members of the PLO was just like the Nazis "making
a selection from the Jewish people." Hillel Goldberg, a Hebrew
University expert on ethics praised by Shipler for his "precision . . . of reasoning," demonstrated his surgical exactness by
saying that "What happened out there [in Sabra and Shatila]
was somehow of a kind with what happened in the Holocaust."
After all these examples, one is ready to believe the Arab
writer who explains to a surprised Shipler how he came to use
Treblinka as a metaphor for the "West Bank": "An Israeli
friend of mine told me about this." Shipler himself at first
"boils and rages" over the Arab equation between Ansar
detention camp and Auschwitz, but he is helped to over-
come his indignation by the radical Israeli journalist Cordelia
Edvardson, herself a Holocaust survivor. She explains to Shipler (as she was later to explain to readers of the *Washington
Post* in October 1983) that the Arabs' use of the slogan "Ansar
is Auschwitz" was nothing more than the imprisoned terrorists' search for a Palestinian history.[15] But not even she was

sufficiently prodigious an explainer to show why this search can take place only amidst the ruins of European Jewish history.

In the arts too, the Holocaust has been exploited by certain Israelis for the purpose of besmirching their countrymen in general or their political opponents or religious fellow-citizens in particular as Nazis. It might be argued, as Norma Rosen has done in an important essay called "The Second Life of Holocaust Imagery,"[16] that the associative habit of artistic metaphor, which discovers likenesses in things apparently unlike, can serve to extend awareness and understanding of the Jewish tragedy during World War II. More often than not, however, making Jews into metaphors is a licentious habit serving pernicious ends. In Israel as elsewhere it reveals not merely the intellectual vulgarity and lack of distinction that pervade modern culture but the will to deceive through outrageous hyperbole.

In 1985, for example, a show by the Haifa Painters and Sculptors Association entitled "Israeli and Palestinian Artists Against Occupation and for Freedom of Expression" advertised itself in the stridently gaudy red, white, and black of the Nazi flag. How better to enrage Jews in the Jewish state, especially in a building located on Zionism Avenue? The Nazi-style posters were more suitable than their designers had imagined, for the scandalous center of attraction of the show was a painting by one Harold Rubin depicting a Nazi thug with "Jewish" features and a Star of David on his hat, twisted (in the unsubtle style of Arab and Russian cartoons that appeared after the Six-Day War) into a swastika. The hoodlum's hand is raised in the Nazi salute, and the painting is labeled "Judenjugend," i.e., the Israeli Hitlerjugend.[17] One had only to look at this painting and a few others like it to understand why the exhibit's organizers had chosen for it so ungainly a title: anyone who voiced a protest about the antisemitic intent of such works as Rubin's could be derided as an enemy of free expression. Israeli antisemites have derived at least one benefit from the Enlightenment: they know how to advocate, when it suits them, a tolerance so capacious that it tolerates fanatical intolerance itself.

At least one major Israeli cultural institution has virtually based itself upon the unrelenting pursuit of the Israeli-Nazi equation. In the article mentioned earlier, the Israeli humorist Dosh singled out the Haifa Municipal Theatre as the most consistently successful exporter of Israeli antisemitism to a world eager for something better than the shoddy goods turned out by Europeans, who had greater experience in anti-semitic production but few fresh ideas and little sense of immediacy to their subject, Jews now being in short supply in Europe. The productions of the Haifa Company have been received with acclaim in Berlin, in Chicago, in Washington, in Edinburgh, despite the fact that no serious literary critic would place the company's playwrights on a level with Israel's many distinguished poets and novelists; and few critics would rank them above mediocrity. Whence, then, derives their astonishing success in the theatrical centers of the world? The answer is that the Haifa Municipal Theatre specializes in Israeli-produced antisemitism, and also—an added attraction of a curious kind—government-supported antisemitism, since the theatre receives large public support from the Cultural Division of the Ministry of Culture and Education, support so generous that the company puts on productions, as one critic wrote, "over-lavish even by Western standards."[18] When the Jewish community of Frankfurt protested in 1985 the Fassbinder play titled *Trash, the City and Death*, one of the protesters held aloft a poster reading "subsidized antisemitism." He might well have offered it to his coreligionists in Dusseldorf who have twice had occasion to protest against Haifa Theatre productions staged in that city as antisemitic, or at least powerful encouragements to antisemitism.

The reasons why these Israeli theatrical productions find favor with foreign audiences eager for new lethal ammunition to fire at Israel are not far to seek. Yehoshua Sobol's *The Soul of a Jew* recounted the career of the half-deranged Otto Weininger, an Austrian Jewish antisemite. The play offended many Israelis when it was first performed in October 1982, but was far more warmly received at the Edinburgh Festival, where it supplied the opening program in summer 1983. Sobol had already indicated his curiosity about Weininger in *Night of the Twentieth* (1976), a play about young Jews who (in the third aliyah) leave their homes in Europe for the express purpose of driving the Arabs out of their homes in Palestine, a play that ends by showing a degenerate Jew about to open fire on an Arab village. But this play about a psychotic Viennese-Jewish antisemite seemed the very thing for the Haifa company to produce in 1982 when the Lebanese War was raging and much of Europe was fulminating against the evil inclinations of the Zionists.

In the course of *Soul of a Jew*, Weininger insists frequently on the incompatibility of Judaism and Zionism, with special emphasis on the loathsomeness of the former. "You have to understand," he tells a Zionist character named Clara, "that Judaism is an abyss in the Jewish soul. It is bound to devour what we try to build upon it." Some of his anti-Jewish reflections are less "philosophical": "From time immemorial Jews have never done a thing that does not pay off in hard cash." But mainly it is the contradiction between Zionism and Judaism that he insists on, as in his final speech before shooting himself: "Zionism aspires to goals totally opposed to the spirit of Judaism. It needs to oppose and conquer Judaism from within, rid itself of Judaism once and for all. . . . " At one point Weininger even goes so far as to say something favorable about Zionism, calling it "the last remnant of nobleness left in Judaism." But this line appears only in the original Hebrew and had mysteriously disappeared when the play reached Scotland.

The familiar techniques of literary apologetics have been practiced by Sobol's defenders among the journalists and assistant professors. Weininger, they argue, is a literary invention, and why suppose that the author would put his own ideas in the mouth of a lunatic, any more than Swift put his own ideas in the mouth of the narrator of *A Modest Proposal* or *Tale of a Tub*?

Unfortunately, Sobol himself has endorsed Weininger's definition of Judaism, for it seems to him a potent weapon in his struggle against the religious Jews of Israel. "I think Judaism is taking over Zionism," he said in commenting about the play. Referring to the (to him) deplorable elements of both Diaspora Jewry and Israeli religious nationalists, he continued: "Weininger, just as Zionism was beginning, saw where things would lead. If, 35 years after the establishment of the state,

there isn't massive immigration, then Weininger's claim is perti-
nent." All of this authorial "interpretation," like many of
Weininger's speeches, might be used to buttress the claim that
Sobol is really defending Zionism in its pristine form against
the incursions of religious obscurantism. But Sobol himself
has made this a difficult task for even his nimblest apologists.
What, asked an interviewer, was his underlying purpose in
recreating the world of *fin-de-siècle* Viennese Jewish antisemitism? "We're used to seeing Zionism as a healthy thing. I want
to show that Zionism is a sick flower which grows in sick
soil." Since the title of his play in Hebrew—*nefesh yehudi*—
implies a generalization—i.e., the soul of any Jew, the Haifa
rabbinate might have been forgiven for seeing Sobol's portrait
of his misogynistic, antisemitic, sexually perverted protagonist
as a celebration of "blasphemy and deformity, depravity and
Jewish self-hatred."

In the same tumultuous year, 1982, a theatre in Tel Aviv,
not wishing to be outdone by Haifa in shocking the Jews,
staged Hanoch Levin's *The Patriot*. This play is about a man
eager to flee Israel's endless wars and ruinous inflation, who
invests in land in Israel's administered territories, hoping to
make a profit if a settlement should be built there, and a still
greater profit if the government should dismantle the settlement and pay compensation. The play is replete with the or-
thodoxies characteristic of the herd of independent thinkers
who comprise Israel's theatrical establishment: religious Jews
are hypocrites, perverts, and sadists; Israeli parents are sending their children to war in order to make financial profit;
and—this above all—Jews have become Nazis. Hanoch Levin's
The Patriot became the first play ever to have been banned in
its entirety by the Israeli Film and Theatre Censorship Board.
The scene which caused Levin most trouble with the censors
was the one in which the patriot must kick an Arab shoeshine
boy to maintain the standards of Jewish settlers in Judea and
Samaria. The scene ends with the boy cowering in fear before
the patriot's gun, a scene choreographed to refer to the famous
picture of a Jewish boy in Europe cowering before the Nazis.[19]
Coming a close second in its power to offend was a scene in
which Jewish sabbath candles are used as instruments to torture Arabs.

The newspaper *Ha'aretz* conceded that *The Patriot* "may indeed seriously harm the basic values of the nation, the state and Judaism," but opposed censorship in accord with standard liberal dogma. People unacquainted with Israeli life need perhaps to be apprised of the curious fact that Israeli liberals go well beyond John Stuart Mill in their readiness to accommodate libel and sedition. Mill wrote that in every permanent political society there must be "in the constitution of the State something which is settled, something permanent, and not to be called in question: something which, by general agreement, has a right to be where it is, and to be secure against disturbance."[20] In a Jewish state established three years after the end of World War II that "something" might be thought to include the conviction that a Jew is not a Nazi, that Zionism is not racism, and that the victims of the Holocaust were Jews and not Arabs. But so far Israeli liberals have decided otherwise, with what consequences we may one day see.

In April 1984, the Haifa players gained more of the peculiar success that comes with scandal by staging Yehoshua Sobol's play *Ghetto*. The English translation of this Holocaust musical is introduced by an Israeli critic named Uri Rapp who declares—appropriately enough, given what follows—that "historical accuracy is unimportant in a work of art." The play's hero is an anti-Zionist Jew named Herman Kruk who belongs to the socialist Bund party. Its chief Nazi, Kittel, turns out to be not just a great admirer of Jews (Gershwin is his favorite composer), but a Talmudic scholar whose mind was formed not in Tubingen or Heidelberg but in the Hebrew University of Jerusalem. He is also, needless to add, a devotee of Zionism, particularly of the Revisionist Zionism of Jabotinsky.[21] The Jews of the Vilna Ghetto are shown as eager to develop a commercial enterprise out of mending German uniforms, and to carry out roundups (*Aktionen*) and selections. Jacob Gens, the Nazi-appointed Jewish chief of the ghetto, offers the following apologia for his conduct: "In order to spare some Jews their clear conscience I had no choice but to plunge into the filth, leaving my own conscience behind." For the Bundist librarian Kruk, the clear sign that Gens is the dutiful puppet of the Nazis' evil intentions is his "Zionist" speech requiring Hebraization of the ghetto. Any such encouragement of Jewish national feeling demonstrates that the Nazis have "succeeded," since "Nationalism breeds nationalism."

Sobol's Holocaust musical was soon exported to Germany and performed at the Freie Volksbuhne of Berlin in June 1984. It was nominated by the German Critics Poll of *Theater Heute* as best foreign play of the year in 1985, and Peter Zadek's German production was chosen as best show in Germany for 1985. Many German reviewers spoke gleefully of how the play depicted Jews as "accessories to the Holocaust," and one wrote that "*Ghetto* depicts how incredibly easily the Jews allowed themselves to be pushed into the role of victims, sometimes to the point of virtually obscene collaboration with the perpetrators."[22] At the party celebrating the premiere of *Ghetto* in Germany, the hosts showed an unerring instinct for the level of taste displayed by Sobol himself: they served cupcakes in the form of the yellow star. At another reception for Sobol during his company's 1985 tour of Germany, the director of a leading German theatre thanked his Israeli guests for having appeared there: "The works of Yehoshua Sobol," he asserted, "will help us to better forget Auschwitz." But then, caught by the embarrassment of unintended candor in words too true to be good, he corrected himself: "better understand the meaning of Auschwitz."

Having done so much to assure Europeans, especially Germans, that the Jews of Europe cooperated actively in their own destruction and were not morally distinguishable from the Nazis, who were themselves crypto-Zionists, the Haifa Theatre had now to demonstrate that the evil spirit of Nazism found its continuator not in Europe at all but in the very state that had given lodging to those who survived the Holocaust, the state of the Jews themselves. *The Palestinian* (1987) deals with a favorite cliché of contemporary Israeli writing, a love affair between an Arab and a Jew that is doomed to sterility and failure because of the prejudices and hostility of that convenient culprit "society," especially its Jewish sector. The Jews in the play are depicted as, for the most part, ugly, bigoted, brutal, "fascistic." The Palestinian Arab girl in the title role has been so atrociously treated by these Jews that, when asked for her address in one scene, she replies, "Nuremburg Avenue, corner of Auschwitz." The incipient Nazi tendencies of the European

Jews in Sobol's earlier play have now reached their full flowering in Israeli "Nazism." When invited by morbidly curious journalists to interpret his own play, Sobol, with characteristic intellectual delicacy, said that he was warning of the "danger of fascist tendencies in Israeli society" and, in a rhetorical question meant to implicate everyone but himself, asked "How much anti-Semitism do we carry within ourselves?" If we were to generalize from the example of Sobol, the answer would have to be plenty.

In Germany, once again, many reviewers interpreted the play in the spirit of the Zionism-Racism resolution passed by the UN when Kurt Waldheim directed that august body; and they drew from it the lessons that Sobol intended. One praised it for showing "the existing reality of Zionism" and the way in which "the Israelis behave as a master race . . . towards the Palestinians." Another praised Sobol for having boosted German morale by "knocking the Jews from their pedestal of being taboo" and "showing them without their halo." Sobol had courageously displayed the "ugly" Israeli and had been unabashed about having this nasty specimen "express his fascist attitudes." Henryk Broder, to whose excellent discussion of the play's reception in Germany I am indebted, described how, at the premiere in the newly renovated Bonn theatre, the audience burst into frenzied, frantic ovations and "showered Sobol with cries of bravo." Were they in ecstasy over the dramatic or lyric power of a play that the more sophisticated and reserved German literary critics variously described as "artistically and politically mindless, even embarrassing," "sentimental and trivializing," and "spewing kitsch"?[23] Or were they expressing their gratitude for being released at last from whatever burden of guilt they might have felt for their country's role in the greatest crime of the century, released, moreover, by an Israeli Jew who assures them that the spirit of Nazism has moved to the Middle East and taken up residence among the Jews themselves? Some Germans, to be sure, were less grateful for a play that presented Jews in something like the way they had once been depicted in Nazi propaganda: all-powerful, aggressive, greedy, brutal. These ungrateful Germans were, of course, the Jews. The Jewish community of Dusseldorf, which had already protested vociferously in 1985 against the antisemitic flavor of *Ghetto*, now appealed to the Haifa Municipal Theatre not to perform *The Palestinian* there. Antisemitism, they argued, was already doing very well in Germany, and there was no need to carry coals to Newcastle. The theatre's board of directors, after endless wrangling, finally acceded to the Dusseldorf Jewish community's request in May of 1987. While the Dusseldorf Jews were wondering whether it was for such things as the Haifa Municipal Theatre that we needed a Jewish state the play was being performed elsewhere in Germany as well as in Holland and Belgium.

In February of 1988 the PLO's Madison Avenue branch contrived a scheme to send to Israel a ship intended "to echo the voyage of the *Exodus*." The event was laden with a great force of symbolic revelation, but what it revealed was not what its designers intended. The real *Exodus*, as some may still recall, was in 1947 carrying 4550 Jewish survivors of Nazi death camps, and was turned away from Palestine by the British who then ruled there. This year's Arab imitation of the *Exodus* carried 135 terrorists deported over the years from Israeli-administered territories—the sweepings from the gaming tables in Monte Carlo, the cafes in Paris and Rome, the lecture platforms of countless left-wing groups; they were accompanied by 300 journalists and 200 assorted well-wishers, among them Israeli Jews.

What moved each of the groups on this ship of knaves and fools to participate in the charade, the symbolic effort to recreate Palestinian Arabs as Jews? For what the *New York Times* (February 16) referred to as the "scores of minor Western dignitaries and journalists" the equation of Arabs with Jews and, in consequence, of Israelis with Nazis, affords a welcome escape from any lingering feelings, however faint, of responsibility for what their countries did, or allowed to be done, to European Jewry. As for the Palestinian Arabs, they have long been consumed by resentment that the Jews should have permanent ownership of all that Holocaust suffering which they themselves would very much like, retrospectively, to share. Palestinian Arabs suffer from what might be called "Holocaust envy," a feeling so strong that it prevents them from seeing that their compulsive desire to appropriate a history that is not their own is itself powerful proof of just how contrived and artificial is the Palestinian sense of national identity. A movement that can conceive of itself only as a mirror image of its Jewish enemy is an anti-nation that derives much of its purpose and meaning from the desire to destroy and replace a living nation.

But what moved the Israelis who wanted to participate in this PLO publicity stunt? What does it say about their sense of identity as Jews that they can confirm or discover it only by allying themselves with Arabs who are pretending to be Jews and who are constantly accusing the Jewish state of being essentially Nazi? Many plausible if not wholly convincing motives suggest themselves. The bitterness of Israeli leftists over having lost what had begun to seem their ownership of government in the 1977 election to people they considered their cultural inferiors has never abated. Indeed, it has been nurtured by the inducements of fame and fortune available to Israelis willing to denounce their country and countrymen as Nazis. I have already alluded to the desperate search for an explanation of the unrelenting hostility, for over four decades, of Israel's neighbors. It is an old law of Jewish history that external aggression, if maintained long enough, will exacerbate the tendency of the more timorous Jews to blame other Jews for the general misfortune of the community. Thus Yehoshua Sobol explains Arab unwillingness to accept the Jewish state by charging that Judaism is essentially "barbaric" and therefore by its nature a provocation: the Jews always, he says, "bring destruction on themselves by provoking great powers."[24]

The desperation of Israelis who resort to antisemitism as a means of explaining the world signifies the failure of dogmatically secular Zionism to provide Israeli Jews with a culture and an inner world of their own. If secular Zionism had succeeded in its intellectual and spiritual aims as well as it had in its territorial and political ones, none of its offspring would today resort to their enemies' travesty of the Holocaust as a means of understanding their own past. It is no accident that the Holocaust is so large a bone in the collective throat of Israel's most militantly secular party, the Citizens' Rights Movement. The flamboyant Shulamit Aloni's colleagues have not lagged behind their leader in expressing the wish to transfer the cherished badge of victimhood from Jews to Arabs. In

March 1989 Citizens' Rights Knesset member Ran Cohen told a group of Palestinian Arabs that he and his fellow leftists had "come to help save you Palestinians from the 'pogroms' of the occupation."[25] Six weeks later, CRM Knesset member Yossi Sarid reluctantly expressed regret that French President François Mitterrand had met with Yasser Arafat on Holocaust Memorial Day, "not because it means anything to me,"[26] but because it fed the fire of critics of the idea of Israeli negotiations with Arafat, which Sarid eagerly supported. How inconvenient and bothersome that the burden of Jewish memory should keep Jews from breaking bread with the chairman of the leading organization of Jew-killers in the world!

Jewish tradition holds that 600,000 Israelites witnessed the giving of the Law at Sinai; and historians record that in 1948 657,000 Israelites witnessed and participated in the birth of the State, a birth that took place only a few years after the greatest dying in the history of the Jewish people. Was not this a miracle? Was not the absorption, within just two years, of another 600,000 people—and this in the midst of severe economic hardship and in the wake of a war that had destroyed one percent of the population—a miracle? Were not the revival of Hebrew and the ingathering of the exiles miracles? The age of miracles is not past, but if you teach your children for two or three generations that God is incredible and revelation impossible, some of them will eventually fail to see miracles that take place before their very eyes, miracles in which they themselves have participated. Light is a quality of matter, but blind people don't see it.

CHAPTER 4

Professor of Terror

PART ONE: *Edward Said on "Collaborators"**

Since the *intifada* began in December 1987 scores of Palestinian Arabs have been murdered as "collaborators" with Israel;
in the spring of this year [1989] the murder rate began to
increase sharply. Even by the standards that obtain in the Arab
world, the murders have been unusually brutal: the lucky victims were shot to death; the unlucky ones were tortured,
raped, then hacked or bludgeoned to death. On June 8, for
example, the Israeli press reported that "the naked, blood-
stained body of Samir Abu Ras, 30, was found chained and
hanging from an electricity pole outside the casbah. Palestinians said Abu Ras, who was known as a 'collaborator,' had
been killed with hatchet blows."

The alleged offenses of the victims include working or
shopping in Israel, selling land to Jews, giving information
to Israel security forces, and expressing interest in the latest
Israeli proposal for elections. Despite the fact that early in
1989 Arafat threatened the life of Bethlehem mayor Elias Freij
for proposing a truce that would make elections possible—
"whoever thinks of stopping the *intifada* before it achieves its
goals," declared Arafat, "I will give him ten bullets in the
chest."—Israeli and foreign journalists continue to ask whether
the killing of "collaborators" in the administered territories
and the threat of killing in the Galilee are done on the ini-

---

Reprinted from Commentary, *August 1989, by permission; all rights
reserved.*

46

tiative of local freelance operators or on orders from the PLO abroad.

The answer to this question may be found in a most unlikely place: the spring issue of *Critical Inquiry*, a journal of literary theory published by the University of Chicago Press. Amid the moldy futilities that typically fill the pages of this quarterly we find a simmering incendiary charge by Professor Edward Said, full of that lurid illumination that always seems to attend any expression of the intellectual's desire to rule the world.

Said, who holds an endowed chair in English and comparative literature at Columbia University, and is also a member of the Palestinian "parliament in exile," has written extensively about a novelist whose great insight into modern political life, as it happens, has precisely to do with the special attraction of intellectuals to terror. Joseph Conrad, in *The Secret Agent* (1906), describes the "pedantic fanaticism" of a professor whose thought "caressed the images of ruin and destruction"; and he analyzes the longing of another (untenured) intellectual to create "a band of men absolute in their resolve to discard all scruples in the choice of means," chief among them "death enlisted for good and all in the service of humanity."

But Said, whose double career as literary critic and ideologue of terrorism is a potent argument against those who believe in the corrective power of humanistic values, has swallowed Conrad without digesting him: knowledge is one thing, virtue another. In *Critical Inquiry* Said offers a so-called "Response" to an article appearing in the same issue by Robert J. Griffin, a member of the English Department at Tel Aviv University. Griffin, a fairly recent Ph.D. from Yale, whose own essay is a carefully reasoned rejoinder to a still earlier screed by Said in the same journal on the subject of Zionism as racism, is treated by his respondent in language like this:

> Who is this Robert J. Griffin who has never in his life written a published word on Palestine, and is only . . . the author of two (or is it three? [in fact, it is neither]) . . . articles on Dr. Johnson? . . . Who is this creature? . . . He should atone for the crimes he defends and keep decently silent until (if he is a human being) he either joins the

real opposition to real occupation or, if he is (as I suspect) a political invention, dissolves himself. . . . [1]

This (and much more) from the Parr Professor of English and Comparative Literature at Columbia, where Lionel Trilling once taught and exemplified the meaning of sweetness and light in culture.

Evidently thinking of his own prose as a verbal equivalent of the weapons wielded by his colleagues on the Palestine National Council (PNC), Said spills ink to justify their spilling of blood:

> When Farouk Kaddoumi or Abu Iyad say that collaborators would be shot or that "our people in the interior recognize their responsibilities"—passages quoted by Griffin— surely even he must be aware that the UN Charter and every other known document or protocol entitles a people under foreign occupation not only to resist but also by extension to deal severely with collaborators. Why is it somehow OK for white people . . . to punish collaborators during periods of military occupation, and not OK for Palestinians to do the same? (641)

Anyone familiar with Said's longstanding habit of confidently reciting the most preposterous falsehoods will not be surprised to learn that the UN Charter includes not one word about resistance to foreign occupation or killing "collaborators." I have searched without success for the unnamed "document or protocol" that would have "entitled" diehard followers of, for example, Tojo or Hitler to execute Japanese and Germans who cooperated with the American occupation forces in the aftermath of World War II. One can understand Said's desire to combine his craving for forbidden fruit with his craving for legality, for the ultimate "right," the right to murder— legally, no less. But if he and his colleagues in Arafat's inner circle claim this right in their dealings with Palestinian Arabs, what may we imagine them to have in mind for the Jews?

For it must be remembered that Said is not merely another dryasdust professor and ideologue but a member of the Palestine National Council, the leading spokesman for the PLO in the American news media, and one of Arafat's closest advisors. Who can forget last November's television images of this intellectual-in-ordinary to the king of terror, whispering (who knows what?) into his master's ear at the conclusion of the PNC meeting in Algiers?

A writer who has alleged that Jews are not truly a people because their identity in the Diaspora has been entirely a function of external persecution, or that the Holocaust served to "protect" Palestinian Jews "with the world's compassion," or that before 1948 "the historical duration of a Jewish state [in Palestine] was a sixty-year period two millennia ago,"[2] cannot easily outdo himself in misrepresentation. And it is true that much of Said's essay in *Critical Inquiry* follows the well-trodden paths of professional Israel-bashers, who can validate Palestinian Arab nationality only by reinventing Palestinian Arabs as the shadow selves of Jews. Thus, Said alleges that Zionists "were in touch with the Nazis in hopes of emulating their Reich in Palestine"; that Israeli "soldiers and politicians . . . are now engaged in visiting upon non-Jews many of the same evil practices anti-Semites waged against Holocaust victims"; and that Ansar III (a detention center in the Negev for security prisoners) is "a concentration camp" (**644, 636, 646**).

But the Israeli-Nazi analogy, now a mere ripple on the dead sea of antisemitic commonplace, also proves insufficiently blatant for Said. "Israel's occupation," he announces, "increased in severity and outright cruelty, more than rivaling all other military occupations in modern history" (**641**). Something new at last! Israel is even *worse* than the Nazi occupiers of Europe— and, one presumes, the Soviet occupiers of Afghanistan, the Syrian and PLO occupiers of Lebanon, the Jordanian occupiers of the "West Bank" who, subsequent to their occupation, destroyed about 10,000 Palestinian Arabs while suppressing the "Black September" uprising of 1970–71.

Said's essay not only answers the question of whether the PLO and PNC have renounced terror in dealing with their internal opponents; it also sheds light on a secondary mystery, about Said himself. Some of his critics have wondered how he could constantly bewail the "racist" stereotyping of Arabs by Western "Orientalists" and yet insist, relentlessly, that "there are no divisions in the Palestinian population of four million.

We all support the PLO."[3] A pedestrian mind might well ask why, if every single Palestinian Arab belongs to a monolithic body with one will, acting and thinking in perfect unison, Said and his friends are so busy about "deal[ing] severely with collaborators"? The answer is perhaps to be found in a sentence in this new essay which says that "every Palestinian, without significant exception, is up in arms against the laws of the Jewish . . . state" (645). The dead and the terrorized are, after all, *in*significant exceptions.

One mystery remains. What impression will Said's advocacy of the short and ready way of dealing with "collaborators" make upon the readers of *Critical Inquiry?* Many are literary theorists who have laid aside not only their old copies of I. A. Richards's *How to Read a Page* but also their old understanding of literature as an art meant to encourage moral awareness and humane understanding. Immersed in what the novelist Malcolm Bradbury calls the latest designer philosophies, they are hard put even to see the tautologies and absurdities in such notions as "postmodernism" and "intertextuality." Can such people be expected to recognize that the organization represented by this bloody-minded intellectual spokesman is an unlikely partner for negotiating a two-state solution in western Palestine? One wonders, but, alas, not for long.

PART TWO: *Edward Alexander Replies to His Critics**

People who complain that good causes attract bad advocates should be comforted by the evidence so abundantly provided by Edward Said's acolytes that bad causes attract even worse ones. For many months, hardly a single issue of the *New York Times* has been without an item about the gruesome torture and murder of Palestinian Arab "collaborators" by PLO agents. Arafat himself has announced that "Ten are the bullets of the Revolution. Nine of them are for the collaborators and one for the Zionists." On September 10, after a flurry of killings not "approved" by the underground tribunal, a leaflet from the *intifada* leadership itself said the killing was getting out of hand and urged that "all cadres of the hit teams and popular committees must use control so that we don't lose our discipline because this would allow the enemy to use this phenomenon both in the field and in the media." Nevertheless for Marianne McDonald (University of California, Irvine) the whole business is "a collection of gossip," for Richard Falk (Princeton University) only "alleged violence," and for Richard Gallo a figment of my "moral indignation." Said's explicit call for "dealing severely with" and "punishing" collaborators is for Gayatri C. Spivak (University of Pittsburgh) "words for Palestinian solidarity."

Carol Bardenstein, still worse off at Dartmouth College in rural New Hampshire, does not seem to have seen the *Times* in twenty-five years, since she thinks the allegation of a certain lack of charity by the PLO in the *Jewish* direction entirely a matter of "hypothetical" conjecture about an "imaginary world." Apparently she has never heard about the Munich massacre of 1972, or the 1974 attacks on the school children of Ma'alot and the mothers and babies of Kiryat Shemona, or the 1978 massacre of thirty-five passengers on a Haifa-Tel Aviv bus, or, in this decade, the shootings at the Rome and Vienna airports, or the attack on fifty Jewish teenage campers in Brussels, Rome, and Istanbul, or the countless other manifestations, right up to the present, of the PLO definition of every Jewish civilian everywhere as a legitimate target of PLO bombs and bullets. Or perhaps she did hear of these little unpleasantnesses attending the daily life of Jews in Israel and elsewhere, but viewed them as instances of what Said calls "the microscopic grasp that Arafat has of politics, not as grand strategy, in the pompous Kissingerian sense, but as daily, even hourly movement of people and attitudes, in the Gramscian or Foucauldian sense."[4] Brave readers of Foucault's *Madness and Civilization* will recall that he said he wanted his books to be "Molotov cocktails." Evidently, through the agency of Said, the Frenchman's wish is being posthumously realized.

Said's chivalrous defenders call to mind Cicero's saying that there is no absurdity that human beings will not resort to in order to defend another absurdity. But the absurdities in these letters are less striking than their tone and tenor. On the one hand we have windy panegyrics for this "accomplished and dedicated family man" (McDonald), this "courageous and compassionate person who [*sic*] many of us value" (Falk), this "champion . . . of moderation" (Yerach Gover [Jewish Theological Seminary], Ella Shohat [CUNY/Staten Island], and Bruce Robbins [Rutgers]). But the counterpoint to these eulogies is a violence of language suggesting precisely the moral disorder that permeates Said's own piece in *Critical Inquiry*. Mr. Gallo finds himself awash in "moral dung"; Miss McDonald pronounces me to be the pride of Adolf Eichmann; Stephen Menick discovers that I am "a self-hating intellectual"; the grieving diagnosticians of *Critical Inquiry* call me "demented"; the Israeli/American-Jewish trio of Shohat and company allege that I "disqualify" Said's scholarship because of his Arab "blood"; and Miss Bardenstein, with an imagination still more lurid and sanguinary, finds in my remarks on Said's claim of a legal right to murder an "antisemitic" caricature of "a bloodthirsty monster, fangs bared and dripping with freshly drawn Jewish or collaborating Palestinian blood." Beautiful and touching words, fit tribute to a writer who in the essay in question dismissed one opponent as a subhuman criminal and the writing of another as a "piece of filth," and whose rude, slanging, head-shaking, filibustering TV performances have made him the scourge of adversaries still burdened with vestiges of civility.

Readers of these letters by Said's apologists will have noticed something more than the usual amount of professorial preening and flaunting of "credentials," as when Barbara Harlow (University of Texas) tells us that "I write to you as a professor of English myself," or the Shohat-Robbins-Gover trinity announce themselves "teachers of the humanities." This is probably not an accident. On August 21, not long after my article appeared, Abdeen Jabara, president of the American-Arab Anti-Discrimination Committee, sent an urgent letter to academic sympathizers, urging them to respond to my "unconscionable piece." The organization, whose national advisory committee includes, among others, Said himself, Richard Falk, Mohammad Ali, Noam Chomsky, and Jesse Jackson, told recipients of the letter: "We were outraged by this attack against Dr. Edward Said and feel that the most effective response is to ensure that individuals with professional credentials such as yours respond directly to the magazine." This may explain the peculiar warning from the blustery (but insecure) Miss McDonald that "many of my friends and colleagues will be writing you with similar indignation." Similar indignation, similar oily sycophancy, and similar prostitution of "professional credentials." It is not a pretty picture.

Not one of the professed belletrists among Said's defenders seems capable of understanding my statement that Said's "double career as literary scholar and ideologue of terrorism is a potent argument against those who believe in the corrective power of humanistic values." Mr. Menick construes this to mean "don't listen to English professors." Miss McDonald takes it to be an assertion that Said "must be a terrorist because he wrote about . . . Joseph Conrad." Professor Spivak, who has been so successful in her struggles against "culture-centrism," "ethnocentrism," and "gender-centrism" that she now wanders through the world of ideas without compass or guide, believes that my confession of waning faith in literature as a means of encouraging humane understanding is an attack on Said's "professional distinction." Miss Shohat and her colleagues, who to problems that demand surgical precision bring the instruments of butchers, allege that I am a sort of Hesperidean dragon guarding the treasures of the wisdom of the West against Arab intruders. Since I have done so poor a job of making myself understood by these humanists, let me quote a more articulate writer on the very same subject. In 1980, Cynthia Ozick wrote (*New Leader*, 11 August): "If, years ago when I was in graduate school, someone had told me that it was possible to be steeped in Joseph Conrad and at the same time be a member of the 'National Council' of a world-wide terror organization I would have doubted this with all the passion for civilization and humane letters that a naive and literature-besotted young person can evidence. I know better now. Professor Said has read *Heart of Darkness*, and it has not educated his heart."

In my essay I gave grudging credit to Said for having passed beyond the commonplace, formulaic analogy between Israelis and Nazis, Arabs and Jews, to plumb new depths of licentious originality by alleging Israel's "occupation" to be even worse than that of the Nazis. His imitators have not caught up with the master. Miss Bardenstein, Miss McDonald, and the Israeli-Jewish triad are still mired in the old inversions, turning Said into a Jew whose critics are "anti-Semitic," affixing the label "Nazi" with the regularity of Homeric epithet to every mention of Israel.

From their letters, I suspect that few of Said's defenders took the trouble to read through his *Critical Inquiry* essay of the spring. A possible exception is Richard Falk, who is a bit nervous about Said's "intemperate, even excessive" language, and whose deep silence on Said's fakery with respect to the UN Charter is, from a scholar of international law, more eloquent than speech. Said claimed that "the UN Charter and every other known document or protocol [!] entitles a people under foreign occupation not only to resist but also by extension to deal severely with collaborators." Yet Shohat and company brazenly declare that Said "never said" that the UN Charter mentions collaboration, and then go on to argue that "the United Nations," basing itself on articles 1 and 55 of the Charter (which say exactly nothing on the topic), has conferred upon people under occupation the right to murder collaborators. This maneuver, very similar to Arafat's trick of periodically declaring that he accepts Security Council Resolutions 242 and 338 (neither of which refers to Palestinians or the Palestinian question) "in the context of all UN resolutions relevant to the Palestinian question," puts one in mind of Swift's statement: "I never wonder to see men wicked, but I often wonder to see them not ashamed." Do Shohat and her friends really suppose that the readers of *Commentary* do not know the difference between a legal document such as the UN Charter and the hodgepodge of General Assembly resolutions (neither binding on the Security Council nor capable of altering the Charter), pushed through by the automatic Arab-Communist-Third World majority, that condemn Zionism as racism and blame Israel for every evil on the globe?

Neither the UN Charter nor any other legal document authorizes civilians to murder for political or any other reasons except self-defense. The Charter, which Said explicitly invokes in *Critical Inquiry* as the PLO's license for ideological murder, deals only with the international use of official force, which it forbids except in the exercise of a state's right to self-defense,

or uses authorized by the Security Council. Article I of the
Charter lists four broad purposes of the UN: to maintain peace
among nations; to develop friendly relations among nations
"based on respect for the principle of equal rights and self-determination of peoples, and to take other appropriate measures
to strengthen universal peace"; to achieve international cooperation in solving economic and social problems; and to serve
as a forum for harmonizing the action of nations in the at-
tainment of these ends. The Charter of the UN has nothing
to say about domestic civil wars or insurrections against the
recognized governmental authorities of a nation or region.
There is no way, even for the disciples of a (reconstructed)
deconstructionist, to convert the Charter, which is designed
to achieve and protect the peace, into a document authorizing
aggressive war.

Israeli and American Jews making the case for the PLO
remind one of Johnson's proverbial dog walking on his hind
legs: it is not done well, but you are surprised to see it done
at all. Said, of course, thinks otherwise, and has awarded high
marks to Ella Shohat for her pseudo-scholarly acrobatics. Indeed, he ranks her study of "Zionism from the Standpoint of
Its Jewish Victims" (1988) on a par with the works of his
other "good" Jews: Noam Chomsky and Israel Shahak. Perhaps
this (well-deserved) tribute explains Shohat's beggarlike gratitude for the miserable bones of condescension thrown to hungry Jews in Said's scandalous book *The Question of Palestine*.
Nine years ago, in the pages of this magazine, Hillel Halkin
wrote of the lines quoted by Shohat that four brief passages like this in a book of 265 pages that excoriated Zionism and ridiculed the Jews as a people without a history, a
culture, a religion, a language, were not exactly a convincing proof of Said's sympathetic understanding of Jews or Zionism. The rapturous embrace of Said's book by certain Jews
shows the truth of Ruth Wisse's observation that "simple self-
respect . . . has been eluding the Jews collectively since the
dawn of modernity."

Shohat and her colleagues are also a bit confused in locating the source of "the Orientalist prejudice that all Palestinians are terrorists by definition," since it was Said, not I,
who wrote that "there are no divisions in the Palestinian popu-

lation of four million. We all support the PLO." Nowhere in the letters by Said's supporters do I find any willingness to acknowledge the human status of the 150 Palestinian Arabs who have been murdered during the *intifada* by the PLO—and murdered, in many cases, precisely because they were interested in the "dialogue" that Shohat and friends claim to desire so passionately. (Bertram Korn, who rightly expresses outrage at Said's assertion that there is "democracy" in the Palestinian refugee camps, should be alerted to the possibility that this lethal form of tyranny by the majority is what Said means when he speaks of Palestinian Arab democracy.)

I commend the editors of *Critical Inquiry* for their tremendous diligence not only in discovering the passage I quoted from *The Secret Agent* but even in unearthing the secret that I "align" myself with *Commentary*. Yet I venture to think that this talent for abstruse research would have been put to better use in exercising editorial control over contributors (including board members) who tell willful untruths such as would be detected by a normally attentive sixth-grader. I regret that I cannot give these self-pitying editors more credit for having mitigated the offense of dullness by the notoriety of scandal in twice opening their pages to Said's exposition of the Goebbels-like paradox that Zionism is racism.

Boundary 2, if we can judge by the pugnacious flailings of the editor of this University of Pittsburgh journal, shows less inclination than *Critical Inquiry* for recondite investigation. Nothing daunted by Said's apologia for murder, Paul Bové has (for once) fallen victim to an idea—the deluding and (to him) flattering idea that "the pro-Israeli, Zionist forces" have conspired with the "hypocritical" Arnoldian humanists "to defend the exclusion of the powerless from the privileges of the powerful," and (somewhat contradictorily) to wrest "political and cultural authority" from Mr. Bové and his friends. Since Mr. Bové belongs to a critical school (the Heideggerian branch, significantly) that has no interest in the relation of theory to empirical evidence, it is probably futile to remark that I never mentioned Arnold in my essay. Had Mr. Bové read *Culture and Anarchy*, he would know that Arnold was indebted to Swift's *Battle of the Books* for the phrase "sweetness and light."

(He might even have benefited from Arnold's observation that the spider in Swift's fable, with his modernism, self-love, and pugnacity, represents liberalism.)

Still, Mr. Bové is surely right to set himself and Said in opposition to sweetness and light, beauty and intelligence—not because they are, as he imagines, the special property of the "powerful," but for the very opposite reason. "The men of culture," wrote Arnold, "are the true apostles of equality . . . who have labored to divest knowledge of all that was harsh, uncouth, difficult, abstract, professional, exclusive; to humanize it, to make it efficient outside the clique of the cultivated and learned." Now *there* is an ideal by which to judge *Critical Inquiry* and *boundary 2* and a few other journals that validate Proust's reference to "the fatal progress of aestheticism which ends by eating its own tail."

I am grateful for the amplifications and refinements of my argument from several correspondents. Mordechai Nisan usefully points out that the search for "collaborators" is an unsavory, self-destructive tradition among Palestinian Arabs, going back to the Night of the Long Knives in the Arab Rebellion. Arthur M. Newman provides a superb analysis of the nihilism that leads Said so effortlessly from deconstructive literary criticism into apologetics for terror. Thus, Said has complained that "So much of the current discussion and representation of terrorism simply *assumes* the disinterestedness, detachment, and objectivity of the author. Yet it is a truism of contemporary interpretive theory that no such position can or ever did exist." Unlike Said (or Paul Bové), I do not see the question of whether (for example) machine-gunning the infants in a kibbutz nursery is or is not terrorism as an abstruse intellectual problem presenting a thousand difficulties of optics and relative perspectives. But even if it were, Said conveniently forgets that a thousand difficulties do not add up to one single doubt, that in fact difficulty and doubt are incommensurate. One may encounter a thousand difficulties in working out a mathematical problem without doubting that a particular answer is the true one. Said is hardly the first scribbler of modern times to fall into this jejune error of relativism; but for him it is the thin end of the wedge that opens the way—as David

Bar-Illan notes in his letter—to encourage and justify terrorism while constantly declaring that you oppose terrorism and never practice it.

Drs. Wyman and Rittenberg, Mr. Karetzky, and Professor Werman deplore the extent to which anti-Israelism has become a smelly orthodoxy of American intellectual life. Professor Werman specifically wonders what so scurrilous a political attack as Said's on Griffin is doing in a literary journal. The answer is not far to seek. The editor of *Critical Inquiry*, W. J. T. Mitchell, gave a lecture at Bar-Illan University in Israel in November 1987 on the topic "Landscape and the Aesthetics of Colonialism." In it he used one of the propaganda photos from Said's *After the Last Sky* to suggest that an Israeli apartment block overlooking a "picturesque" Arab village had produced a "fractured landscape" that forced on a viewer the question of "who 'owns' this landscape." To Mitchell's political statement Professor Harold Fisch reacted by referring to the terracing on the Judean hills—a landscape entirely created by Jews during the Second Temple period and largely neglected and allowed to fall into disuse by the Arab "colonizers" after their conquest in the seventh century, until it was restored by the returning children of the ancient Israelites. Now, the PLO's burning of the National Park on the Carmel in September, referred to in Werman's letter, provides Mitchell with a much more powerful example of a "fractured" landscape than Said's. I look forward to his elucidation, in a forthcoming issue of *Critical Inquiry*, of how it shows the kind and intensity of Palestinian Arab devotion to and ownership of the Holy Land.

Let me end by offering some encouragement to Drs. Wyman and Rittenberg, who bemoan the fact that in America psychotics can pass as sociologists, apologists for terror as humanists. In France, which often establishes precedent for our literary theorists, the structuralist critic Louis Althusser, while he was undergoing psychoanalysis by Jacques Lacan in 1980, strangled his wife. He was subsequently judged mentally incompetent to stand trial. These things, as George Eliot used to say, are a parable.

CHAPTER 5

The Wit and Wisdom of Alexander Cockburn

PART ONE: *Countries Deserving Rape**

On January 21, 1980, the left-wing weekly *Village Voice* carried the following defense of the Soviet invasion of Afghanistan: "We all have to go one day, but pray God let it not be over Afghanistan. An unspeakable country filled with unspeakable people, sheepshaggers and smugglers, who have furnished in their leisure hours some of the worst arts and crafts ever to penetrate the occidental world. . . . If ever a country deserved rape it's Afghanistan. Nothing but mountains filled with barbarous ethnics with views as medieval as their muskets, and unspeakably cruel too." These touching words (and thousands more like them) were written by Alexander Cockburn, the Anglo-Irish expatriate journalist whose voice has struck a specially responsive chord in Seattle-area leftists. Several times in recent years (and twice in recent months) Cockburn has been brought here to regale his acolytes with visions of the prospective "rape" of yet another country: Israel. The title of his latest (December 9) Seattle lecture is "Palestine, the Middle East, and U.S. Foreign Policy." There is no such country as Palestine, but since neither Cockburn nor his sponsors wish to soil their lips with the name of a country whose existence they deplore, "Palestine" is the preferred euphemism.

Who is the man lately become the guru of such Seattle

Reprinted with permission from Seattle Times, *6 December 1989.*

friends of progress as (to name a few of his sponsors) the National Lawyers Guild, CISPES, American-Arab Anti-Discrimination Committee, and the Lesbian Work Group? In an autobiographical essay, Cockburn tells how he recognized that journalism was his destiny. He recalls that his father, Claud Cockburn, a U.S. correspondent for the London *Times* who specialized in sending his paper reports that were total fabrications, also showed a remarkable flair for lying in his private life. Once, his son remembers, the father tried to extricate himself from a humiliating situation by telling young Alexander a bold-faced but imaginative lie: "It was a fine try, and . . . I felt . . . the powerful urge to become a journalist, since only a journalist . . . could have conceived such a preposterous story at a moment's notice and within moments recounted it with such vibrant conviction."[1]

Since his arrival in this country in 1972 Cockburn has been faithful to his original conception of the journalist as someone who recites preposterous falsehoods with bravado. His dogged defense of Stalin is a case in point. The massive revelations in the Soviet Union itself in recent years about the millions killed during the Stalin era have silenced even the most intrepidly "revisionist" historians. But not Cockburn. Gorbachev may have forsaken the struggle to deny that the death toll of Stalin's victims between 1926 and 1939 was about 20 million, and a new textbook prepared by the Soviet Union for its secondary schools may tell young Russians that 40 million people were killed or "repressed" by Stalin, but Cockburn, last of the true believers, remains—so to speak—more Catholic than the pope. In the *Nation* of March 6, 1989, Cockburn grudgingly admitted that some people "had an awful or terminal time of it between 1927 and 1953," but minimized their numbers, saying they probably amounted to some tens or hundreds of thousands. Although the mass graves opened almost weekly nowadays in the Soviet Union suggest that Cockburn suffers from "terminal" untruthfulness, he continues to allege that the historians (such as Robert Conquest) who have chronicled Stalin's crimes are mere tools of "Ukrainian Nazi propaganda."

Neither Ukrainians nor historians should feel unduly aggrieved by Cockburn's application of the "Nazi" epithet to

them, since he is one of those leftists who would be rendered
virtually speechless if deprived of the "fascist" and "Nazi" label
for people and ideas he dislikes. He has called Baden Powell,
the founder of the Boy Scouts, "the *echt* British fascist"; he
has likened President Reagan's media role during a national
crisis to "master of ceremonies in electronic equivalents of a
Nuremberg Rally"; and he has compared real-estate develop-
ers in Miami Beach to "the Goths massing before Rome, or
Bomber Command proceeding toward Dresden."

It is noteworthy that, as the late Henry Fairlie pointed
out, when Cockburn needs a World War II analogue for the
Goths, he chooses the hated Americans and British. To those
who practice Goebbels-like inversions, everybody is potentially
a Nazi except the Nazis themselves. Thus, Cockburn's illiterate
fulminations against the Hebrew Bible are invariably aimed at
depicting the Jews (and not the Nazis)as the "chosen people . . .
of genocide." In March 1986, when Gore Vidal (in the *Nation*)
attacked American Jews as "fifth columnists," "guests" who
have no interest in becoming "assimilated Americans" and
don't respect their "host country," Cockburn came to the defense of his colleague's antisemitic screed by assuring readers
that "the Nazis approved of Zionism" (*Nation*, 21 June 1986).
None of the *Nation's* numerous resident experts on racism had
the temerity to ask Cockburn to explain the view of Zionism
expressed by a Nazi named Adolf Hitler. In *Mein Kampf*, Hitler
wrote: "While the Zionists try to make the rest of the world
believe that the national consciousness of the Jews finds its
satisfaction in the creation of a Palestinian state, the Jews again
slyly dupe the dumb *goyim*. It doesn't even enter their heads
to build up a Jewish state in Palestine for the purpose of living
there; all they want is a central organization for their international swindle." Such words may be music to Cockburn's in-
ward ear; but do they really express "approval of Zionism"?

In August 1982, when Israel was being battered by virtually the entire press, Cockburn complained that "the cowardice of almost all American reporting on Israel has long been
a source of wonderment," and that for thirty-four years it had
been impossible to find in American papers or TV reports
"any indication that Israel might have behaved in a manner
other than beneficial . . . to humanity at large." His explanation

for the "wonderment" was very similar to Hitler's feverish imag-
ining of the Jewish global conspiracy: "It was plain that the
U.S. press was . . . obediently catering to Zionist fantasies" (*New
Statesman*, 27 August 1982). (Claud Cockburn would have been
proud of his son's flair for the preposterous falsehood.)

A year and a half later, the fiercely independent and dis-
obedient Cockburn was "suspended indefinitely" by the *Village
Voice* for taking a $10,000 "fee" from the Institute for Arab
Studies, an offshoot of the PLO. At this moment, he was
absorbed by the *Nation,* ever eager to show itself deserving of
the appellation conferred on it by William Buckley as "the
cesspool of opinion journalism." After bringing more than a
few spoonfuls of his own to this fetid basin, Cockburn has
navigated it in the manner of a basilisk, exhaling poison at all
those "unspeakable," stubborn, retrograde little nations that
object to being "raped" by the Communist juggernaut (and
its journalistic sycophants).

PART TWO: *Cockburn, Two and a Half Years Later, Strikes
Back; and Edward Alexander Replies**

11 August 1992

Mr. Victor Navasky
Editor
The Nation

Dear Mr. Navasky:
    In an autobiographical essay, Alexander Cockburn has told

---

**Although my letter was written on August 11, within a few days of
the appearance of Cockburn's article, it required nearly six months of
hectoring letters from me, some including mention of the dread word
"lawyer," before the* Nation, *on 15 February 1993, printed a part of
what I had written. Its editor cut out all my references to Cockburn's
grosser factual errors and neglected to use ellipses to indicate that
segments of the letter had been omitted. Some parts of the letter printed
here in its entirety appeared in the* Nation, *and some parts appeared
in* Congress Monthly.

how he recognized that journalism was his destiny. His father, the U.S. correspondent for *The Times* of London who specialized in sending his paper reports that were total fabrications, tried to extricate himself from a humiliating domestic situation by telling young Alexander an imaginative lie. "It was a fine try, and . . . I felt . . . the powerful urge to become a journalist, since only a journalist . . . could have conceived such a preposterous story at a moment's notice and within moments recounted it with such vibrant conviction." Cockburn's libelous attack on me in the August 17/24 *Nation* shows how loyal he remains to his father's ideal of the journalist as a person who tells wilful untruths with aplomb.

After more than two and a half years of brooding over an essay he claims I published about him in "the obscure venue of the *Seattle Post-Intelligencer*, a paper whose editors have felt no compunction about publishing, without checking, his deranged polemics," Cockburn has gathered his mental energies for a retaliatory strike. I have never published a word about Cockburn in the *Post-Intelligencer*, whose obscurity, by the way, encompasses a circulation more than twice that of the *Nation*. I did publish a piece on him in the larger Seattle paper, the *Times,* on 6 December 1989. If Cockburn thinks it strange that, when he comes to Seattle for a series of lectures, a critical essay should be published in the local press (rather than, say, the *New Statesman*), and is shocked that the paper in question should print an essay about his august person without first requesting his imprimatur, I suggest he study the domestic manners of Americans more closely.

Cockburn does manage to locate correctly an essay ("The Holocaust . . . and Me") I published in 1990 in the *Congress Monthly*, but says (repeatedly) that that journal is published by the World Jewish Congress, which it is not. This "error" is not accidental. Cockburn has on several occasions been corrected for making it (see, e.g., *Nation*, 27 August and 24 October 1988). But he remains confident that incessant substitution of "World Jewish Congress" for American Jewish Congress will sound very like "World Jewish Conspiracy" and thus acquire irresistible appeal to a sizable segment of *Nation* readers (Gore Vidal, for example).

But these (and several other) demonstrations of filial piety toward his father's journalistic ideal in his eruption of August 17/24 are secondary to his allegation that I have been writing "Nazi apologetics." He quotes part of a sentence from a literary review in which I endorse the (perfectly conventional) scholarly view that among all peoples living under Nazi rule the Jews alone were singled out, by plan and policy, for total annihilation. Neither in that essay nor anywhere else have I denied Nazi persecution, sometimes extending to murder, of Poles, homosexuals, Gypsies. In the case of the Gypsies (Romani), the word "genocide," in the sense defined by Raphael Lemkin in 1943—humiliation, dehumanization, forcible, even murderous denationalization of a group—is appropriate. But since some Gypsy tribes were protected, since individual Gypsies living among the rest of the population were not hunted down, and since many Gypsies served in the Nazi army, most scholars have distinguished between genocide of the Gypsies and the Holocaust, the campaign to murder every single Jew. (The relevant scholarly journal is called *Holocaust and Genocide Studies*.) Of course, I recognize that this may be a distinction too subtle to be encompassed by what the poverty of the English language compels me to call the mind of Alexander Cockburn (whose expertise in such matters has long rested on his claim that "Stalin did not plan or seek to accomplish genocide").

Now it requires such considerable mental agility to leap from my denial that Hitler was bent on murdering every last member of virtually every identifiable group except ethnic Germans to the conclusion that I write "Nazi apologetics" that one wonders how Cockburn could have managed it without help. In fact, he has not. These febrile lucubrations have been cribbed, nearly verbatim, from another of the *Nation*'s favorite experts on the Jewish question, somebody who can teach even Cockburn a thing or two about how (to) *épater les Juifs*: Noam Chomsky. On August 19, 1991, Chomsky (on the electronic mail USENET network [soc.culture.Jewish newsgroup]) referred to the very same passage from my essay and described it as "pro-Nazi apologetics." Electronic mail is, of course, a truly "obscure venue" and would constitute abstruse research for an English dilettante like Cockburn, but it is safe to guess that Chomsky laid the fruit of his own labors in the lap of Cockburn (who is also indebted to Chomsky for the McCarthyite reference to Americans for a Safe Israel as "a sponsor of the late Meir Kahane"). Since readers of the *Nation* are familiar with Chomsky's sweaty defenses of the real "revisionists," the neo-Nazis like Faurisson, I shall refrain from comment on the Goebbels-like inversion of his *tu quoque* argument: i.e., you people who say that the Holocaust did occur, that the Jews were singled out for total destruction, are the true Nazi apologists.

Since Cockburn takes umbrage at my use of the word "oppression" to refer to the experience of black slaves, I suggest he take up his complaint with the authors of the old Negro spiritual that epitomizes the experience of slavery in the words "oppressed so hard they could not stand." Still, I am glad to recognize Cockburn in his new found role as champion of the oppressed. Some of us still remember the unregenerate racist Cockburn and his apologia for the Soviet invasion of Afghanistan, "an unspeakable country filled with unspeakable people, sheepshaggers and smugglers, who have furnished . . . some of the worst arts and crafts ever to penetrate the Occidental world. . . . If ever a country deserved rape, it's Afghanistan. Nothing but mountains filled with barbarous ethnics with views as medieval as their muskets."

Let me conclude by admitting that I have not always been correct in my estimate of Cockburn. Once, in a discussion, I referred to him as a "gutter journalist." "Oh, no," said my disputatious interlocutor, "he is a sewer journalist." I now stand corrected.

Sincerely yours,

Edward Alexander

CHAPTER 6

Praying for Nazis, Scolding Their Victims: Archbishop Tutu's Christmas Message to Israel*

On the day after Christmas, Archbishop Desmond Tutu, Anglican Primate of South Africa and holder of the Nobel Peace Prize, standing before the memorial at Yad Vashem in Jerusalem to the millions of Jews murdered by Hitler, prayed for the murderers and sermonized the descendants of their victims. "We pray for those who made it happen, help us to forgive them and help us so that we in our turn will not make others suffer" (*New York Times*, 27 December 1989). This, he said, was his "message" to the Israeli children and grandchildren of the dead.

Moral obtuseness, mean spite, and monstrous arrogance do not make for sound ethics and theology. Neither Tutu nor the Israelis he lectured can "forgive" the Nazi murderers. Representatives of an injured group are not licensed (even by the most unctuous of preachers) to forgive on behalf of the whole group. In fact, forgiveness issues from God alone. The forgiveness Tutu offers the Nazis is truly pitiless because it forgets the victims, blurs over suffering, and drowns the past.

No one familiar with Tutu's long record of hostility to Jews, Judaism, and Israel will be surprised that he is far less moved by the actuality of what the Nazis did ("the gas

*Reprinted with permission from Seattle Times, 18 January 1990.

chambers," he once said, "made for a neater death" than apartheid resettlement policies)[1] than by the hypothetical potentiality of what, in his jaundiced view, Israelis *might* do. His speeches against apartheid return obsessively to gross, licentious equations between the South African system and Jewish practices, biblical and modern. "The Jews," Tutu declared in 1984, "thought they had a monopoly on God" and "Jesus was angry that they could shut out other human beings" (*Hartford Courant*, 29 October 1984). Tutu has been an avid supporter of the Goebbels-like equation of Zionism with racism. He has alleged that "Jews . . . think they have cornered the market on suffering" (Shimoni, 51) and that Jews are "quick to yell 'antisemitism' " because of "an arrogance of power—because Jews have such a strong lobby in the United States" (*New York City Tribune*, 27 November 1984). He has repeatedly declared that (as he told a Jewish Theological Seminary audience in 1984) "whether Jews like it or not, they are a peculiar people. They can't ever hope to be judged by the same standards which are used for other people" (Religious News Service, 28 November 1984).

Certainly Tutu has never judged Jews by the standards he uses for other people. Although South African and American Jews are more, not less, critical of apartheid than the majority of their countrymen, Tutu in 1987 threatened that "in the future, South African Jews will be punished if Israel continues dealing with South Africa" (*Courrier Austral Parlamentair*, February 1987), and in 1989 warned that black-Jewish relations in America would "continue to suffer until Israel repudiates its involvement with South Africa."[2]

Israel's trade with South Africa is about 7 percent of America's, less than a tenth of Japan's, Germany's, or England's. But so far Tutu has not threatened South African or American citizens of Japanese, German, or English extraction with punishment. Citizens of Arab nations supply 99 percent of the one resource without which South Africa could not survive: oil. Tutu has made countless inflammatory remarks about Israel's weapons sales to South Africa (consisting mainly of naval patrol boats to protect international shipping lanes) but has said almost nothing about South Africa's main Western arms supplier, France, which has also built two of South Africa's three nuclear reactors—the third being American. He has been just as silent about Jordan's sales of tanks and missiles to South Africa.

Tutu's insistence on applying a double standard to Jews may explain an otherwise mysterious feature of his anti-Israel rhetoric. He once asked Israel's ambassador to South Africa, Eliahu Lankin, "how it was possible that the Jews, who had suffered so much persecution, could oppress other people" (*Jerusalem Post*, 11 November 1989). On another occasion, in 1984, he expressed dismay "that Israel, with the kind of history . . . her people have experienced, should make refugees [actually she didn't] of others" (Religious News Service, 28 November 1984). In other words, Jews, according to Tutu, have a duty to behave particularly well because Jews have suffered so much persecution. The mad corollary of this proposition is that the descendants of those who have *not* been persecuted do not have a special duty to behave well, and the descendants of the persecutors can be excused altogether for behavior it would be hard to excuse in other people.

This perverted logic may explain not only Tutu's decision to pray for the Nazis while berating the descendants of their victims, but also his espousal of the PLO, whose leader, Yasser Arafat, is both the biological relative and spiritual descendant of Haj Amin el-Husseini, the Mufti of Jerusalem who actively collaborated with Hitler in the destruction of European Jewry in World War II.

Rabbinical tradition, however, provides a simpler explanation of Tutu's eagerness to "forgive" the Nazis while excoriating the descendants of their victims: "Whoever is merciful to the cruel," the rabbis warn, "will end by being indifferent to the innocent."

CHAPTER 7

The Holocaust . . . and Me*

In Piotr Rawicz's powerful novel *Blood from the Sky*, the narrator-protagonist, Boris, is urged to take up "the vocation to be witness" to the murder of the Jewish people of Europe. But when, having survived the carnage, he turns to the task of testimony, he finds that the "I" who lived in the town and endured prison and torture hardly exists in the man who puts pen to paper. "When a whirlwind comes along," he cynically concludes, "one must make the most of it, exploit it, start writing at once, lying at once." Indeed, after the Holocaust, "the 'literary manner' is an obscenity by definition."

The difficulty that even Holocaust survivors face in testifying to, or representing in a literary imitation, an unprecedented abomination, does not seem to have troubled more than a few of the twenty-seven contributors to David Rosenberg's egregiously titled *Testimony: Contemporary Writers Make the Holocaust Personal.*[1] This book testifies to nothing so much as Rawicz's acrid definition of the literature that tries to "personalize" the Holocaust as "the art, occasionally remunerative, of rummmaging in vomit." Indeed, one uneasy contributor (Gordon Lish) confesses: "Yes, I am being paid for this. . . . If it looks as if anyone is possibly ashamed of this, then just chalk it up to strictly looks" (415). The title *Testimony,* in its pretentious appropriation of an idea that has acquired historical and moral resonance for Jews, was offensive enough when I began reading the unrevised proofs of the book in unadorned paper covers. But only when the finished product arrived, lavishly illustrated, on dust jacket, title page, and chapter openers,

---

Reprinted with permission from Congress Monthly, vol. 57, no. 4 (May/June 1990), copyright 1990 American Jewish Congress.

with details from *Curtain for the Torah Ark* (Italy, 1643–44),
did the full horror of the book's blasphemous vulgarity reveal
itself.[2]

The Torah ark curtain proclaims that this testimony has
an almost sacred quality, intended to call to mind Exodus
25:16: "And thou shalt put into the ark the testimony which
I shall give thee." But what we actually find in this five-hun-
dred-page monument to egoism is (with a few exceptions)
much closer to the profane than to the sacred, much more
akin to the advertiser who offers "to personalize your paper
towels" than to the moral heroism of which Hannah Arendt
wrote when she referred to the testimony of "one man [who]
will always be left alive to tell the story." The common reader's
most frequent reaction to the responses given by Rosenberg's
twenty-seven contributors to his questions about how their
lives and writing careers have been shaped by the Holocaust
will be: "Who cares?" Who cares about the failed marriages
of Anne Roiphe or Alfred Kazin, or the Ashanti circumcision
of Leslie Fiedler's grandson? Who cares that Leonard Michaels'
"life was a mess" (11) when he heard Arendt give a lecture,
or that Daphne Merkin was hospitalized at age eight for psychi-
atric observation because she thought of her father (a German
Jew) as "a Nazi manqué" (18), and of her mother as Ilse
Koch? Who cares that "God became the God of the Holocaust" for Anne Roiphe in "the year of my puberty" (135),
or that she thinks she married a non-Jew because of the Holocaust? Who cares that Fiedler resents people who wrongly assume that he is a Jew?

Worse still than the mawkish, self-pitying, licentious equations between their Lilliputian "personal" disturbances and the
torture and murder of European Jewry are the "ideas" of these
literary scribblers. Here ignorance and arrogance are in full
flower. Most exploded fictions about the Holocaust—ranging
from the notion that not only Jews but also Poles, Communists, and homosexuals were chosen by the Nazis for total
annihilation, to the imbecile description (by Phillip Lopate)
of the majority of the Jewish victims as "religious peasants"
(293) to the tale about body fat being reduced into soap—is
dredged up repeatedly, apparently to the satisfaction of the
book's editor. Contempt for Israel is rife among these writers,

and, despite the fact that Israel is the only country in the world whose neighbors (with the relatively recent exception of Egypt) have for forty-five years denied her right to exist, many of Rosenberg's testifiers see another Holocaust in prospect for virtually every group except the Jews. Several "worry" about Latin America or the omnipresent "Palestinians"; and E. M. Broner's uncurbed benevolence embraces nothing less than "the earth . . . in mortal danger" (279). Conjectural speculation about how Zionism *might* "grow into a fanatical passion" (thus Geoffrey Hartman [431]) like the nationalism that laid waste European Jewry is more in evidence than simple respect for the Jews who actually died. One hopes that Daphne Merkin's tongue will cling to the roof of her mouth next time she wants to allude to "overweight Jewish women standing before open pits, covering their pubes with their hands" (18).

Rosenberg reports that the working title for *Testimony* was "Sheltered Lives." Alan Lelchuk, in one of the few good essays in the book, modestly explains what this means: "Over here, in America, a small Jewish boy was following the Dodgers and listening to 'The Shadow' and 'The Green Hornet' and playing boxball on the sidewalk, while, over there, in Europe, the game was the killing of Jews. Such was history" (254). The book's most riveting (and learned) essay, by Susanne Schlotelburg, rejects *Testimony*'s premise, arguing that "to ensure remembrance the Holocaust would have to be made transpersonal rather than personal," and that those who are not bound by *akedah* or *brith* are no more likely to remember the Holocaust than the Crusades (353). Most of the book's contributors, however, remain just as sheltered from the Holocaust now as their predecessors (and sometimes they themselves) were in the 1940s. Thus Leslie Fiedler, like some curious insect preserved in amber from the pre-Holocaust (or pre-Dreyfus) period, holds forth about how his "love of all humanity, including whose who have long persecuted us," leads him to urge Jews "to cease to exist in their chosenness for the sake of a united mankind" (229). It never occurs to Fiedler that, as Emil Fackenheim has written, after the Holocaust a commitment to Jewish survival is precisely "a testimony to life against death *on behalf of all mankind.*"[3]

Outdoing even Fiedler in his mercifulness toward "those

who have long persecuted us" and (no easy task) far outdoing all other contributors in the gross, the flagrant, the blatant, is the tooth-baring Phillip Lopate. Lopate seethes with hatred and rage—not against the Nazis (in fact, he speculates on the "youthful idealism" of the SS and praises Reagan's laying a wreath on the SS tombs at Bitburg as a gesture of "old-fashioned Homeric nobility" [294]) but against the Jews. These include the middle-class victims, "lined up in their fedoras and overcoats" (293), his own mother, who was "erotically excited" by blue numbers on the arms of survivors, and those he derides as "Holocaustians" (287), including Yehuda Bauer, Elie Wiesel, and the late Lucy Dawidowicz.

Too obtuse to understand that the uniqueness of the Holocaust consists neither in the number of Jews killed nor in the degree of individual suffering but in the fact that Hitler's was a war against the Jews, that Jews occupied the central place in his mental universe, that Jews alone were singled out for total destruction, and that European Jewish civilization *was* totally destroyed, Lopate keeps flailing away at Jewish "chauvinism" (299), Jewish "ethnic muscle-flexing" (296), Jewish "tribal smugness," Jewish "pushiness" (307), and Jewish lack of compassion "for the other victimized peoples of this century" (300). He recommends as ultimate wisdom on memorializing the victims of the Holocaust a passage from Avishai Margalit's "brilliant essay" (298) in the *New York Review of Books,* on "The Kitsch of Israel." In this passage Margalit heaped scorn on the "children's room" at Yad Vashem with its "tape-recorded voices of children crying out in Yiddish, 'Mame, Tate.'" It was long ago pointed out by Reuven Dafni of Yad Vashem (and could be pointed out by anyone who had visited the place) that Margalit is a liar, that there is no "children's room" or taped children's voices at Yad Vashem. There is a memorial to the murdered children and a tape-recorded voice that reads their names. Apparently, Lopate's "aesthetic" sense of the fitness of things is more offended by Jewish mourning than by Jewish lying.

Lopate's description of the very word *holocaust* as a Jewish conspiracy in which "one ethnic group tries to compel the rest of the world" to follow its political program, his voracious munching on the "grain of truth" in "the more moderate revisionist historians" (294), and his allegation that Jews have been able to "own the Holocaust" only because of political clout ("There are many more Jews in the United States than there are Ibos or Bengalis" [293]) bring him perilously close to the position of the neo-Nazis. "Before I give the wrong impression," he nervously announces, "let me interject that I am not one of those revisionist nuts who deny that the Nazis . . . exterminated millions of Jews" (286). Lopate might have added that, despite appearances to the contrary, his essay could hardly be called antisemitic since it originally appeared in a Jewish magazine called *Tikkun,* of which, in fact, he was the literary editor.

The reason why so many of the essays in this volume are egocentric, mean-spirited, and vulgar is not far to seek. Most of these American Jewish writers are people for whom the post-Enlightenment Emancipation formula—"Be a man in the street and a Jew in your tent"—seems perfectly natural. Having accepted the disfiguring privatization of Jewish self-definition, they feel no shame in "making personal" a loss that was sustained by the whole Jewish people. When the Yiddish poet Jacob Glatstein, who was also safe in America while European Jewry was being murdered, wrote that "Just as we all stood together/at the giving of the Torah,/so did we all die together at Lublin," he immersed himself in the vast ocean of Jewish civilization. When the contributors to *Testimony* speculate about how the Holocaust has affected their sex life or their politics, they are navigating an enclosed basin.

While reading this wretched book, I learned of the death of Dorothea Krook, Israel's most distinguished literary critic, winner of the Israel Prize for her *Elements of Tragedy,* and one of the country's great, vibrant characters. Doris (as her friends called her) also had a "personal" relation to the Holocaust, but it was expressed in the desire to do something for the Jewish people rather than to contemplate herself. I remember how, several years ago, she came to my office in the Tel Aviv English Department carrying a large shopping bag that held a large manuscript. "I want," she said, "to talk about something *not* literary, something that has preyed on my mind ever since the end of the Second World War." This "something" was the question: "What can *I* do to redeem those who were killed in

Europe, to heal this terrible wound in our people?" Doris had already done more in this direction that all the contributors to *Testimony*: she had resigned her post at Cambridge University to go on *aliyah* to Israel in 1960. But she had long brooded over and, in her last years, immersed herself in a scheme (elaborately articulated in the manuscript) for a "great aliyah" whose motive power would be an appeal to young Jews in America to secure the Jewish future by viewing themselves as "replacements" for those murdered in Europe. One has only to read *Testimony* to see how wildly Doris overestimated the idealism of American Jewry, and how quixotic, even mad, her scheme was. Yet it is worth remembering that it was from a still more mad and quixotic scheme that Herzl's Jewish state arose—and that from the egocentric contemplation of Jewish navels nothing has, can, or will come.

CHAPTER 8

Nelson Mandela and the Jews: The Dickens-Fagin Pattern*

Almost from the moment he was released from detention in South Africa, Nelson Mandela has expressed a powerful attraction to some of the world's cruelest and most ferocious tyrants and terrorists. Of Fidel Castro's Cuba he said, in Angola: "There's one thing where that country stands out head and shoulders above the rest. That is in its love for human rights and liberty."[1] A week later, in Libya, he praised Muammar Qaddafi for his "commitment to the fight for peace and human rights in the world." In New York Mandela planned to participate in an "act of solidarity" with the Puerto Rican terrorists who shot up the U.S. Congress in 1954 as well as with the Puerto Rican gunman who tried to kill President Harry Truman in 1950. The mayor of New York, however, persuaded Mandela that sharing a platform with convicted terrorists was "not a good idea" (*New York Post*, 15 June 1990).

But no one, least of all his Jewish admirers and sycophants, persuaded Mandela to curb his public displays of loyal affection for Yasser Arafat, head of the PLO. In the short time he has been free, Mandela has twice met with Arafat, and has embraced and kissed him with a fervor unmatched even by members of the "Stockholm Five," the Jews who in December 1988 went to Sweden to train Arafat to read George Shultz's

---

Originally published in Jewish Western Bulletin *(Vancouver, B.C.),* 2 August 1990.

lips well enough to qualify him to open discussions (recently suspended) with the U.S. government.

Mandela embellished his embraces of Arafat with the bitterest taunts he could muster for Zionism and the State of Israel. On 27 February 1990, in Lusaka, Zambia, he said that Arafat "is fighting against a unique form of colonialism, and we wish him success in his struggle" (*New York Times*, 28 February 1990). Asked on the following day whether such remarks might perhaps alienate South African Jews, Mandela replied with a contemptuous sneer: "If the truth hurts it is too bad" (*New York Times*, 1 March 1990). (This is a variant of Archbishop Tutu's charming reply to Jews who expressed dismay over his antisemitic remarks: "Tough luck.") He did allow one emendation of his original vilification of Zionism as a *unique* form of colonialism by saying that the Palestinian "struggle" against Israel was just like that of black South Africans against Pretoria. "We are," Mandela said of the PLO, "in the same trench struggling against the same enemy: the twin Tel Aviv and Pretoria regimes, apartheid, racism, colonialism, and neo-colonialism" (*New York Post*, 20 June 1990).

Barring the resurrection of Hitler, it is difficult to think of a figure more likely than Arafat to arouse the loathing of ordinary Jews. If the Jews were a normal, a self-respecting people, Mandela's defiant embrace of this Jew-killer would therefore seem to have been an unlikely way to ingratiate himself with them. Yet hardly had his North American visit been announced than a group of Jewish "leaders," eager to join in the planned love-fest for Mandela and fearful that his trip might be "marred" by Jewish protests, hastened to arrange a meeting with him in Geneva on June 10. A few soft words about recognizing the State of Israel, a few childish semantic tricks such as identifying himself, in the now familiar, immaculate euphemism, as "a critic of the Israeli government," and lo!—the seemingly impossible had been accomplished. Henry Siegman and Robert Lifton of the American Jewish Congress, Maynard Wishner, former president of the American Jewish Committee, Albert Vorspan of the Union of American Hebrew Congregations, Herbert Wander of the National Jewish Community Relations Advisory Council, and (most surprising of all) Abraham Foxman of the Anti-Defamation League professed themselves "delighted" with Mandela and pleased beyond measure by their "warm session with good personal feelings on all sides." All that nasty talk about Zionism as a unique form of colonialism, all that tooth-baring offensiveness, all that slavering over Arafat, were quickly forgotten. Henry Siegman effervescently told the press that "Mr. Mandela is a man of great integrity, with consistent points of view, who sticks to his friends." Would that Siegman could have said the same of himself and his band of self-appointed and self-fascinated emissaries, who mistook "good personal feelings" for diplomatic success, and showed themselves better suited to followership than to leadership (*New York Times*, 11 June 1990).

Mandela does have a lesson to teach Jews, but Siegman and his colleagues are not the people to learn it. When asked why he made such thugs as Qaddafi, Arafat, and Castro his special foreign friends, Mandela replied: "What concerns me is the foreign policy of those countries, especially as it relates to us" (*New York Times*, 20 June 1990). Siegman and his friends know full well that the foreign policy of a South Africa ruled by Mandela as a loyal servant of the largely Communist African National Congress (which includes twenty-seven Communist party members in its thirty-five-person national executive) will be fiercely anti-Israel, yet they have sought to placate Mandela by doing him the favor of conferring a Jewish stamp of approval on his anti-Zionism.

This doing of favors takes us to the heart of the problem of Mandela and the Jews. Why is it, Jews often ask, that so many black leaders—from Louis Farrakhan to Jesse Jackson to Tutu and Mandela—have singled out for hatred the very group, the Jews, that assisted them in their struggle against oppression, both in America and South Africa? The answer to this troubling question is what I call the Dickens-Fagin theory. Literary scholars know that Fagin, the satanic Jew of *Oliver Twist*, was named after a real Fagin, whom the young Charles Dickens had known in the blacking factory where he spent the most wretched period of his life. The only boy who *befriended* young Dickens in that place (where all the other boys beat and bullied him) was named Fagin, whose kindness the adult Dickens repaid in this most peculiar way. So passionate was the young Dickens' desire for the station in life to which he felt entitled, so convinced was he that it was not his destiny to be a wage-slave, that he came to hate the real Fagin precisely for the virtue that he, Dickens, could not bear to accept or recognize in the oppressive world of the factory. Poor Bob Fagin was no more aware than the aforementioned Jewish leaders of the second law of moral thermodynamics, as once stated by Milton Himmelfarb: "If you don't want people to dislike you, don't do them favors."

CHAPTER 9

The Last Refuge of a Scoundrel: Patrick Buchanan's Anti-Jewish Patriotism

PART ONE: *The Rosh Hashanah Sermon**

With a fine instinct for tradition in such matters, Patrick Buchanan timed his latest attack on Jews (20 September [1990]) for publication on the Jewish New Year. Perhaps someone had told him that pogromists in Europe often assaulted Jews at Passover; and certainly he remembered that the Arabs launched the 1973 installment of their forty-two-year-old war against Israel on Yom Kippur, the holiest day of the Jewish year.

Buchanan is a veteran of many struggles with the nefarious Jews in recent years. Having decided that the survivors of Hitler's death camps suffer from "group fantasies of martyrdom" and "Holocaust survivor syndrome," he alleged that the gas chambers could not have killed human beings. How did the budding scientist know this? Simple: "In 1988, 97 kids, trapped 400 feet underground in a Washington, D.C. tunnel while two locomotives spewed diesel exhaust into the car, emerged unharmed" (*New York Post*, 17 March 1990). Buchanan has, however, declined invitations to stand in a gas chamber designed to murder people and find out for himself whether it proves more lethal than accidental spewing of exhaust into a tunnel.

---

*Originally published in Boston Jewish Times, *4 October 1990.*

His resentment of Holocaust survivors led him to become a truculent defender of a whole gallery of Nazi war criminals, including John Demjanjuk ("Ivan the Terrible"), Klaus Barbie ("Butcher of Lyons"), Karl Linnas, who ran a Nazi death camp in Estonia, and other worthies. As Alan A. Ryan, Jr., former Justice Department prosecutor, said: "Buchanan is the spokesman for Nazi war criminals in America. His campaign on behalf of these people is so infused with distortions and misrepresentations of the facts that it's almost impossible to engage in any sort of response. He simply piles lie upon inaccuracy upon surmise upon personal attack" (*Washington Post*, 20 September 1990). Since Buchanan had long vilified lawyers who sought to reopen cases of *Americans* on death row as "bleeding hearts,"[1] his newfound compassion seemed suspiciously selective.

In a *New York Post* column of 16 August 1989 he took up the cudgels against Jews who objected to the presence of a convent and a twenty-foot-high cross outside Auschwitz, the greatest site of Jewish slaughter in history. They were guilty of a "blood libel" against Catholicism (the very church that invented the blood libel), especially if they dared suggest that the Vatican's silence about the murder of European Jewry was less than laudable.

At first glance, Buchanan appears to be some anachronism preserved from the 1950s, when a vocal minority of American Catholics tended to equate Catholicism with the nineteenth-century dogma of papal infallibility, which they mistakenly interpreted as extending beyond matters of morals and faith to politics (especially bad politics). In fact, however, Buchanan aspires to be more Catholic than the pope. Even as he was busily defending Pope Pius XII's behavior during World War II and the outrage of the Auschwitz convent, the present pope pulled the rug out from under him by supporting the 1987 recommendation of four archbishops that the convent be relocated to a more decent place. Although Buchanan has alleged that the U.S. Congress is "Israeli-occupied territory" (*Washington Post*, 20 September 1990) and has even insinuated that Marion Barry's exoneration could somehow be blamed on the bad example set by Israeli courts, some fit of prudence kept him from charging that the pope too had become a Zionist agent.

Now that A. M. Rosenthal (*New York Times*, 14 September 1990) has had the temerity to affix to Buchanan the antisemitic label he so richly deserves (quite as much as the adulterous Hester Prynne deserved her scarlet letter) he has decided to cloak himself in the American flag: "Nothing un-American," he righteously quotes Al Smith, "can live in the sunlight" (*Seattle Post-Intelligencer*, 20 Septembr 1990). He will sally forth as a courageous knight to rescue America from the clutches of alien Hebrews. As Samuel Johnson wrote long ago, "Patriotism is the last refuge of a scoundrel." It is therefore perfectly natural that Buchanan should avail himself of it.

From the beginning of Iraq's invasion of Kuwait, Buchanan the patriot has been contributing to the morale of American hostages in Kuwait and Baghdad by declaring that Saddam Hussein was justified in holding them because the American blockade is an act of war against Iraq. He has been making his patriotic contribution to the morale of our troops by insisting that they have no business to be in Saudi Arabia at all. And now he is trying to make his greatest contribution to national unity in crisis by charging that "there are only two groups . . . beating the drums for war in the Middle East: the Israeli defense ministry and its amen corner in the U.S." (*Seattle Post-Intelligencer*, 20 September 1990). Does this mean that John O'Sullivan, editor of the *National Review*, and Senator Alfonse D'Amato and all the other journalists and politicians who have urged destruction of Iraq's poison gas factories, germ-warfare laboratories, and military installations are crypto-Jews? Does it mean that Syria, Egypt, and Saudi Arabia, which are privately urging the very same action, have recently undergone mass conversion to Judaism, or are under the mysterious control of Jews? If Buchanan really believes that they are, I would very much like to meet this flag-waver and have the opportunity to sell him some choice real estate in downtown Beirut.

PART TWO: *The Yom Kippur Sermon**

The enemies of Israel neither slumber nor sleep; and they follow the Jewish calendar with an attentiveness that our own

---

Originally published in Seattle Post-Intelligencer, *24 September 1991.*

people might well emulate. On the Jewish New Year in 1990 Patrick Buchanan alleged that the only groups "beating the drums for war" against Iraq were Israel and the American Jewish community. Buchanan's dumbfounded readers were left to wonder whether John O'Sullivan, editor of *National Review*, and Senators D'Amato and Gore and all other journalists and politicians urging destruction of Iraq's poison gas factories, germ-warfare laboratories, and nuclear installations were crypto-Jews. Did Buchanan mean that Syria, Egypt, Kuwait, and Saudi Arabia, which certainly seemed to be "beating the drums" for war, were secretly Jewish, or were under mysterious control of Jews?

This year (in his article [*Seattle Post-Intelligencer*, 18 September 1991] attacking U.S. loan guarantees for Israel) Buchanan has struck on the Day of Atonement. In characteristically delicate language, he calls Congress a "parliament of whores incapable of standing up for U.S. national interests" against the "American-Israeli Political Action Committee" (there is, by the way, no such group) and its sinister design to pick the pockets of American citizens in order to pay the cost of absorbing Soviet and Ethiopian immigrants into Israel.

Buchanan's obsession with Jews and their destroyers is of long standing. He has given his support, if not outright endorsement, to the Holocaust deniers. He has vilified Holocaust survivors. In 1977 he chastised American educators for "failing" to show young Americans that Hitler was "an individual of great courage, a soldier's soldier, a political organizer of the first rank."[2] Buchanan was also "credited" by the *Washington Post* with Reagan's notorious speech about German soldiers and SS troops as "victims" of the Nazis, "just as surely as the victims in concentration camps."

For someone who has aligned himself with neo-Nazis who deny the existence of Nazi gas chambers, rewriting the history of the forty-five-year-old Arab war against Israel—as Buchanan attempts now to do—is a mere anticlimax. His Yom Kippur assault on Jewry exploits the usual propagandist's tricks—fraudulent use of statistics ("1.7 million Palestinians now live on 22% of Palestine"), selective quotation, historical distortion, facts without context. Apart from a single reference to Iraq, the Arab nations that have repeatedly waged war on Israel are mysteriously absent from his account. We hear that with the 1967 war large numbers of Arabs were displaced. But who caused their displacement by starting the war? What does Buchanan tell us of Nasser's closing of the Gulf of Aqaba and blockading of Israel on 22 May 1967 or of the 20 May 1967 boast of Syria's defense minister, one Hafez Assad, that his forces had violated Israeli air space "dozens of times," or of Nasser's famous definition (28 May 1967) of Israeli "aggression" (*"As I have said, Israel's existence in itself is an aggression."*), or of the PLO chairman who, when asked on May 31, 1967 what would happen to native-born Israelis if the Arab attack succeeded, answered: "Those who survive will remain in Palestine. I estimate that none of them will survive." Of all this, Buchanan tells us exactly nothing. He believes that lies have long legs, and will be halfway across the country before anyone even tries to catch up with them.

The real struggle over absorption of immigrants into Israel has a moral and psychological source that Buchanan is ethically unfitted to recognize. Even in the midst of Iraq's Scud bombardment of Israel, thousands of Jewish refugees continued to pour into the country from Ethiopia and the USSR. They were greeted with singing, dancing, cakes, embraces, and gas masks. Meanwhile the Arabs were doing all they could—bribing, cajoling, threatening—to choke off immigration. They have been doing this for a century, most notably during the Hitler period. But there is, as Cynthia Ozick has noted, a new psychological element in their meanspiritedness, the element of bad conscience. If Jewish refugees are greeted with love and kindness by their brothers and sisters, the Arabs, by contrast, have dealt with their refugee cousins as if they were human refuse, thrusting them into camps and keeping them there, through generations, as political instruments. What the Arabs have refused to do to help their own people, they will not allow the Jews to do.

An American president—and it is to Mr. Bush that Buchanan addresses his arguments against the loan guarantees—should not make himself the agent of such meanness toward immigrants. Let him leave such vileness to Pat Buchanan, who recently declared in his *Washington Times* column[3] that what has made America "so vulgar, so coarse, so uncivil," is "a flood tide" of nonwhite immigrants who "rolled in from the Third World." The man who believes that the blacks who are ruining his pristine America are immigrants who recently "rolled in" is a natural ally of Arafat and Assad; the president of this country is not.

PART THREE: *Michael Kinsley and Patrick Buchanan: An Unpublished Letter*

9 February 1992

Mr. Martin Peretz
Editor-in-Chief
The New Republic

Dear Mr. Peretz:

Having already demonstrated, to his own satisfaction, that nobody who falls short of explicitly advocating the mass murder of Jews can be called an antisemite, Michael Kinsley now (TRB, 24 February) enunciates the corollary principle that a person who, like Patrick Buchanan, has "warm personal relations" with Jews (especially if they are named Michael Kinsley) is most unlikely to be an antisemite.

I recommend that Kinsley's research into this subject pause briefly over the story of Paolo Orano and Ettore Ovazza. Orano, rector of the University of Perugia (no David Duke, he) published in May 1937 a book called *The Jews in Italy*, which instantly became the bible of Italian fascist antisemitism and the preamble to its racial laws of 1938–39. Ovazza was a leading figure of Jewish fascism, the founder of *La Nostra Bandiera* (Our Flag), which relentlessly attacked Italy's tiny Zionist movement. Orano and Ovazza maintained extremely "warm personal relations" throughout this period; and when Ovazza was recovering from an auto accident, the antisemitic ideologue inquired after his health every day. In the very month that Orano published the book that laid the groundwork for the persecution of Italian Jews, he wrote to commend his "dear and noble friend" for "your position in relation to the Zionism of the Italian 'fascists' of the Jewish faith." The warm personal relation continued until October 1943 when, at the conclusion of Yom Kippur, Ovazza, his wife, and daughter, were shot in the back of the neck and burnt in a furnace, solely because they were Jews and despite the record of fervent opposition to other Jews called Zionists.

Of course there are relevant instances of antisemitic warmth towards deserving Jews nearer to hand than fascist Italy. Yasser Arafat, for example, has often praised "Jewish dissenters" from Zionism for their "courage and moral integrity." But since, given CNN's foreign policy, Arafat himself may some day, for all I know, turn up amiably rubbing elbows with Kinsley in a CNN studio, the Italian example seems a better aid to reflection.

Sincerely yours,

Edward Alexander

CHAPTER 10

Why Jews Must Behave Better than Everybody Else: The Theory and Practice of the Double Standard*

In October of 1989, the annual motion to expel Israel from the United Nations was brought to the floor of the General Assembly by the delegate from Libya. To him fell the privilege of denouncing Israel as an outlaw country unsuited to be a member in good standing of the family of nations. The incident calls to mind a dramatic moment in Philip Roth's novel *The Counterlife* when a metalworker named Buki says: "I am in Norway on business for my product and written on a wall I read: 'Down with Israel!' I think, what did Israel ever do to Norway? I know Israel is a terrible country but, after all, there are countries even more terrible. . . . Why don't you read on Norwegian walls, 'Down with Russia,' 'Down with Chile,' 'Down with Libya'? Because Hitler didn't murder six million Libyans? I am walking in Norway and I am thinking, 'If only he had.' Because then they would write on Norwegian walls, 'Down with Libya,' and leave Israel alone."

But this opening of the UN General Assembly was driven

---

from the front page by something even more calamitous: namely, the Bay Area earthquake. The earthquake interrupted the World Series, and in the aftermath of so much destruction and suffering the question arose, should the games continue? The commissioner of baseball, recognizing the sensitivity of the situation, postponed the third game for eleven days. Several sportswriters noted that this action was in sharp contrast to that of Avery Brundage, chairman of the International Olympic Committee, who, about two hours after eleven Israeli athletes had been murdered by PLO terrorists during the Munich Olympics of 1972, declared that "the games must go on." Brundage's reasoning may have been something like that imputed to Roth's Norwegian graffiti artist, for in 1936 the same Brundage, as chairman of the American Olympic Committee, had insisted that—despite the little unpleasantnesses to which Jews in Germany were then being subjected—he could find no hard evidence that Germany was discriminating against its Jewish athletes, and therefore "the games must go on."

One notable feature of the postmortems on the Israeli athletes in 1972 was the fear expressed by the man in charge of the ABC television crew broadcasting the games. His greatest concern of the moment, he said, was not for the athletes who had just been murdered—not for him such banal emotions—but for what might result from what he called the well-known Israeli propensity to exact an eye for an eye and a tooth for a tooth. He thus became one of the first moralists to establish the by now well-fixed principle that the conjectural potentiality of what Israelis *might* do is a more legitimate occasion for grief than the actuality of what Arabs have *already* done. Thus the *Washington Post*, in the spring of 1984, printed a photo of a dead Israeli woman, slumped in the seat of the bus she had been riding when an Arab terrorist's bomb ended her life, and commented: "A woman was one of three persons killed yesterday when a bomb exploded on an Israeli bus in the latest incident of a growing wave of violence that was expected to raise fears about retaliation against Arabs." In ordinary cases of murder, sympathy is generally directed to the murdered person; when Israelis are murdered, sympathy is directed, with remarkable frequency, either to the conjectural victim of Jewish retaliation or to the murderer himself, who was driven to commit his deeds because he had not been listened to sufficiently.

In February 1978, an ABC-TV program called "Hostage" examined the terrorist use of hostages to achieve political ends. The stars of the program were Palestinian Arabs and their supporters. From start to finish the narrator took it for granted that in any terrorist outrage it is not the victim—the mutilated child or murdered mother—but the terrorist himself who is the injured party, and whose grievances require immediate healing. In November of the same year, Frank Reynolds of ABC justified an hour-long commercial for violence entitled "Terror in the Promised Land" by claiming that the Palestinian Arabs had been forced to kill people because no one would "listen" to them: "To refuse to listen is to strengthen their argument that violence is their only recourse."

Needless to say, those viewers whose memories had not atrophied in the preceding eight months understood just the opposite to be the case: the more they are "listened" to, the more clearly do terrorists recognize the profitability of murder. For in between their two prime-time shows on ABC the Arab terrorists found time to commit some of their most spectacular outrages, including the murder in March of thirty-five men, women, and children, and the wounding of seventy others, on the coastal road near Haifa. Eight years later, in May 1986, by which time the Palestinian Arabs had surely become the most publicized claimants to victim status of any national or ethnic group in the world, Palestinian Arab terrorists butchered Pan Am passengers in Karachi and Jews worshiping in Istanbul. At this moment, Bill Moyers, another advocate of the "listening" theory of terrorism, called for a massive effort to discover, with respect to the killers, "Who are these young men? What's happening out there to rouse their fury?" Since the primary wish of these young louts is to destroy Israel and the Jews who inhabit it and perhaps also the Jews who do not inhabit it, how exactly did Moyers propose to abate their "fury"?

It requires no abstruse research to conclude that there is something irregular, startling, flagrant, and scandalous in the way that many prolific, world-class explainers deal with Israel. It is the way of false moral symmetry and the double standard.

On the one hand, the actuality of crimes that have been committed by Arabs is yoked together, by a perverse metaphorical violence, with the potentiality of crimes that might be committed by Israelis; and, on the other hand, Israel's actual conduct is judged by a standard applied to no other nations, least of all the Arab states.

No more industrious laborer in this Goshen of duplicity can be found than the *New Yorker*'s Middle East expert, Milton Viorst. Viorst hailed the three noes of Khartoum (August 1967: no peace, no recognition, no negotiation) as a major breakthrough for peace because the Arab nay-sayers did not specifically call for the destruction of Israel. (Actually, they did, for they declared the need to recover "all occupied Arab territory.") Viorst has called the incessant terrorist war against Israel, sponsored by states whose combined military might approaches that of NATO, the last resort of the weak against the powerful. He has called the Yom Kippur War launched by the Arabs a limited-objective exercise, not threatening to "Israel itself or to its people." He has alleged, falsely of course, that Rabbi Kook (the first chief rabbi of modern Eretz Yisrael) advocated an *Arabenrein* Israel and a "Jewish jihad." Profoundly troubled by the conjectural potentiality of such anti-Arab actions, he has yet to deplore the actuality of *Judenrein* Saudi Arabia or Jordan, or the grim situation of Jews in Syria, a country he usually depicts as a model of trustworthiness and responsibility. Syria may once or twice have used some aggressive language toward Israel, but, he adds, there are "hawks on both sides." Since Israel deploys forces just outside its northern border in Lebanon, why, he asks, should anyone complain about Syrian occupation of two-thirds of that country, especially since Syria has a conjectural fear that it may one day find "an Israeli army sitting on its western frontier."[1]

Viorst interprets Israeli attachment to Judea and Samaria as a cynical preference for territories over peace; but he defends Egypt's insistence on every inch of the Sinai as not only understandable but admirable. In a November 1989 op-ed piece in the *New York Times*, Viorst concluded that Israel is to blame for the carnage and chaos in Lebanon, which to the untutored eye seems to involve Syrians and various factions of Lebanese Arabs. Why? Because the Middle East crisis can be solved only at an international conference which treats it as "a series of linked problems involving Israel, Syria, Lebanon, and the Palestinians." The United States, so he alleges, endorsed such a conference in 1988 but backed away from it because Israel was opposed. The willful untruth in the absurd claim that the United States ever proposed any such thing (the U.S. hinted at support of a conference but nothing resembling the kind Viorst describes) is less remarkable than the desire to depict Israel as a diabolic vampire with global reach.

As Viorst's tortured lucubrations suggest, international conspiracy is the theme on which the busy virtuosi we call Israelbashers play most of their variations. George Ball, a former undersecretary of state, has blamed Israel not only for the war of 1948—which the Arabs, to judge by their own enthusiastic declarations at the time—surely *thought* they had started, but also for all the subsequent ones. He has also alleged that Israeli intelligence knew that the U.S. Marine barracks in Beirut would be blown up on October 23, 1982, but chose to let the American marines die to provoke anti-Arab feelings. (The same Shiite group bombed an Israeli post several days later, killing 60 Israelis.) He has blamed Israel not only for every dispute with her neighbors and nearly every one among her neighbors but also for the Russian invasion of Afghanistan, the Iran-Iraq war, the Iranian invasion of the American embassy, and the Pakistani burning of its American embassy. He has also laid America's defense and energy problems at Israel's door. In August 1990, Ball blamed Israel for the necessity to defend Saudi Arabia with American soldiers. He once told the readers of the *New York Times* that the failure of American leaders to understand that "no one should expect the Palestine Liberation Organization to give up its commitment to Israel's destruction" showed that the U.S. had "entrusted the shaping of . . . foreign policy to Israel."[2]

When the Iran-Iraq war began, it was not only each of the combatants who blamed "Jews and Zionists" for directing the hand of the other. *Time* magazine was quick to find a source in the State Department to say that the war had begun (and presumably would continue year after year) because of Israel's failure to solve the omnipresent "Palestinian problem." *Time* was less diligent in finding expert comment on the role played in perpetuating the war by all the Arab countries who lined up on one side or the other of the struggle.

In 1984, a time when Israel was seared by war and beset by grave economic difficulties, including a severe shortage of housing, a ruined currency, and rapidly increasing unemployment, the Israeli government was spending hundreds of millions of unbudgeted dollars on the absorption of immigrants from Ethiopia. Some naive Israeli politicians thought that the humane and generous reception of thousands of distressed, penniless, starving black immigrants would give the lie to allegations that Zionism is racism. But Israel's permanent enemies did not view the matter in this light. Assorted Marxists around the world echoed, with local variations, the official statement issued by the Marxist Ethiopian government's foreign ministry that "It is a serious affront to the sensibilities of world public opinion that the current drought and famine in Ethiopia should be invoked as an excuse for the Israeli-engineered . . . massive kidnapping of the Falashas. . . . The entire operation conjures up the revival of the slave trade."

Germany's main TV news program on the first network (ARD) offered a two-part interpretation of the rescue of Ethiopian Jewry. The network's bureau chief in Israel, Peter Dudzig, said the Israelis didn't really want these Ethiopians at all. Else why would they have intentionally leaked news of the airlift? Then came the network's commentator on Israeli affairs, Hans Leschleitner, to call the Israelis racists because—yes—they did indeed airlift the Ethiopian Jews to Israel, and so revealed the "selectivity" and "egoism" of a state and religion that uprooted hungry people from native soil and dumped them in an alien land, all as part of a cynical arms deal posing as "humanitarianism." Once the yellow patch had the word "Jew" inside it, but now it enclosed the label "hungry"; and now the selections and transports were being conducted by the Jews themselves. Was further proof needed that the UN General Assembly and the African Solidarity Congresses had been right to condemn Zionism as racism? Given his remarkable skill in Orwellian inversion, Leschleitner's German viewers must have wondered why he did not identify as the ultimate instance of Israel's racism her failure to ship her own citizens southward to starve along with the Ethiopians.[3]

After international relations, the most-favored realm for application of the double standard against Israel has been civil liberties and human-rights abuses. Journalists who claim unconditional freedom to determine what the public body shall be informed about find themselves uniquely aggrieved by Israeli censorship. During the war in Lebanon, no theme was more relentlessly pursued by the TV networks, especially NBC, than that of censorship—Israeli censorship. John Chancellor complained that "Censorship . . . is getting to be a real problem here." It was not clear why Middle East censorship never became a problem for Chancellor until practiced in the midst of a hard-fought war by Israel. Chancellor did mention, in passing, that Syria "enforces a total ban on stories about its own military," but this did not constitute a problem. Syrian censorship had earlier in 1982 effectively kept TV cameras away from the city of Hamma (the fifth largest in the country) while the Syrian army ruthlessly massacred, with tanks and artillery, between 20,000 and 30,000 of its own, unarmed citizens, guilty of refractory behavior toward the regime. Where then was Chancellor's concern for the American public's right to know? Was he not troubled by the problem that little, if any, attention is paid by his colleagues to slaughters in Arab countries that cannot be photographed although they are known to have happened? His boss, Reuven Frank, president of NBC News, when taxed with this question, replied: "There isn't interest in the Copts or the Kurds, or the massacre in Burundi . . . so you don't cover them." To talk of what "should" be covered suggests moral criteria, which are not his profession's concern. "You cover what you think is interesting to the viewers. I can't imagine anybody getting upset about the Copts."

If Mr. Frank was cool about the Kurds in 1982, his journalistic colleagues were equally "uninterested" when thousands of these people were decimated by Iraqi poison gas in 1988. No doubt, if some enterprising reporter at NBC could discover that the poison gas was manufactured in Tel Aviv, then people would sit up and take notice. Since 1987, Iraq has expelled hundreds of thousands of its Kurdish citizens from their mountain homes and deposited them in the lowlands of Kurdistan and in camps in the desert near the Saudi and Jordanian borders. But, in Reuven Frank's words, *their* plight is not "interesting" to the viewers. Is it remotely possible that the absence of coverage explains the absence of interest?

Some government officials and journalists claim that none of these practices is truly discriminatory because Israel is really part of the West and must therefore expect to be judged by Western standards. But, as Charles Krauthammer has pointed out[4] the relevant Western standard is not that of Britain, France, or America at peace but at war. When any of these countries faced rebellions similar to the *intifada*, they behaved far *more* harshly than Israel has. During the Arab revolt of 1936–39, the British mandatory authorities killed more than 3,000 Palestinian Arabs; in 1939 alone, they *hanged* 109. India, not Western but surely democratic, attacked rebellious Sikhs in the Golden Temple in 1984, killing 300 in a single day. And neither Britain nor France nor India was threatened, as Israel is, with the prospect of being obliterated by her adversaries. (As recently as April 1990, Saddam Hussein, president of Iraq, threatened to "burn" half of Israel with poison gas.) Whatever the sins of Manuel Noriega, he had hardly launched an *intifada* against America when President Bush ordered an invasion that is widely believed to have killed more Panamanian civilians in two weeks (Mr. Bush's critics claim 2,000) than have died in the *intifada* in three years.

Eventually, Israel's Arab adversaries, who also watch TV and read newspapers, began to draw useful conclusions about the double standard. If others could use it so artfully on their behalf, why could they not use it themselves? In consequence, the old calls for driving Israel into the sea, turning the Mediterranean red with Jewish blood, waging holy war against the infidel, abated—in the western field of operations. In November 1989 the *New York Times* Cairo correspondent, reporting Hosni Mubarak's comment that the PLO must have the final say on the Baker plan, called it "an example of Cairo's moderating influence on the PLO." Readers puzzled by this non sequitur were soon enlightened: "The Egyptian Government has been trying to restrain the PLO from using rough language." In the twenty-two Arab states, belief in and practice of Enlightenment principles of secular democracy barely exist. Jordan, whose king is forever holding forth in the United States on which parties Israel should allow to contest elections in the administered territories, rules over a country which has outlawed all political parties since 1957, and which only recently held its first parliamentary general election in twenty-two years. President Mubarak, widely praised for his ten-part proposal for elections in those same territories, shares no authority with the puppet parliament of Egypt.

Nevertheless, it is in the language of the Enlightenment and of secular democracy that the Arab nations now make their case to the West, knowing that it will be music to the ears of liberals. Thus the terrorist group Al Fatah, whose spokesmen repeat "secular democratic state" with metronomic regularity, is an organization whose very name signifies the opening of a country, by conquest, for Islamic rule. Similar duplicity determines the distinction between what Arafat—once he had learned to read the lips of Rita Hauser and George Shultz—said in Geneva at his press conference in December 1988 and what he and his spokesmen say to their own people. In Geneva, Arafat said that after the PLO is granted a seat at an international conference, and after a Palestinian state is established with its capital in Jerusalem, he would be prepared to recognize the right of other nations in the area, including Israel, to live in peace. However intrinsically valueless, this formula was interpreted by the helpful explainers of the State Department and, of course, by most of the professional communicators, as "recognition" of Israel. But when Arafat and his lieutenants spoke in Arabic and to their own people, they took pains to indicate that this new tactic, this "peace offensive," was part of their "phased plan" to achieve the destruction of Israel. Two weeks after Geneva, Rafik Hatshe, of Al Fatah's Central Council, announced that "the phased plan lies at the root of our political approach." The phased plan was first adopted as PLO policy in Cairo in 1974, after the failure to destroy Israel in the Yom Kippur War. It calls for the establishment of a PLO state in any territory vacated by Israel as a first stage. This state will be used as a base for continued "armed struggle," thus inciting a war in which the Arab states will annihilate a small, weakened Israel.

That terrorism itself continues as before while members of the PLO National Council sit in New York hotels and universities sipping coffee with editors of *Tikkun* magazine and members of Israel's Citizen Rights party will surprise no one who recalls that the organizers of the Ma'alot massacre of schoolchildren in 1974 were well-known Palestinian "moderates" who had long been in dialogue with Israeli doves.

We come at last to the question of the theoretical justification offered for the double standard by its practitioners. Many of them have grown tired of denying its existence, and have instead taken to arguing that it really is right that things should be wrong, because the more unfairly Israel is treated, the better off she will be. Anthony Lewis is probably the best-known exponent of this view. About ten years ago, an irreverent reader of the *New York Times* nominated Lewis for the Pete Rose Journalism Award, in recognition of his having written forty-four consecutive columns on the Arab-Israeli conflict which laid all blame for its continuance on the intransigence, brutality, and oppressiveness of the Jews. By now, even the Joe DiMaggio Award (for hits in fifty-six consecutive contests against Israel) would be insufficient recognition of Lewis's unmatched consistency in depicting Israel as a breeding ground of fanatics who have betrayed the high ideals of Jews of the prophetic persuasion, from Isaiah to Brandeis to Anthony Lewis.

Lewis typically deplores Israeli actions not merely because they hurt Arabs. No—he deplores them because they "cannot serve the spirit of Israel, or its true security." Like Brutus brooding over the misdeeds of his beloved Caesar, Lewis has persuaded himself that "in the spirit of men there is no blood." He is therefore not tremendously perturbed by the prospect that it may be difficult to come by Israel's spirit without dismembering Israel. "Yes," Lewis has written, "there is a double standard. From its birth Israel asked to be judged as a light among nations."[5] Of course this preposterous assertion bears no relation to the truth about the Zionist movement, which rejected Jewish chosenness and sought precisely to normalize Jewish existence while gaining acceptance as a member of the family of nations, treated neither worse nor better than others. "Yes," said Jabotinsky to the Royal Commission in 1937, "we do want a state; every nation on earth, every normal nation, beginning with the smallest and humblest who do not claim any merit, any role in humanity's development—they all have states of their own. That is the normal condition for a people. Yet, when we ask for the same condition as the Albanians enjoy, then it is called too much. I would remind you of the commotion that was produced in that famous institution when Oliver Twist came and asked for 'more.' He said 'more' because he did not know how to express it; what Oliver really meant was this: 'Will you just give me that normal portion which is necessary for a boy of my age to be able to live?'"[6] Lewis's formulation is, finally, sinister in its insinuation that Israel has no right to exist unless and until she is perfect, a "light unto the nations," and therefore that she should never had been created in the first place.

In Anthony Trollope's novel of 1855, *The Warden*, a journalist named Tom Towers is described as "walking on from day to day, studiously trying to look like a man, but knowing within his heart that he was a god." In the Bible God Himself keeps saying to Israel: "You only have I known among all the families of the earth; therefore, I will visit upon you all your iniquities" (Amos 3:2). In Lamentations, Jeremiah describes how the enemy has ravaged Jerusalem and butchered her citizens, but conveys God's message that all is the fault of the Jews themselves. If God speaks as if He were a member of Peace Now, always blaming Israel for the aggression of her enemies, why should not the members and advocates of Peace Now speak as if *they* were God? In claiming that his invocation of the double standard to lacerate Israel for her sins arises from his unique love for her, Lewis has actually confused himself with the God of the Hebrew Bible, who also sees Israel as the only responsible party in Middle Eastern conflicts. Worship of one's own mind has rarely led to more flagrant idolatry.

Unless it be in the mind of Lewis's younger colleague at the *New York Times*, Thomas L. Friedman. In his widely acclaimed book *From Beirut to Jerusalem*, Friedman recounts a moment of revelation he had in London while reading the *International Herald Tribune*. He noticed that the paper had spread over four columns on its front page a photo of "an Israeli soldier not beating, not killing, but grabbing a Palestinian." When he sought out the story behind the photograph, he discovered only a two-paragraph item on page two. But the rude blare on the front page blotted out, among other small troubles in the Islamic world, that day's slaughter of several thousand people in the Iran-Iraq war. What, Friedman asked himself, was the explanation of this "lack of proportion"?

His answer was that "this unique double dimension" is attributable to "the historical and religious movements to which Israel is connected in Western eyes." The double standard of journalists covering the Middle East derives, according to Friedman, from their profound immersion in the Bible. Here, at last, is the explanation of the inveterate, obsessive lashing of Israel we have come to expect from G. A. Geyer, Robert Novak, and Nick Thimmesch on the right, or Tom Wicker, Christopher Hitchens, and Alexander Cockburn on the left: "Their identification with the dreams of Biblical Israel and mythic Jerusalem runs so deep, that when Israel succeeds and lives up to its prophetic expectations, it is their success too." It is because these journalists—most of whom must have been surprised to learn from Friedman of their profound identification with biblical Israel—view the world from a biblical perspective that they see the Jews as the central, decisive actors in the cosmic drama. Consequently, "what the West expects from the Jews of the past, it expects from Israel today."[7]

Is it possible that Thomas Friedman really believes that what the West expected of the Jews of the past was the perfection of so-called prophetic morality? Can this really be the same "West" whose Christian leaders, from the time that Christianity became the state religion of Rome in the fourth century, hounded and persecuted Jews because they had murdered or continued stubbornly to "deny" the Son of God, and whose secular leaders expelled them on racial grounds or stood by passively while the Nazis murdered them en masse? Most people, including, I suspect, the very journalistic colleagues whom Friedman depicts as daily engrossed in devotional exercises, will remember that "the West," far from thinking of the Jews benignly and ideally, has viewed them as deicides dancing obscenely at the foot of the cross, crafty and diabolic vampires draining the blood of Christian children for their Passover matzot, and, in the words of Martin Luther, "torturers and persecutors of Christians all over the world."

In only one respect is Friedman right about the unchanging great expectations of the West from the Jews. Despite the fierce persecutions to which they were subject, the Jews for two thousand years did not resort to preventive attack, armed resistance, or retaliation. One of the reasons for Zionism was the desire to flout these great expectations of endless passivity. If Friedman wants an explanation for the double standard of journalists, he should seek it in their disappointment in that department. But he prefers to believe, with Anthony Lewis, that the more unfairly Israel is attacked, the better this will be for the Jewish soul. The ostensibly flattering practice of applying the highest standards of responsibility and guilt to Israel alone has practical consequences that readily indicate its special attractiveness to apologists for Palestinian Arab irredentism.

Of course, the theorists of the double standard are lying through their teeth both in what they assert about Jewish expectations of the West and Western expectations of the Jews. Having begun with the words of a Philip Roth character, let me end the same way, especially since Roth's characters are usually wiser than their author on the subject of Israel: "The fellows who say to you, 'I expect more of the Jews,' don't believe them. *They expect less.* What they are really saying is, 'Okay, we know you're a bunch of ravenous bastards, and given half the chance you'd eat up half the world. . . . We know all these things about you, and so we're going to get you now. And how? Every time you make a move, we're going to say, "But we expect *more* of Jews, Jews are supposed to behave *better*."' *Jews* are supposed to behave better? After all that has happened? Being only a thick-headed grease monkey, I would have thought that it was the *non-Jews* whose behavior could stand a little improvement. Why are *we* the only people who belong to this wonderful exclusive moral club?"

CHAPTER 11

Multiculturalism's Jewish Problem *

Prior to May of 1991, the advocates of multiculturalism and diversity at University of Washington had encountered the Jewish question but once, and had not answered it very adroitly. In the spring of 1990 the university's faculty-student Task Force on Ethnicity met to put the finishing touches on a proposal that would compel every student at the university to devote one-quarter of the Humanities and Social Science credits required for a bachelor's degree to Ethnic Studies courses. The stated purpose of such courses and of the Ethnic Studies Requirement (ESR) would be to "sensitize" the American majority toward this country's minority groups and in this way combat racism. The Task Force had already denied most-favored minority status to such "white" candidates as Italian and Irish Americans; now it was the turn of the Jews to be measured.

Although someone unschooled in the ways of diversity training might suppose that such questions as whether the Jews are a minority in this country and whether antisemitism is a form of racism are hardly intricate, they aroused intense debate. All the minority student groups present—African-American, Native American, Asian American, and Chicano/Latino—vigorously opposed the inclusion of Jews and antisemitism in the Ethnic Studies curriculum because Jews are not "people of color." The students seemed genuinely bemused by the idea that people not in their political party should have the temerity to invade their turf and poach on the (very considerable) spoils

Reprinted with permission from Congress Monthly, *vol. 58, no. 7 (November/December 1991), copyright 1991 American Jewish Congress.*

of their anticipated victory. Their recommended solution—eventually approved by the committee—was to substitute the term "people of color" (a term linguistically analogous to "jeans of blue") for the term "minorities" wherever it appeared in committee documents.

The prize for semantic juggling was won not by the students, however, but by the two professorial representatives of the Ethnic Studies program itself, both of whom had also presided over Afro-American Studies. One—Professor Joseph Scott—said that he could not assent to the inclusion of Jews and antisemitism in the proposed scheme of courses unless other "Semitic" peoples, most particularly the Palestinian Arabs, were also included. Another, Professor Johnella Butler, opposed inclusion of Jews because Jewish persons are not necessarily of "Semitic descent" and "antisemitism is not institutionalized in this country."

These remarks brought a raising of the collective eyebrow and even some tittering. For it appeared that of the 37,000 who teach and learn at the University of Washington, virtually the only ones ignorant of the fact that antisemites hate Jews and not "Semites" were the professors of Ethnic Studies, the officially designated historians and exorcists of racism and promoters of multiculturalism. Some uncharitable observers, to be sure, suspected that if you touched the delicate, exotic fruit of this professorial ignorance, it would quickly lose its bloom and turn out to be not so much ignorance of the history as guilt of the sin of racism. Could the spiteful introduction of Palestinian Arabs into a discussion of American minorities be innocent? Could the assertion by a grown-up and heavily degreed woman that institutional antisemitism (as if that were the only kind) is absent from this country be indicative less of a susceptibility to balderdash than of a desire to make up for that absence?

Almost exactly a year later, the leaders of the campus campaign against racism were afforded a splendid opportunity to practice what they preach. On 22 May 1991 one Abdul Alim Musa, speaking under the auspices of the Associated Students of the University of Washington (ASUW), the Black Students Commission, International Muslim Student Association, and another Muslim organization mysteriously labeled

CHAM, delivered a vituperatively antisemitic speech that lasted nearly two hours. In it he alleged that—I quote from the detailed account in the 24 May issue of the *University of Washington Daily*—America is "controlled by an influential Jewish community, determined to keep minorities repressed and powerless," that Jews, "instead of Americans," exercise "control of American domestic policy," and that "the Yahuds are the enemy of humanity." He also gleefully predicted a second Holocaust in this country, in which Jews will be slaughtered in a popular uprising.

A few letters to the student paper questioned the appropriateness and legality of using mandatory student fees to sponsor a racist agitator whose views most students must deplore. But the sponsors of the speech were entirely unrepentant, and this despite the fact that two of them, the Black Students Commission and the ASUW, had been among the most intrepid supporters of the Ethnic Studies Requirement antidote to racism described above. Indeed, at the very moment when some people were complaining of the ASUW's sponsorship of a racist, the president of the ASUW (Heidi Wills) was busily excoriating faculty who opposed the latest, revised version of ESR (called APR, for American Pluralism Requirement) for their insensitivity to the problem of racism.

The silence from other devotees of diversity at this institution, the cover of whose general catalog was during these years adorned by a picture of members of the "major" minorities as well as the political symbols of sexual minorities, was equally impressive. For years the university had been assured by its president, William Gerberding, as well as by assorted deans, that morality was advancing on a broad and invincible front, slaying the dragons of racism, sexism, classism, looksism, and every other affliction capable of causing outbreaks of ismitis among aspirants to victimhood. It did not require a very refined sensibility, much less diversity and sensitivity training, to recognize Musa's speech as a racist screed of the most flagrant kind. Yet not a single one of the entrepreneurs in the diversity industry seemed capable of recognizing the racist beast when it stared them in the face. The officially designated battlers against racism had nothing to say. The aforementioned professors of Ethnic Studies, it appeared, were better at train-

ing people to keep a sharp eye out for the touch of racism
that can be detected in a casual opinion or slip of the tongue
than in recognizing the thing itself.

And what of the administration? When the associate vice
president for student affairs (Stephen Nord) was asked for his
reaction to the Musa affair by physics professor Edward Stern,
he made light of the matter, saying that "only a few Jews"
were concerned about it. Despite its moral squalor, the view
that only Jews should be disturbed by Jew-hatred is not un-
usual, and would hardly be worthy of remark unless it came,
as in this instance it did, from the very man whose office—
Student Affairs—carries the multiculturalist banner to every
corner of the university in the form of posters and advertisements proclaiming that the University of Washington "Values
Diversity," and of sensitivity-training workshops. Indeed, one
of the better-publicized projects of the Student Affairs office
was a specially-designed sensitivity-training course for the president of the university himself. In May of 1990 he had been
guilty of what could fairly be called a racial slur—thoughtless
rather than malicious, but a slur nevertheless—against a His-
panic student at an awards dinner. Although he apologized
repeatedly, once in front of a howling mob, for the offense,
Gerberding's penance was deemed incomplete until he had
agreed to submit to a regimen of sensitivity-training that
would teach the racism out of him.

It therefore seemed appropriate, in the aftermath of Musa's
widely publicized speech, to expect some response from our
newly sensitized president. And so, in an open letter to Gerberding published in the *Daily* on June 5, I and my colleague
Alexander Pettit asked: "Will you . . . as a beneficiary of the
latest designer methods in diversity training, give us a little
guidance in this matter, preferably in the form of an unequivo-
cal condemnation of Musa's speech and of its unrepentant sponsors?" Neither then nor at any time since was there a reply
from Gerberding, either to our letter or to private requests
from other faculty that he use the moral authority inherent in
his position to criticize the antisemitic speech of Musa and
the granting of university support to racist agitators.

This episode at Washington follows a pattern well established at our universities. The multiculturalists do not recog-

nize antisemitism as a form of racism. After all, their wise men have decreed that only "people of color" can be the targets of racism and that these same "people of color" are, no matter how consumed with hatred they may be, protected, by virtue of their pigmentation, from being racists themselves. This wonderfully convenient and self-serving doctrine may, along with all the traditional political attractions of antisemitism, help to account for the special obsession with the Jews that besets so many of the laborers in the diversity vineyard.

A few examples should suffice to indicate the pattern. At Duke University, "multiculturalism" is the official ideology, its principles set forth in a manifesto called "Duke's Vision." By way of instilling that vision, Duke requires all incoming freshmen to take a test, in which they must answer yes/no or agree/disagree to a series of statements, all so heavily loaded that any student who had examined two or three newspaper stories about "political correctness" would know what answer was expected by Big Brother (and Big Sister too). Prominent among the statements asking to be knocked down is: "Jewish students should support all the policies and actions of Israel." There is, however, no statement saying: "Black students should support all the policies and actions of the African National Congress."

In June of 1991, Thomas Sobol, New York's commissioner of education, received a report prepared by a committee of twenty-four educators which urged much greater curricular emphasis on the roles of nonwhite cultures in American life. The report aroused controversy largely because of its obsession with "race" as "a cultural phenomenon, not a physical description," and its dogged adherence to the doctrine that "the information-dominant approach to the social studies curriculum fails as a vehicle for multicultural education. . . . "[1] This manifesto of the multiculturalist movement also pays special attention to the Jews, here the dead ones. Perhaps in order to illustrate what is possible to those who discard the tiresome old "information-dominant approach" in favor of titillating ignorance, the Sobol report includes a six-page "annex" by Professor Ali Mazrui of the State University of New York at Binghamton. In it he argues that the term "holocaust" should not be reserved to describe the Nazi murder of European Jewry but should "remain a general metaphor" embracing the oppression of American Indians and black slaves as well.[2] The Jews, in Mazrui's view, must not be allowed to monopolize all that beautiful suffering which other groups would very much like (ex post facto) to share.

The "Afrocentric" branch of the multiculturalist crusade seems to carry the burden of a special mission with regard to the Jews. At City College of New York, the flamboyant Leonard Jeffries, former chairman of Black Studies and long-time theorist par excellence of the pigmentational theory of culture, teaches his students that "rich Jews . . . financed the slave trade."[3] On 20 July 1991, during a two-hour lecture at the aptly named Empire State Black Arts Festival in Albany, he treated his audience to an unwholesome stew of warmed-over Afrocentric pieties and raw Jew-hatred. Russian Jews in this country, he declared, have, from their Hollywood head-quarters, in collusion with "their financial partners, the Mafia," presided over "a financial system of destruction of black people." Thomas Sobol, who had previously used Jeffries as an expert consultant on multiculturalist matters, said he found his erst-while expert's remarks "very unfortunate"; but the director of the SUNY African-American Institute, Dr. A. J. Williams-Myers, defended the speech and said that it was the *New York Post*, which had first reported it, that was guilty of "race-baiting."[4]

At Columbia University, Khallid Abdel Muhammad, a Louis Farrakhan disciple, was invited by the Black Student Organization to speak on "Afrocentricity." He began his learned discourse by emphasizing his bravery in speaking at "Columbia Jewniversity" in "Jew York." The rest of his speech contained more ugly references to Jews. Afterwards a Jewish student wrote to the Columbia *Spectator*: "I have an idea. As a white, Jewish American I'll just stand in the middle of a circle comprising . . . Khallid Abdel Muhammad and assorted members of the Black Student organization and let them all hurl large stones at me. . . . I gather this will be a good cheap method of making these people feel good."[5]

On the opposite coast, at UCLA, the African-American student newsmagazine *Nommo*, in February 1991, carried an article validating and extolling the *Protocols of the Elders of Zion*, the Czarist secret police forgery of 1905 which portrayed a

Jewish conspiracy to control the world. Multiculturalists seem to have a lively interest in the *Protocols,* one of the most lethal antisemitic tracts of this century. Andrew Sullivan reported in the *New Republic* of 26 November 1990 that at the Second National Conference on the Infusion of African and African-American Content in the High School Curriculum, held in Atlanta earlier that month, not one but several "vendors [were] selling *Protocols of the Elders of Zion.*" (New York's Commissioner Thomas Sobol was among the conference's featured speakers, but does not appear to have expressed any views for or against the *Protocols.*)[6]

Nommo embellished the original *Protocols* with the clichés of Afrocentrism: "a small group of European people have proclaimed themselves God's 'chosen' by using an indigenous African religion, Judaism, to justify their place in the world." In addition to resurrecting this old forgery, the journal also printed a new one, a letter extolling anti-Jewish hatred as "good for Hitler . . . good for Stalin and . . . good for *Nommo.*"[7]

One notable feature of these antisemitic outbursts by the Afrocentric multiculturalists is a stunning carelessness about substituting "Zionist" for "Jew," something that sophisticated antisemites have been doing for decades. Often it is only after the untutored zealots have embarrassed their sponsors that the public will be told it should have heard "Zionist" whenever "Jew" was uttered. After the Musa speech aroused a furor at the University of Washington, David Grim, the director of public relations(!) of the International Muslim Student Union which had sponsored him explained that the speech had been "anti-Zionist," not anti-Jewish. His letter, which may well merit a place in some future museum tracing *fin-de-siècle* developments in antisemitism, in effect announced that if only *Mein Kampf* (a work heavily indebted to the aforementioned *Protocols*) could be reprinted with "Zionist" substituted for "Jew" in every instance, it would be an edifying, unexceptionable moral-political tract. At UCLA, the public-relations cover-up was less delicate: in June, *Nommo*'s entertainment editor, Darlene Webb, bade farewell to her readers with an extended salvo at "cave-dwelling (Khazar mountains, to be exact) white, zionist fucks."[8]

What is it that attracts the multiculturalists to antisemitism? After all the verbal fireworks and excrement-flinging at UCLA, a short and ready answer was supplied by a local sage named Janet Hadda, professor of Yiddish and head of the Jewish Studies Program. "You're dealing with something they [blacks] use to organize their view of themselves and the world. It's not simply a matter of hating—it's a belief structure."[9] To which one might reply that if antisemitism is indeed "a belief structure" then the sooner it is torn down the better. Tearing it down, however, would require heavy blows from "the information-dominant approach," i.e., that old-fashioned disinterested pursuit of the truth that, according to the multiculturalists, "fails as a vehicle for multicultural education."

If the Jewish speck blots out the truth and also the glory of the world in the eye of the multiculturalist, the reasons for his distortion in vision may be even less flattering to him than Professor Hadda's liberal condescension suggests. The minorities enlisted in the multicultural campaign understand, just as well as the cynical University of Washington administrator cited above, that "only a few Jews" will protest antisemitism. Impoverished minorities therefore connect themselves with the soundest philistine impulses of the comfortable majority when they attack the Jews. As Ruth Wisse has written, "the aggression of antisemitism against an absurdly small minority ensures that it cannot be countered by opposition in kind, and its focus on a particular group—the Jews—makes it irrelevant to those who are not Jews."[10] The multiculturalist hostility to Jews expresses too the ancient tendency of majorities to bully minorities. If this sounds paradoxical, it should be noted that the Sobol report urging greater curricular attention to non-white cultures actually repudiates the once-cherished label of "minority," arguing that what appear to be minorities in the United States are really majorities in the world. But this can hardly be said of the Jews. Since 997 out of every 1000 people in the world are *not* Jews, they may be left as the only American minority, subject to the whims, jealousies, and frenzies of the new union of minorities for whose human and civil rights they fought, whether disinterestedly or in the expectation, now proved mistaken, that this support would be reciprocated.

CHAPTER 12

Some of My Best Friends Are Antisemites: William F. Buckley's Dilemma*

In May of 1991, in the pages of *Commentary*, I wrote that "From so acute and interesting a mind as William Buckley, Jr.'s one might have expected better than vapid remarks about [Patrick] Buchanan's 'insensitivity' and A. M. Rosenthal's 'over-sensitivity.'" Not long afterward, the seminal mind of America's post-Second World War conservative movement set himself to consider in detail not only the controversy involving allegations of Buchanan's antisemitism but the increasing extent to which, in this country, the twentieth century's most successful and lethal ideology can now be espoused without cost. His considerations resulted in a 40,000-word essay that takes up nearly the entire 30 December 1991 issue of *National Review*.[1] The five-part composition, full of valuable matter but also rambling, digressive, and ill-constructed, evaluates the charges of antisemitism that have been brought against three right-wing parties, Joseph Sobran, Buchanan, and the *Dartmouth Review*, as well as against the leftist Gore Vidal and his sponsors at the *Nation*. A conclusion rounds off the essay and also validates its otherwise incomprehensible title—"In Search of Anti-Semitism"—by naming James Freedman, president of Dartmouth, as "the principal malefactor of the season" (62)

Reprinted with permission from Congress Monthly, *vol. 59, no. 3 (March/April 1992), copyright 1992 American Jewish Congress.*

because (and here Buckley is right on the mark) he inflated the prank of one mischievous student into a racist plague at the college.

Of course, Buckley was moved to this effort by forces more profound and compelling than any little rebuke of mine. As long ago as the 1950s he was working conscientiously to purge the American conservative movement of antisemitism. In 1958, for example, he declared that the writers on the masthead of his *National Review* who were also on the masthead of the antisemitic *American Mercury* would need to retire from one masthead or the other. For a long time Buckley seemed to have this "problem" well under control. In 1986 he could justifiably claim that institutional antisemitism had during the previous fifteen or twenty years found its (proper) home in the political left, that "in England, anti-Semitism (disguised as anti-Zionism) is the property of the political Left" and that in America "The *Nation* magazine exhibits the same kind of toleration toward anti-Semitism . . . that it shows to Fidel Castro" (24).

But in recent years Buckley has had to deal with the alarming discovery, made gradually and reluctantly, that some of his best friends and closest colleagues are antisemites or (his preferred formulation) have said and done things that reasonable people construe to be antisemitic. The trouble began at the *National Review* with the senior editor Joseph Sobran, whose quaint, febrile, demonic lucubrations about Jews nearly relegate the effusions of Buchanan and Vidal to the category of garden-variety antisemitism. In one column, Sobran deplored the pope's visit to a synagogue because it might lead people to forget the persecution visited by Jews upon Christians over the centuries. In another apoplectic eruption, he charged that the *New York Times*, that famously Zionist newspaper, had endorsed the military strike against Libya because bombing served the Zionist cause. Sobran did not, of course, object to all Jews; and by way of proving his freedom from what Buckley calls "ethnic allergy," he declared that Noam Chomsky was "a true Israelite, in whom there is no guile" (27). And so on, ad nauseam.

Buckley never admits that his colleague is an antisemite, only that he "went cuckoo," that is, became obsessed on the subject of Israel, became licentious in dealing with facts, and was "not industriously curious to uncover refutations of his burgeoning case against Israel" (28). Buckley is also more likely to say "That isn't exactly correct" when confronted by one of Sobran's outrageous distortions than "This is a bold-faced lie." But this verbal coddling of his "highly esteemed and beloved colleague" did not prevent Buckley from taking the necessary action to dissociate the magazine from Sobran's views, to chastise and eventually expel him. In July 1986 Buckley rebuked Sobran in a lengthy editorial in the *National Review*. In it he declared that "the structure of prevailing taboos respecting Israel and the Jews is welcome," that any reader of Sobran's columns on Israel and Jews "might reasonably conclude that those columns were written by a writer inclined to anti-Semitism," and that it was "of first strategic and tactical importance" for the right to discard its "old prejudices" (23–24). Four years later, when the Gulf Crisis drove Sobran altogether beyond the reach of reason (to say nothing of Buckley's cherished "right reason") Buckley dropped him as senior editor, though he could continue to write on topics outside of his obsession.

Still seeking an answer to his central question of "what is anti-Semitism these days," Buckley moves from Sobran to Buchanan, the political journalist and TV commentator whose omnipresent hyena grin seemed (to cable subscribers, at least) unavoidable on any channel lower than 36 on the dial—until he transferred his operations to the New Hampshire presidential primary. Buckley presents Buchanan as an "iconoclast" fatally addicted to "mischievous generalizations" (32–33). But it is not Buchanan's smashing of idols so much as his adoration of them that ignited his rage against the Jews.

Most of Buchanan's litany of complaints against Israel and Jews, and his tedious whining about how his voice is being "stifled" (perhaps on the one night of the week when he was not on TV) could have (indeed much of it did) come out of the pages of the *Nation*, especially the fierce mouthings of Alexander Cockburn. In fact, Buckley correctly points out that Michael Lerner's fundraising letter for *Tikkun* "could have been signed by Joe Sobran or Pat Buchanan" (39); he might have added the highly revealing fact that most of Buchanan's ardent defenders when he was accused of antisemitism were leftists. What Buckley fails to point out, though no one is better suited than he to do so, is that the distinctive note in Buchanan's anti-Jewish polemic is resentment of "caustic, cutting cracks about my church and popes from both Israel and its amen corner in the United States" (*Seattle Post-Intelligencer*, 20 September 1990). Buchanan, who [as noted earlier in this book] tends to make Catholicism coextensive with the nineteenth-century dogma of papal infallibility, was outraged by Jewish criticism of Pope Pius XII's derelictions during World War II and of the convent constructed outside of Auschwitz. But when the present pope decided to support the 1987 recommendation of four archbishops that the convent be relocated, he decided that his combat with the Jews required him to be still more Catholic than the pope.

If Buchanan's personal history is examined with the care usually bestowed on presidential candidates, several paradoxes of his life will soon be common knowledge. He is a devotee of law and order who was expelled from Georgetown University for assaulting a policeman; a fierce opponent of birth control who is childless after twenty years of marriage; a vituperative critic of Jews as shirkers of military service who has himself never served in the military; a person who one week reminisces nostalgically about his golden youth in "the old America, where ancestry did not count" (*New York Post*, 29 December 1990), and the next week asserts that "we [are] more shocked when a dozen people are killed in Vilnius than a massacre in Burundi because they are white people. That's who we are. That's where America comes from."[2]

This last pellet of Buchananite intellection calls to mind yet another relevant topic ignored by Buckley: namely, the basis of Buchanan's presidential campaign. It is none other than the hope that millions of Americans will interpret his unsubtle hints as follows: "This is the guy, the only guy, who will put the niggers and the yids in their place." Although Buckley comments at length about George Bush's sinister remarks at his press conference of 12 September about the thousand Jewish lobbyists besieging the one, poor "lonely little guy in the White House," he never notices in the speech or its aftermath what Buchanan saw at once: the ease with which an unscrupulous politician can awaken and exploit that notoriously light sleeper called antisemitism.

Instead of dealing with these more immediate questions Buckley wanders off in (endless) pursuit of red herrings, principally the "question" of whether, as Sobran, Buchanan, Vidal, Cockburn, and their countless Jewish epigones assert, with steam-engine regularity, antisemitism has been unfairly redefined by the wicked Zionists to mean any criticism of Israel, and this in order to silence such brave critics. It is amazing that a writer of Buckley's intelligence and, on occasion, even wisdom can spill ink over this allegation. Everybody knows that a critic need not be an enemy; and yet "critic of Israeli policies" has become one of the most baneful euphemisms of contemporary discourse.

Several dozen leftists place an ad in the *New York Times* (13 March 1988) calling for "dismantling" the state of Israel as an act of "minimum justice," and they are referred to in the ensuing controversy as "critics of Israel." Alexander Cockburn calls the God of the Jews "a deity of savagery urging his chosen people to acts of genocide," sprinkles the word "Nazi," like some condiment or popular seasoning, over nearly every reference to Israel, and charges that the whole U.S. press must cater to "Zionist fantasies"; instantly he is denominated, by his charitable journalistic colleagues, "critic of Israeli policies." Gore Vidal describes Judaism (this in *Playboy Magazine*) as "an unusually ugly religion," and depicts American Jews as fifth columnists in the country of their birth who should be required to register with the Justice Department as agents of a foreign power. He too, instantly, is blandly labeled "critic of Israel." George Ball, former undersecretary of state, has likened Israeli soldiers in the 1948 War of Independence to Nazi soldiers in Poland, equated Israel's use of tear gas in responding to the *intifada* with the Nazis' use of poison gas, depicted the pro-Israel lobby (AIPAC) as more ruthless than the KGB, and, in the words of Edward Luttwak, relentlessly depicted "one small country as the sum of human iniquity": he is a charter member of "the critics of Israel." As for the Jewish-imposed silence of which the "critics of Israel" all complain, it is the noisiest ever known. Their articles appear in the press and their faces on the screen with killing regularity; the royalties from their books continue to be paid, the gravel walks of their villas continue to be rolled. So long as they carry on as "critics of Israel," Buckley need not expend undue labor "in search of antisemitism." (His surprising susceptibility to balderdash on this topic of inordinate Jewish influence is evident in his ready acceptance of the egregious Mike Wallace's accusations against AIPAC for its role in the 1988 Rhode Island election, accusations effectively exploded by the *National Review*'s own expert on Jewish matters, Professor Jacob Neusner.)

Buckley's weaknesses in dealing with antisemitism are usually imputable to lack of a sense of the history of his subject. To say, as he does, that he is not offering a history of anti-semitism, is one thing; to write as if it has no history prior to this century, is another. If he had been alive to precedents, he would have recognized that Buchanan's major blasts at Israel and its "amen corner" did not appear just by accident on Rosh Hashanah in 1990 and on Yom Kippur in 1991. A livelier awareness of the links between old-fashioned religious Jew-hatred, going back to Church Council edicts of the fourth century, and modern antisemitism would also have saved him from such embarrassing utterances as the following: "The anti-Semitism of days gone by obviously manifested itself in other ways [than anti-Israelism], ranging (with Hitler's awful exception) from exclusion from certain country clubs to immigration barriers." More important, it would have made him more keenly aware than he seems to be of the underlying meaning of the fact that Israel is the only country in the world whose "right to exist" is considered a legitimate subject of discussion by otherwise respectable people.[3]

But we should not be overly censorious of Buckley. It is, after all, less important that Buckley should recognize Buchanan as a spiritual descendant of all those (from Origen to John Henry Newman) for whom Judaism "in the fullness of time came to naught" than that he should recognize him, as he does, as a menace to the body politic, and should propose action on the basis of that recognition. Buckley notes in his conclusion that Buchanan's survival, like Gore Vidal's, shows that "anti-Semitism with Israel as its focus is no longer professionally suicidal" (56). Moreover, and this is of crucial importance, Buckley rejects the view that antisemitism should be exclusively the concern of Jews, or that they should be the ones responsible for removing antisemites from the public forum. "It would not have been inappropriate," he says, "for newspaper editors who publish Pat Buchanan to decline to publish those of his columns that touched on Jewish or Israeli questions, pending evidence that he would more carefully observe the civilized distinctions" (62). One may wish that Buckley had arrived at this conclusion—whether about Buchanan or Sobran or Vidal—by a less winding and hesitant path; but when we compare his course with that of his fellow-editors at the *Nation* or the *Village Voice* or *Chronicles*, we may well say: better this way than not at all.

CHAPTER 13

What the
Holocaust Does
Not Teach*

"World Jewry has a special responsibility." This hectoring trumpet call blared forth from the midst of a *New York Times* op-ed piece (9 November 1992) by Flora Lewis entitled "Save Lives in Bosnia." Jews, she argued, had acquired this special responsibility to Bosnian survivors of Serbian camps because their own ancestors had experienced concentration camps; now they had the opportunity "to show that concentration camps provoke the solidarity of victims of persecution." For Lewis, the lesson of the Holocaust is that Jews now have a responsibility to behave particularly well because their ancestors suffered so much persecution. The unstated corollary of this argument (as Conor Cruise O'Brien once pointed out in another context) is that the descendants of people who have not been persecuted do not have a special responsibility to behave particularly well, and the descendants of the persecutors of Jews can be excused altogether for behavior that would be very hard to excuse in other people. That is perhaps why Lewis went on to give specific instructions to Jews to offer Bosnian Muslims refuge in Israel in order to show "that the Jewish state does indeed want to get on in peace with its Muslim neighbors." Since the ancestors of these Muslim neighbors did their very best to choke off Jewish immigration to Palestine during World War II, it follows, according to Lewis' immaculate logic, that

---

Reprinted from Commentary, February 1993, by permission; all rights reserved.

these Arab neighbors should now not only be excused for their recent attempts to keep Soviet and Ethiopian Jews from reaching Israel, but should also be offered this conciliatory gesture (which can be expected to have a mighty impact on nations that have always treated *Arab* refugees like human refuse).[1]

If this seems rather a peculiar lesson to extract from the Holocaust, it is sobriety itself when compared with some that have been expounded by even more nimble interpreters. In Israel, one of the few places in the world where the "special responsibility" of Jews is discussed more frequently than in the editorial pages of the *New York Times,* the new minister of education, Shulamit Aloni, has taken it upon herself to reverse the direction of that country's study and commemoration of the Holocaust. A generation ago, Israel's greatest writers, from Uri Zvi Greenberg on the right to Abba Kovner on the left, exhorted their countrymen to look backward and reflect upon the impetus they had received from the experience of the Nazi murder of European Jewry and the callous indifference of the nations of the world to the Jewish catastrophe, and to consider their responsibility to redeem the dead. "From the promised land I called you," wrote Kovner to the murdered children of Europe, "I looked for you/among heaps of small shoes./At every approaching holiday." Gershom Scholem justified the choice of the Star of David for the Israeli flag precisely because "under this sign [the Jews] were murdered," and "the sign which . . . has been sanctified by suffering and dread has become worthy of illuminating the path to life and reconstruction."[2] In 1970, he predicted that the reaction to the Holocaust, "when it comes, could be either deadly or productive. We hope it will be productive; that is why we are living here, in this Land."[3]

But Mrs. Aloni, the Israeli version of what East European Jews used to call "a cossack in a sukkah," has deplored the stress upon the Holocaust as regressive and nationalistic. "I do not take pictures of the backside of history," she declared on Israeli Radio. "The Ministry of Education must be concerned with the future." Even before her elevation to office, Aloni had frequently denounced Holocaust education in Israel because it taught children that "the Nazis did this to the Jews instead of the message that people did this to people." If Mrs. Aloni has her way in the Israeli schools, then the Nazi murder of the Jews of Europe, a crime of terrifying clarity and distinctness, a crime based on the principle that every European must be able to prove that he is *not* a Jew in order to claim the right to live, will become for young Israelis a blurred, amorphous agony, an indeterminate part of man's inhumanity to man.

Do the ratiocinations of Lewis and Aloni confirm the wisdom of replying to the question of what we learn from the Holocaust with the dismissive quip: "Nothing, I hope"? The late Lucy Dawidowicz would not have thought so. In her post-humously published collection of essays, *What Is the Use of Jewish History?* she returns frequently to this question, most notably in "How They Teach the Holocaust" and "Could America Have Rescued Europe's Jews?" The former, a survey of how the Holocaust is taught in American secondary schools, shows that some American Holocaust curricula have already achieved the condition to which Aloni would have the (puta-tively Jewish) Israeli schools aspire. One used excerpts from *Mein Kampf* not just to show that "racist hatred extends to all groups that are 'others'" but to give the impression that blacks and not Jews were Hitler's primary targets. The most pervasive failure of these curricula, Dawidowicz discovered, was omission of the long history of antisemitism, with the term itself gen-erally subsumed under the generic "racism" and "prejudice."[4]

Dawidowicz never doubted that we study the history of the murder of the European Jews not only to mourn and remember them, but to try to understand and learn lessons from the past. The past could not, however, instruct those who asked it the wrong questions. The unrelenting ferocity of her attack on the historian David Wyman, who in *The Aban-donment of the Jews* asked the question "Could America Have Rescued Europe's Jews?", arose not so much from a desire to defend Roosevelt and American Jewry from allegations of com-plicity in the Holocaust as from a flinty political realism. Not for her the imagined otherwise of what she derisively labeled "preaching history" (176), which made moral judgments on the basis of the *ought* rather than the *is* of history.

The real question to ask, she insisted, was how the country called Nazi Germany could have quickly gained dominion over Europe and readily enlisted both its own citizens and other peoples into mass murder of the people called the Jews. Judicious answers to *this* question, she asserted, would suggest the lessons to be learned from the Holocaust. The first was the infectious power of antisemitism, especially when embodied in the state; the second was the importance of a strong military (for if the pacifists, appeasers, and isolationists had not first had *their* way in England and America, Hitler would not have had *his* way in Europe); the third, "one which every Jewish child now knows" (177), was the necessity of Jewish political power and a Jewish state for Jewish survival.

Those who reject these lessons have a vested interest in opposing study of the Holocaust or distorting its history. Given Shulamit Aloni's insistence that it was not the Nazis who murdered the Jews but "people [who] did this to people," it would not have surprised Dawidowicz (or, for that matter, Gershom Scholem) to learn that Aloni has also blamed Jews for arousing antisemitism in Poland by displaying the flag of the Jewish state at Auschwitz and for other Holocaust-related activities "which create the feeling that we were victims and that we have to be strong." Apparently, the wisdom Dawidowicz attributed to every Jewish child has not yet reached every Jewish adult.

2

Dawidowicz observed that the lesson most frequently taught by high-school Holocaust curricula centered on the theme of moral choice between obedience to authority and following the dictates of one's own conscience. The standard examples used to exhort the students to beware of the consequences of blind obedience and conformity were the invocation of the "superior orders" justification by Adolf Eichmann at his trial in Jerusalem and by Lt. William L. Calley at his court martial for having shot to death unarmed Vietnamese civilians at My Lai in 1968 (78).

No historian of the Holocaust has demonstrated more powerfully how hollow and meretricious are the claims of Nazi criminals that they could not disobey orders without risking the penalty of execution or imprisonment in a concentration camp than Christopher R. Browning in *Ordinary Men*, a study of the role of Reserve Police Battalion 101 in the "Final Solution" in Poland. "In the past forty-five years," Browning writes, "no defense attorney or defendant in any of the hundreds of postwar trials has been able to document a single case in which refusal to obey an order to kill unarmed civilians resulted in the allegedly inevitable dire punishment."[5] Browning's luminously intelligent and finely written book is based on the investigation and prosecution of 210 of the nearly 500 men of Reserve Police Battalion 101 conducted, between 1962 and 1972, by the Office of the State Prosecutor in Hamburg. (About 125 of the testimonies were substantial enough to enable Browning to construct his narrative of the battalion's history and to analyze its internal workings.)

The unit was sent to Poland in June 1942 to murder those Jews who lived in cities smaller than Warsaw or Lodz. Its members were men too old for the German Army, middle-aged family men of working-class and lower-middle-class background from the city of Hamburg. They were also ordinary in that few had had prior military service, only five were members of the Nazi party, and none was an SS member. Ranging in age between thirty-three and forty-eight, all had been molded in the pre-Nazi era, and all were from a social milieu that, according to Browning, had been anti-Nazi in its political culture. "These men would not seem to have been a very promising group from which to recruit mass murderers on behalf of the Nazi vision of a racial utopia free of Jews" (48). Despite these disadvantages, however, these "ordinary men" did very well indeed in their extraordinary task: before they were finished, in May 1943, this little band of brothers had murdered at least 38,000 Jews and sent 45,000 other Jews to their death in Treblinka.

They began their work in July 1942 in the Polish village of Jozefow, about thirty kilometres south and east of Bilgoraj. They were ordered to round up 1800 Jews and, after separating the male Jews of working age for shipment to a camp, to murder all women, children, and elderly people. Before they began, however, their commander, Major Wilhelm Trapp, "made an extraordinary offer: if any of the older men among them did not feel up to the task that lay before him, he could step out" (2). About a dozen men did step forward; they turned in their rifles and were told to await a further assignment from the major. Trapp himself, according to the postwar recollections of some of his men, complained about his orders and wept bitterly; and while he complained and wept his men turned to the task of murder. The battalion's representative of the healing arts offered them expert medical instruction in how to administer a "neck shot" to the victims. At this point, with a clearer notion of just what their work would entail, several more policemen dropped out; others did not take up Trapp's offer until they had killed several people and, failing to master the technique of the clean or surgical neck shot, spattered themselves with the brains and blood of their victims.

Only twelve members of Battalion 101 availed themselves of the opportunity to drop out of the firing squad at once. Most of those who found shooting helpless Jews a nasty, unbearable piece of work dropped out early in the slaughter, but some did not do so until they had murdered 10 or 20 Jews. Ultimately, or so Browning concludes from the (no doubt self-serving) postwar testimony of the policemen, between 10 and 20 percent of those assigned to the firing squads sought release or evaded the shooting by more surreptitious methods. But this means that between 80 and 90 percent of the men called on to shoot Jews continued to do so until the 1500 Jews of Jozefow were no more.

" 'Why did this happen to us?' one of the men asked. 'Jozefow was a home of Torah.' 'It was God's will,' a second answered. 'But why? What sins did the small children commit? They were buried alive.' 'The hill behind the synagogue shook for three days.' " This survivor's account of the mass murder of Jews in Jozefow comes not from Browning's book about the Holocaust in 1942 but from I. B. Singer's *The Slave* (1962), a historical novel about the Chmielnicki massacres of 1648, the most terrible that had up to that time befallen Diaspora Jewry. Set alongside Browning's narrative, how telling and instructive are these few lines! They lend a voice to those who are entirely silent in his account, which includes no testimony from survivors but relies entirely upon the slaughterers for its picture of Jozefow (and other abattoirs in Poland); and for the slaughterers, "the Jews remained an anonymous collective"

(153). The passage also reminds us that one element of the Jews' unpreparedness for Hitler's assault on them was their view of him as another Chmielnicki, a part of the ancient cycle of destruction and deliverance; they had survived Chmielnicki, and they would, they supposed, survive the new Haman as well. Thousands of individuals might die, but could he destroy a whole people?

After the Jozefow massacre, Major Trapp faced the problem of widespread demoralization both in his willing killers and in his shirkers and evaders. Therefore, two changes were introduced in most (but not all) of the battalion's subsequent operations. Henceforth, they would involve ghetto clearing and deportation rather than outright murder; and deportations would be undertaken jointly by 101 and the Trawnikis, the SS-trained auxiliaries from the Soviet territories. This division of labor proved an effective psychological anodyne. Most killing was removed to the death camps, and the worst "on the spot" killing was done by the Trawnikis. Nevertheless, when the time came for the members of 101 to kill once again, they had "matured" into efficient and hardened executioners.

At every stage, Browning stresses, the order police had a considerable degree of choice about joining the killing squads. To some extent, this latitude was a function of the eagerness with which many Germans participated in hunting down and killing Jews. One policeman recalled how "often there were so many volunteers that some of them had to be turned away" (128). Another policeman remembered how news of an imminent shooting action in Lukow moved a visiting entertainment unit of Berlin police to a perfect frenzy of volunteerism: "The [musicians and performers] . . . heard of the pending shooting of the Jews. They asked, indeed even emphatically begged, to be allowed to participate in the execution of the Jews. This request was granted by the battalion" (112). This surfeit of intrepid killers may explain why even Himmler, while insisting that "the Jews shall . . . one day disappear in accordance with the wish of the Fuhrer" (136) and extolling obedience in general, could be lenient with the individual killer "whose nerves are finished, one who is weak. Then one can say: Good, go take your pension" (74–75).

If the members of Battalion 101 were indeed "ordinary

men," then, says Browning, their actions are relevant to all the rest of us who consider ourselves ordinary. "I must recognize that in the same situation, I could have been either a killer or an evader—both were human . . . " (xx). Browning does not lapse into the moral confusion of saying that since we are all potential criminals we should forgive what the killers of 101 did to the Jews. No: we may all be potential criminals, but between the hypothetical potentiality of what one person (or nation) might do, and the actuality of what the German killers of Battalion 101 did do, there remains a yawning chasm. What then, given the relative ease with which one could evade this duty, led some of the policemen to cease shooting, and what led the rest to continue?

Browning notes that even 20 or 25 years after the events of 1942–43 those who did opt out of the firing squads cited sheer physical revulsion as their prime motive, "but did not express any ethical or political principles behind this revulsion." In Browning's view, however, this does not mean that such principles had atrophied. "Given the educational level of these reserve policemen, one should not expect a sophisticated articulation of abstract principles" (74). Is it possible that Browning is too charitable here? Every man can know (and we hope that most do know) the difference between a just and a wicked action. Such knowledge has little to do with "abstract" questions about church articles, sacerdotal authority, apostolical succession. Does any religious system make moral decisions a mystery to be comprehended only by a few persons of sublime genius? Does one need to be Bishop Berkeley to grasp and articulate the meaning of "Thou shalt not murder"? If Browning is willing to believe the testimony of the policemen who claim to have evaded shooting, why should he doubt them when they cite nausea or nerves or colitis as their reason? Most of the evidence he presents suggests that diseases of the liver had more sway than the terrors of conscience over the small number of non-"shooters."

And what moved the great majority of battalion members who did continue with their shooting in the months after Jozefow, often with an appetite that makes one understand anew what Lionel Trilling meant when he said that the Holocaust revealed "a cannibalism more literal and fantastic than that which Montaigne ascribed to organized society"?[6] The wife of one Lieutenant Brand remembered the policeman who reported to her husband one morning in Poland: " 'Herr Leutnant, I have not yet had breakfast.' When my husband looked at him quizzically, he declared further, 'I have not yet killed any Jews.' " One policeman recalled his comrades joking at lunch, which they ate just after a shooting action. "I remember as especially crass that one of the men said now we eat 'the brains of slaughtered Jews' " (127–28). Only the witness failed to find meat and drink in the joke.

In his classic story of an ordinary, representative man, Tolstoy wrote that "Ivan Ilych's life had been most simple and most ordinary and therefore most terrible." How can ordinariness become terrible? Why did the most ordinary of the ordinary men of Battalion 101, the 80 to 90 percent who continued to shoot Jews when they could have chosen not to, behave as they did? In his final chapter, Browning considers a variety of explanations, ranging from theories of social psychologists about obedience to authority, to the persuasiveness of antisemitic propaganda and the pressure to conform.

Of all the explainers summoned by Browning to testify in this belated trial of the members of 101, Primo Levi is by far the most astute. Yet Browning's presentation of Levi's idea of a "gray zone" of ambiguity encompassing both criminals and victims in regimes of terror is somewhat askew and misleading. Browning says that Levi "dared to suggest that this zone encompassed perpetrators as well" (187). That is technically true; but Levi's whole emphasis is on the *distinction* between the Jews and their killers. "I do not know, and it does not interest me to know, whether in my depths there lurks a murderer, but I do know that I was a guiltless victim and I was not a murderer. . . . to confuse [the murderers] with their victims is a moral disease . . . precious service rendered . . . to the negators of truth."[7]

It must be emphasized that Browning is *not* one of those people (Archbishop Tutu comes to mind) inclined to spray forgiveness indiscriminately in every direction but the Jewish one. Nevertheless, the lessons that Levi drew from the Holocaust fit the evidence so skilfully assembled by Browning better than Browning's own conclusions do. Levi, in "The Gray

Zone," recalled how in July 1944 400 Jews from Corfu refused, without exception, to serve in the Auschwitz sonderkommando, "and were immediately gassed to death." This was the true state of compulsion following an order, a rigid either/or, immediate obedience or death. The alleged state of compulsion invoked by Nazis brought to trial "could have been resolved (actually often was resolved) by some maneuver, some slowdown in career, moderate punishment, or, in the worst of cases, the objector's transfer to the front."[8]

Of the various explanations proffered for the compliance of the great majority of Battalion 101 with instructions to murder, Browning favors conformity. This, in his view, played the greatest role because it set "the norms of the battalion" in opposition to "the demands of the conscience" (185). Yet if Browning cannot produce convincing evidence that conscience was at work in the dissenters, how can we believe that it put up much of a struggle in the conformists? Perhaps, as Saul Bellow's fictional Dr. Sammler argued (against Hannah Arendt), "Banality is the adopted disguise of a very powerful will to abolish conscience." Since the Nazi regime had done precisely this, the absence of conscience in individual policemen of this regime was indeed "ordinary." That such ordinariness can be terrible is not a modern discovery. It is inherent in the ancient doctrine that there is such a thing as a national or state conscience, and that judgment will fall upon a sinful nation. When Abraham could not produce ten righteous men in Sodom and Gomorrah, those cities were destroyed by fire from heaven. Something similar happened to Nazi Germany.

3

Browning's book is very much a product of what in Holocaust studies might be called the school of Hilberg. This is not only because Raul Hilberg (to whom *Ordinary Men* is dedicated) was, in 1982, the first person to call attention to the central role of the Order Police in the Final Solution, but because it is based almost entirely on German archival sources and is not about the Jews but about the destroyers of the Jews. When it appeared in 1961, Raul Hilberg's massive *Destruction of the European Jews* was widely recognized as the definitive and comprehensive history of the Nazi destruction process and the machinery of destruction. It was the first study based upon the entire unindexed collection of Nuremburg documents. Its incisive analysis embraced, in addition to those who, like the Einsatzgruppen and Order Police, killed their victims "personally," the huge network of desk-killers, drawn from all the professions, in the German administrative bureaucracy. Thorough as it was in documenting the unique Nazi system of destruction, the book insisted, in one of its many classic utterances, on a continuity between ancient religious Jew-hatred and Nazi antisemitism. "The missionaries of Christianity had said in effect: You have no right to live among us as Jews. The secular rulers who followed had proclaimed: You have no right to live among us. The German Nazis at last decreed: You have no right to live."[9] Not the least of the book's virtues was that Hilberg wrote of the most appalling events in a detached, understated, ironic style, often with a kind of lethal innocence that moved the reader to react far more strongly than he would have done to impassioned rhetorical fireworks.

But not everybody was satisfied. The destruction process was presented by Hilberg from the point of view (in the technical sense) of the destroyers, not the victims. The victims, moreover, were described as having "plunged themselves physically and psychologically into catastrophe." Perhaps the harshest of Hilberg's critics was Lucy Dawidowicz, who in her book *The Holocaust and the Historians* (1981) accused the eminent political scientist of "profound ignorance of Jewish history."

Now Hilberg has brought out a collection of discrete, self-contained essays called *Perpetrators Victims Bystanders.*[10] Much of the first third of the book amplifies (and may depend upon our awareness of) the pervasive lesson elaborated in his seminal study of 1961: that, although it was decentralized, the Nazi campaign against the Jews was a vast interlocking organism involving the ministerial bureaucracy, the armed forces, industry, and the Nazi party, and embracing every component of German life, every stratum of society. Some of the representative chapters tell, with a stress upon individual personalities, how old bureaucrats, new bureaucrats, physicians and lawyers, were absorbed into the organism.

Both the amount and the nature of the attention given to the Jewish victims in the book's second section may serve to blunt some of the criticism of Hilberg's past views on this subject. His treatment of the Jewish leaders, for example, is now measured and relatively sympathetic and "understanding," closer to that of Isaiah Trunk than to the denunciations of Hannah Arendt. His chapter entitled "The Unadjusted" studies four forms of Jewish "nonconformity": suicide, hiding, escape, and resistance. He notes that Jews often had to pass up opportunities to escape because of their responsibility to members of the family who would be left behind. Whether such observations will suffice to mollify his critics it is hard to say, especially since the "old" Hilberg is still present in criticisms of the Jewish councils for desisting from psychological warfare, or in such observations as this: "The rhythm of compliant behavior, practiced over the centuries, was not about to break at the sight of a ditch" (179).

Hilberg says that the chapters of this book are "modules" and may be read "in any number and any order" (xii). That is to say, the book is a small encyclopedia of the Holocaust, but with its departments of knowledge unorganized either by the antiphilosophical principle of the alphabet or by a dominant idea or closely knit argument. Readers will find in Hilberg a reliable and shrewd guide to the main topics of Holocaust research, and one still capable of the cold contempt for the killers and their protectors that has always characterized his work.[11] But the book does not offer a comprehensive, unified interpretation of the Holocaust. For this one would do better to turn back to Hilberg's great book, either in its original version or the 1985 revision, or to Dawidowicz's *The War Against the Jews 1933–1945* (1975, 1985) or to the Israeli scholar Leni Yahil's magisterial and meticulously integrated *The Holocaust: The Fate of European Jewry, 1932–1945.*

In reading Hilberg's new book, we get a sense, once again, of the Holocaust as historical actuality, moral quagmire, theological stumbling block. But for a sense of the Holocaust as the seething cauldron of unedifying controversy it has now become, we must turn to Dawidowicz. The majority of the essays (gathered from the last decade of her life) in her posthumous volume deal with the Holocaust, and their titles alone often indicate their embattled nature: "Lies About the Holocaust," "The True History of Babi Yar," "History as Ideology" (originally "Perversions of the Holocaust"), "Indicting American Jews." More than any other professional historian in America, she was willing, in her work, to dirty her hands in combat with the vast underworld of charlatans who hold forth on the subject of the Holocaust:[12] the deniers of the Holocaust (and their influential friends, including two recent presidential candidates, Buchanan and David Duke); the "functionalist" explainers away of Nazi intentions; the Germanophiles; the relativists; the universalizers; the "appropriators" (who wish to distribute Holocaust suffering more evenly); and the legions of Israel-haters who see the Holocaust as what Hitler called Zionism itself: a way to "slyly dupe the dumb *Goyim.*"

Scholars generally prefer to deal with controversies that involve the fruitful, if often noisy, conflict of half-truths. Dawidowicz set herself the more onerous, Sisyphean labor of rolling back the onslaught of malicious calumnies. She did this partly out of her sense of obligation to restore the honor of her profession, whose derogation of responsibility she had documented in *The Holocaust and the Historians*. The first "revisionist" work on World War II, she points out, was written by the reputable English historian A. J. P. Taylor, whose argument that Hitler had not planned a general war at all "soon became the banner under which a swarm of Nazi apologists, cranks, and anti-Semites rallied" (85). Her fellow historians, by averting their eyes and noses from the mephitic effluvia emanating from the fever-swamps of neo-Nazism or the cesspools of left-wing opinion journalism, thought they could escape defilement. But they were wrong. In 1980, the *American Historical Review,* the journal of the American Historical Association, published a respectful review of a book inspired by the Holocaust deniers; and the Organization of American Historians, after selling its membership list to the *Journal of Historical Review,* the publication of the American Holocaust deniers, was at a loss to understand what it had done wrong. Still later, Dawidowicz found that the foul unwholesomeness was seeping into books published by university presses.

Dawidowicz liked to quote Cicero's laws for historians: "The first . . . is that he shall never dare utter an untruth. The second is that he suppress nothing that is true." But finally it was something more than her loyalty to the historian's ideal that moved her to smite hard and throw back the liars and calumniators. It was her sense of obligation to the murdered Jews of Europe, the very personal lesson she had learned from the Holocaust. Once, when she and I were discussing how indecent, when viewed from the perspective of the Holocaust, was the ambition of the nineteenth-century German-Jewish founders of *Wissenschaft des Judentums* "to give Judaism a decent burial," I said that it sometimes seemed to me that certain contemporary practitioners of Jewish history were hoping to do the same for the State of Israel. She scolded me for being exaggerative and intemperate, but nevertheless added that nobody could write genuine Jewish history without *ahavat yisrael,* love of the Jewish people, and promised to send me a copy of her lecture on this subject. Illness prevented her doing so, but the lecture is now the title essay of *What Is the Use of Jewish History?* Its central message is this: "Some people think that the professional historian's personal commitments—to his people, his country, his religion, his language—undermine his professional objectivity. Not so. Not so, as long as historians respect the integrity of their sources and adhere strictly to the principles of sound scholarship" (19). These monitory words still serve as a guide to learning the very particular *and* the very universal lessons the Holocaust never ceases to teach us.

CHAPTER 14

The Nerve of
Ruth Wisse*

"Ruth Wisse is worth a battalion." This I heard from a graduate student of mine at Tel Aviv University with some expertise
in military matters, being a colonel in the Israeli army. Her
remark, astute in 1988, seems in retrospect positively prescient
as a characterization of Professor Wisse's heroic new book, *If
I Am Not for Myself . . . The Liberal Betrayal of the Jews.* For
Wisse (an eminent Harvard scholar of Yiddish literature and
longtime contributor to *Commentary*) is ever mindful of the
obligations of warfare, obligations that, she contends, Jewish
liberals have dodged: "The defense of Israel against the Arabs,
as against earlier anti-Semites, would require of liberals the
kind of sustained exertion in the realm of ideas and political
action that Israelis have had to manifest in the military defense
of their country. Instead, many liberals sacrifice the Jews to
liberal pieties and find that Israel is no longer a worthy cause."[1]
Ruth Wisse, more than anyone else I know, has shouldered
her obligations in this war, though she is always mindful of
the fact that she is fighting on the North American, and not
the Israeli, front.

Unlike the numerous Jewish critics of Israel's alleged short-
comings who have sought to formulate Israeli foreign policy
and even make and break Israeli governments from the safety
of Oakland or Cambridge, she has always acknowledged the
secondary, supportive role of Diaspora Jewry. The controlling
metaphor of her many-sided discussion of the relation between

---

*Reprinted from Commentary, *May 1993, *by permission; all rights
reserved.*

Israeli and Diaspora Jews is that of the divided Jewish family trying to care for mother and father. Some of the children stay at home while others go off on their own. These parents, especially when they are besieged by illness, are the State of Israel, and the children who stay by their side, that is to say, the Israelis, "are forever on guard. . . . We all dream of a cure or . . . of long periods of remission. In the meantime, however, those in Israel and those not in Israel know which of them carries the heavier share of the filial burden" (115). But it is a paradox of Jewish life, as the Yiddish writer Chaim Grade once observed, that the lighter a burden becomes, the harder it is to bear. This may help to explain why liberal Jews increasingly opt out of the struggle.

The Jews of Israel have been able (so far) to throw back the Arab attempt (begun in 1948 and continued to this day) to destroy the state; but the Jews of the Diaspora have everywhere, since 1967, been in confused retreat before the Arab ideological onslaught against Zionism itself, an onslaught which can claim conquests among the Israelis themselves. Wisse's book seeks to explain why the Arabs have, since 1967, succeeded in turning upside down the world's (especially the liberal world's) view of the "conflict" between themselves and the Jews in the Middle East.

She argues that the master stroke of the Arabs' strategy was to expand their war from the battlefield, where they had failed to live up to their own traditions of military prowess, to the realm of ideas, in which Jews were alleged (mistakenly, it would now appear) to be adept. "Zionism . . . was declared racist because it deprived Palestinian Arabs of *their* homeland" (12). Having refused to admit a Jewish state into a region they designated as exclusively theirs, the Arab nations now accused the Jews of refusing to accept an Arab ("Palestinian") state; having launched several wars, perpetrated countless terrorist attacks, and maintained an international boycott, the Arabs now accused Israel of aggression for defending itself. Beset by guilty conscience for the way they had exploited Arab refugees they themselves had created and continued to treat as human refuse, they now blamed Israel for this condition of homelessness. Their charge that the creation of Israel was a crime against an Arab people acccused the Jews for the very fact of their national existence and thus justified all the physical harm the Arabs might do to Israel.

By inverting the terms of their struggle against Israel, by shifting from the aspiration to "turn the Mediterranean red with Jewish blood" (the battle cry of 1967) to the pretended search for a haven for the homeless, the Arabs were transforming the rhetoric of their opposition to Israel from the Right to the Left, and making a calculated appeal to liberals. The fundamental premise of Wisse's argument is that this appeal has succeeded because when liberals are forced to choose between abandoning their faith in the progressive improvement and increasing enlightenment of the human race, and abandoning the Jews (whose continuing persecution by their enemies seems to call that faith into question), they will abandon the Jews. It will always be easier, she argues, to blame or discredit the Jews, "a very tiny people" (10), than to come to their defense. Since the Jews of Europe were destroyed, either liberalism had been wrong to trust in rationality and progress or rationality and progress had somehow got out of control.

Wisse is by no means the first to remark that liberalism has a "Jewish problem." In 1878 the shrewd English novelist George Eliot observed that, among her contemporaries, "anti-Judaic advocates usually belong to a party which has felt itself glorified in winning for Jews . . . the full privileges of citizenship." Like Wisse, she observed the paradox of "these liberal gentlemen, too late enlightened by disagreeable events," routinely blaming the Jews themselves for the inability of liberalism to protect them. Eliot also foreshadowed Wisse in noting how Jews alone, of all modern peoples, were not allowed by liberals to transfer their declining religious identity to the new "religion" of nationalism: "Why," asked Eliot, "are we so eager for the dignity of certain populations of whom . . . we have never seen a single specimen . . . while we sneer at the notion of a renovated national dignity for the Jews?"[2]

If ideological liberals became unsympathetic to the fate of the Jews because it contradicted their sanguine view of the world, the tenacity of the Arabs' rejection of Israel and their campaign—aggressively pursued in the universities and schools, in the churches, in the news media, in the publishing houses, in the professional organizations—to destroy Israel's moral image was bound to cause the mass defection of Jewish liberals too from Israel. For if ideological liberals in general were unsympathetic to the fate of the Jew because it contradicted their worldview, Jewish liberals had the additional motive of seeking to escape from the negative role in which they were being cast by the alleged misdeeds of Israel.

Why is it, asks Wisse, that there is no ethnic, racial, or religious minority in America, besides the Jews, many of whose members obsessively and as publicly as possible, disclaim responsibility for the alleged misdeeds of their own people and land? Why don't Polish-Americans have an organization lobbying against aid to Poland in the way the Jewish Peace Lobby and New Jewish Agenda lobby against Israel and on behalf of the PLO? Why don't American Catholics negotiate with Britain on the conflict in Ulster as American Jews like the lawyer Rita Hauser "negotiate" with the PLO? The answer is that the more the (famously illiberal) Arab nations and organizations have been able to discredit Israel in the eyes of liberals, "the more Jews outside Israel tried to win back their own popularity by proving their innocence. The paradoxical political behavior of American Jews could . . . be described as the desire to dissociate oneself from a people under attack by advertising one's own goodness" (34).

But it is not only American Jewish liberals who have fallen victim to the Arab war of ideas. Wisse also indicts those Israelis who, under the political pressure generated by the attack on their country's legitimacy, have acquired the habit of differentiating between two Zionisms, the pure and good Zionism of ingathering versus the evil Zionism of expansionism (to .02 of the Middle East). Israel's intellectuals most petted in the West, she argues, are those who in their writings have acquiesced in the erasure of geographical perpsective and obscuration of historical fact that characterize anti-Zionist propaganda and have twisted the Jewish reality to fit liberal stereo-types. Among the Israeli writers who have failed to temper self-criticism with self-respect, she singles out David Grossman, who in his chronicle *The Yellow Wind* incorporates the ultimate Arab improvement upon old-fashioned antisemitism—namely, the transfer of the symbols and terms of Jewish history and national consciousness to the Palestinian Arabs, so that they can "replace" the Jews.

If I Am Not for Myself begins with a letter from the author to a friend who has left Canada (where Wisse herself used to live and teach) to settle in Israel. Wisse then appears to change course and abandon her epistolary structure for a series of discrete chapters about the varied aspects of the liberal surrender to force and betrayal of the Jews to the will of their enemies. Wisse is herself a kind of liberal, but a liberal "tempered," as Matthew Arnold once said of himself in the introduction to *Culture and Anarchy*, "by experience, reflection, and renouncement." For this reason, and because every chapter returns, in its own way, to what she calls "the connecting dramatic link between moral courage in personal life and in politics" (xiii), the whole book takes on a highly personal—or, better, familial—tone, and may be read as an extended, if sometimes brokenhearted, love letter.

Never has a book so relentlessly as *If I Am Not for Myself* unmasked the evasions, the flummery, the toad-eating, the cowardice parading as courage, the abandonment of one's own people glorifying itself as transcendence of Jewish parochialism, that have long characterized a certain species of Jewish liberalism. Never has a book shown such surgical precision in cutting through the cant of "moral strutters" (80) who, by making Israel's existence contingent upon its being a "light unto the nations," licentiously equate the divine election of the Jew to receive the Law with the antisemitic choice of the modern Jew as the prime target of international discrimination.

Nor is Wisse merely "negative" in her approach. She persistently and passionately celebrates the implicit universalism of Jewish "parochialism" as against the repressiveness of universalist idealism; she shows how Jewish nationalism, not Jewish socialism, has been the powerful force of liberation in this century; and she demonstrates how, in contrast to the absurd (and implicitly racist) notion of a *Jewish* socialist or a *Jewish* humanist, the traditional, halakhic idea of a Jewish way of life is open to all people alike, a "tree of life" to those who will take hold of it.

If I Am Not for Myself is a triumph of moral reasoning, a necessary and indispensable utterance on the contemporary Jewish condition, a work of true elegance of mind. How then can it be that another elegant mind—one of the most elegant it has been my privilege to know since we were in college together several decades ago—has excoriated this book as "scurrilous," "perverse," "tendentious," "strident," "unpleasant," and (with hammering insistence) "paranoid"?

The author of this attack, Robert Alter, is, like Wisse, a regular, veteran contributor to *Commentary*. A professor of Hebrew and comparative literature at Berkeley, he has, in his studies of the Hebrew Bible, given us new eyes with which to read the ancient texts, and in his general literary criticism has done much to restore our waning faith in literature as a means of encouraging humane understanding. He has also been the foremost interpreter of modern Hebrew literature in this country, and introduced to American readers many of the Israeli writers attacked by Wisse. He has, moreover, long been a committed, active Zionist (who in 1991 had the distinction of being singled out for vilification by Noam Chomsky's fanatically anti-Zionist followers in the San Francisco Bay Area.)[3]

Yet despite the shared values and Jewish commitments that might have led some to expect a different outcome, Wisse's book touched a raw nerve of anger in Alter, who in his lengthy essay-review in the *New Republic* of 30 November 1992[4] could not find in it even one sentence of redeeming value. He chastised her for indicting all criticism of Israel as "motivated by a sick or cynical complicity with the enemy"; for failing to distinguish between leftists and liberals, anti-Zionist propagandists like Chomsky and "staunch friends" like the sociologist Nathan Glazer; for indicting modern Hebrew literature on the basis of half a dozen texts; for misrepresenting the character of Arab hostility toward Israel as continuous with European anti-Semitism; for forgetting, in her zeal to attack liberalism, that the liberal democracies have not only conferred great benefits upon the Jews of the West but also destroyed the lethal antisemitism of the Hitler and Stalin regimes; and, finally, for flouting the heroic aspiration of Zionism to "normalization," which means, among other things, dispensing with Diaspora Jewry's "pathological" fears about omnipresent enemies. It is precisely to such a pathology that Alter ascribes Wisse's alleged failures of discrimination and balance. He ac-

cuses her of suffering from a deranging obsession which he en-
capsulates in the statement: "Wisse is convinced that every day
is Masada" (28).

This imputation of "Masada"-like paranoia to an opponent
must remind Alter's admirers of an earlier unfortunate episode
in his uniquely distinguished career. In the July 1973 issue of
Commentary, Alter published "The Masada Complex,"[5] an article that was provoked by the columnist Stewart Alsop's accu-
sation that Israel (in the person of Prime Minister Golda Meir)
was, by failing to respond positively to alleged Egyptian "over-
tures," "creating its own Masada." Meir had retorted to Alsop:
"We do have a Masada complex. We have a pogrom complex.
We have a Hitler complex." Stepping back from this confronta-
tion, Alter traced the paradoxical development of the Israelis'
image of the mountain fortress in the Judean Desert where
the last stand of the Jewish rebellion against the Roman legions
took place in 73 C.E.—a rebellion that ended in suicide rather
than submission.

The paradox, he noted, lay in the fact that Masada had
come to symbolize what the Jewish state should *not* be ever
again—that is, faced with the choice between submission and
suicide. The large role played in the development of Israel's
image of Masada by Yitzhak Lamdan's 1927 poem of that
name led Alter to express his unease with the link between
literary and political images in Israel. He granted that the antecedents of political Zionism were literary, but neglected to add
that *all* research of theoretical politics proceeds on myths, and
that, as Lionel Trilling used to say, "the value of any myth
cannot depend on its demonstrability as a fact, but only on
the value of the attitudes it embodies . . . and the actions it
motivates."[6] Alter particularly deplored the application to politics of the poetic process because it is conducive to "cognitive
conservatism," whereas "the political imagination has to be
rigorously empirical" (23). Golda Meir, in linking Holocaust,
pogroms, and Israel's state of siege in summer 1973, might,
Alter feared, have had her political thinking muddled by poetry. That was perhaps why she failed to see that Israel was
by so much the dominant, virtually omnipotent, power in the
region that she could very easily "afford to negotiate out of a
position of strength" (24); and Alter urged "greater flexibility

and more readiness for diplomatic risk-taking than the Israelis
have so far evinced" (24).[7]

Three months after Alter urged Israel to jettison its "Masada" myth, the Arabs, who had certainly not dispensed with
their myths,[8] launched the Yom Kippur War and very nearly
overran the state of Israel. The correspondence about Alter's
"Masada Complex" in the October *Commentary* must have
reached the hands of readers as 1400 Syrian tanks were racing
down the Golan Heights (to be met by a total of 180 tanks
of the omnipotent Israelis) and 80,000 Egyptian troops were
besieging 500 Israeli defenders along the Suez Canal.

Nothing daunted by this misstep, or by second thoughts
about what the Israeli writer Hillel Halkin has called the ethical
indelicacy of American Jews advocating "risk-taking" for Israeli
Jews but not for themselves, Alter has now decided that Ruth
Wisse's mode of coming to Israel's defense is almost as great
a danger to the state as he once thought Golda Meir's siege
mentality to be. He accuses Wisse too of lacking a sense of
history when she sees the Arabs as continuators of the Nazis,
and takes special umbrage at her statement that "The Arab
charge that the creation of Israel is a crime against an Arab
people has much in common with the earlier Christian charge
that Jews denied the Son of God, or that of the Nazis that
Jews polluted the Aryan race" (Wisse, 33). Although Alter
readily grants that the Arabs have constantly "used" antisemitic
ideas in their propaganda, he insists that their hostility to the
Jews is not "rooted" in antisemitism because it depends not
on fantasies but "on observed behavior of the Jews" (31), i.e.,
the modern Jewish settlement of Palestine.

But surely, one might argue, the antisemitism of European
Christendom also began with "observed behavior of the Jews"
before it evolved into something more pathological. As Alter
himself wrote in an article of 1991: "The Jews *did* emphatically
reject the divinity of Jesus, the truth of the Gospels, and the
authority of the Church, just as they were denounced for doing
in anti-Judaic exhortation."[9] The fully developed tree is not
reducible to its root. Even if one believed Alter's astonishing
statement that "The Israeli-Arab conflict is a conflict of two
peoples over one land" (31), one might ask whether the Jews
compelled the Arabs to transform a "normal" political conflict

into an antisemitic crusade, forced them to collaborate with Hitler in the 1940s and with neo-Nazi organizations in the 1990s, forced them to disseminate the *Protocols of the Elders of Zion?*

Alter's charge that Wisse has a "frozen view of history" (because she sees anti-Zionism as continuous with antisemitism) invites not only the strenuous denial which she has made in her reply to his attack[10] but a *tu quoque*. Thus, Alter indicates, quite rightly, that the designers of Israel's military defense and many of her political leaders since the *yishuv* were themselves "liberal" in the broad sense of the term. But his fierce defense of contemporary Israeli liberals and leftists takes no account of how that tradition has changed since the 1977 election, when the Labor party lost control of what it had come to consider its ownership of government to people it viewed as cultural inferiors. During those fifteen years in opposition, the Israeli left built up a terrific energy of resentment against the state, against religious Jews, in some quarters against Zionism itself. The Dayan of Israeli politics is no longer Moshe, but his daughter, the novelist and Knesset member Yael, who runs to meet with Arafat in order to signal her support of sanctions against her own country. The Benvenisti of Israeli culture is no longer the proud historian of Eretz Yisrael, David, but his son, the sociologist Meron, who travels the world to tell receptive audiences that Israel is "the master-race democracy." The Abba Eban who in 1980 could mockingly congratulate George Ball, former undersecretary of state, for appearing on a TV program for six minutes "without blaming Israel for whatever he was talking about" would in 1990 feel no qualms about accepting appointment as George Ball Lecturer at Princeton University.

It is with some trepidation that I venture any criticism of Israeli intellectuals, since one of Alter's most bitterly stated objections to Wisse concerns her criticisms of such Israelis from the left and center, "including many who have stalwartly served in three or more wars and have seen friends and comrades perish in combat" (28). How far, one wonders, is Alter willing to go in extending this exemption from moral responsibility on grounds of military service? Should it be granted to Matti

Peled, a retired major general, after all, who is a long-time favorite on the pro-PLO lecture circuit? Is Alter certain that Ilan Halevy, designated several years ago by the PLO as its Israeli representative to the Socialist International, and the Haifa professor who has made a career out of declaring that "Zionism's original sin" can only be expunged by Israel's extinction, and the Israelis who sign *New York Times* ads calling for "dismantling the state" as an act of "minimum justice" have not done *their* military service? It is one of the great achievements of Zionism that the kind of Jew who in this country ends up as a conscientious objector in the American Friends Service Committee will in Israel serve in the army. But that should not make us forget that there is more than one kind of courage. The Yiddish writer S. Ansky recalls how, during his travels in war-torn Galicia, he encountered one Dr. Shapira, who ran medical services in a village whose Jews were reeling from a Cossack pogrom. He offered her money to take care of them, but she rejected it irately. "This intelligent woman, who exhibited the most remarkable bravery in operating under fire, didn't have the courage to declare herself a Jewess and to defend her persecuted brothers."[11]

Of no group of liberal-left Israelis is Alter more defensive than certain writers, especially the novelists Amos Oz, A. B. Yehoshua, and the aforementioned Grossman. In her chapter on "The Ugly Israeli," Wisse asserts that anti-Zionism now affects even Israeli attitudes toward Israel in precisely the way antisemitism once affected Jewish attitudes toward Jewishness. "Despite the transforming presence of a Jewish country, intellectuals and writers in Israel today, like their diaspora counterparts of the 1930s, try to separate their own 'progressive' desire for an independent homeland from the 'reactionary' desires of their fellow Jews, in order to escape the Arab politics of hatred" (146). She analyzes two stories, S. Yizhar's "The Prisoner" (1948) and A. B. Yehoshua's "Facing the Forests" (1963), to illustrate her argument that what admitted Israeli literature into the liberal cultural mainstream of the West was its tendency to judge Jewish behavior by the severest standards without taking any account of omnipresent Arab hostility.

Of the first story (about mistreatment of an Arab prisoner

by Israeli soldiers), Wisse stipulates explicitly: "I don't mean
to suggest, not even slightly, that this [admittance into liberal
Western culture] was Yizhar's consideration in writing" (153).
Nevertheless, Alter does not so much confute her analysis of
the stories as upbraid her for questioning the motives of their
authors, just as, according to him, she questions the motives
of all her opponents. He shows no interest in her suggestion
that readers of Yehoshua's tale (about an Arab who, with Jewish
help, burns a Jewish national forest to the ground) might have
included the Arabs who, showing that life can imitate art,
burned down the Carmel forest in 1989; but he himself presents Irgun forces as virtually armed with the (cognitively conservative?) verses of rightist poet Uri Zvi Greenberg when they
attacked Arabs in the village of Deir Yassin in 1948.

The chemistry of human motivation is subtle, especially
if we allow for the distinction between conscious and uncon-
scious motives. But numerous Israelis of the type for whom
Alter speaks have been perfectly open about their consuming
interest in being read, accepted, and influential abroad. Avishai
Margalit, the ideologue of Peace Now, stated some years ago
that "an article in the *New York Times* is much more influential
than the same article published here" (*Jerusalem Post*, 10 March
1989). More recently, left-wing Israeli apologists for the scandalous decision to award the Israel Prize to Professor Yeshayahu
Leibowitz (intrepid purveyor of the Israeli-Nazi equation) justified the action as "a special way of telling the whole world
that we are one of the most . . . democratic societies" (*New York
Times*, 5 February 1993).

But something much more serious than the pursuit of
fame or fortune and the gratification of vanity is involved in
the appeal of the Israeli writers to liberals abroad. Alter says
correctly that the Zionist pioneers wanted to "tak[e] control
of their own destiny under the conditions of national auton-
omy enjoyed by other peoples" (32–33). Yet in February 1988
(as Wisse points out) some of his own favorite Zionist exem-
plars—Oz, Yehoshua, the poet Yehuda Amichai, and the journalist Amos Elon—published a strident manifesto in the *Times*
demanding that "all friends of Israel in the United States . . .
speak up" against Israeli policy in the disputed territories. Even

now, when the "moderate left Meretz party" (30) for which, according to Alter, these writers worked in the last election campaign is part of the Rabin government, we read how one of its ministers (Shulamit Aloni) approved James Baker's "Fuck the Jews" eruption as "a legitimate expression," and another declared, after the Bush-Baker downfall, that "Baker was good for Israel because he pressured us to make concessions. . . . without massive U.S. intervention we will be stuck."[12] The desire to escape the consequences of national self-determination by inviting foreign domination may be consonant with "moderate" leftism, but can it really be called Zionism?

The Israeli writer and specialist on Zionism, Dan Vittorio Segre, does not share Ruth Wisse's view that anti-Zionism is an extension, refinement, and dramatization of antisemitism. But he does say that it has a powerful, neurotic logic of its own, "a logic that has inspired a worldwide campaign of hate against 4 million Jews who have created a state on a territory smaller than the island of Sicily."[13] If Segre is right, then the complacent disparagement of Wisse's engaged, passionate attempt to get at least Jews to resist anti-Zionism seems irresponsible, if not worse.

As it happens, nobody has described the danger of a self-criticism that is not tempered with self-respect and political honesty better than one of the writers Alter defends, the novelist A. B. Yehoshua:

> When I saw the depths of crazy self-hatred to which some of my leftist friends had sunk, I started thinking. I decided that I would judge Israelis by the same standards as I judge the rest of the world—not by absolute standards. . . . I'm afraid of this self-hatred, because I know that it can be exploited. When Englishmen or Frenchmen hate themselves—and some do—it doesn't put their countries at risk. They're in their countries unconditionally. Whereas here, self-hatred is always connected to something else. . . . [14]

That Yehoshua himself, who uttered those words in 1987, has so notably failed to achieve the perfection of his ideal should not detract from its desirability. On the contrary, his failure testifies to the extremity of a predicament in which many Jews find themselves today and to which, it grieves me to say, my old friend and intellectual guide Robert Alter has now contributed his mite. But to this same agonizing predicament Ruth Wisse has responded with unmatched clarity and courage.

CHAPTER 15

Michael Lerner: The Clintons' Jewish Rasputin

In May 1993 a flurry of newspaper and magazine articles revealed that Hillary Clinton's crusade to bring the reign of virtue to a selfish and benighted America was to be carried out under the spiritual tutelage of Michael Lerner, the Jewish leftist "thinker," self-promoter, and editor of *Tikkun* magazine, a publication itself dedicated (according to its official motto appearing in each issue) "to heal, repair and transform the world." Lerner, it turned out, had visited the White House to instruct the first lady in "the politics of meaning" and also of "caring and sharing." "As Michael Lerner and I discussed," Mrs. Clinton gushed, "we have to first create a language that would better communicate what we are trying to say, and the policies would flow from that language."[1] To people not beguiled by Lerner, his "language" is redolent less of mind than of pudding and corn-mush. "I proposed that the Clinton Administration establish a policy where, for any proposed legislation . . . there would have to be written first an Ethical and Community Environmental Impact Report . . . to report how the proposed legislation or new program would impact on shaping the ethics and the caring and sharing of the community covered by that agency." "The 1970s and '80s in the U.S. were dominated," Lerner has written, "by this belief that the individual had only him/herself [rather than "the system"] to blame if s/he faced a life that was unfulfilling."[2] (Although a very slovenly writer, Lerner is a diligent gender warden and pronoun policeman.) Insofar as readers could penetrate the

New Age pseudo-jargon that emanated from this odd couple, it appeared that Lerner had promised to distill for Mrs. Clinton the essence of the ethical ideas of the Bible for application to public policy. She had, moreover, proved a ready pupil, one who could say to him, with characteristic elegance, at a White House reception: "Am I your mouthpiece or what?"[3]

Who, everybody began to ask, was the Clintons' new "guru"? Journalists with poor memories or a weak instinct for research mistakenly referred to him as being—prior to his elevation by the Clintons—"welcomed virtually nowhere."[4] In fact, however, he had been a favorite of the news media ever since he began, in 1986, to promote the "Palestinian" cause within the Jewish community, where his name has been a familiar one since the late 1960s, partly for his aggression against that community itself, partly because of his involvement in radical causes generally.

In the fall of 1969 Lerner commenced his open battle with what he likes to call "the Jewish establishment" of "fat cats and conformists" in an article entitled "Jewish New Leftism at Berkeley" in *Judaism* magazine. It included such utterances as the following: "The Jewish community is racist, internally corrupt, and an apologist for the worst aspects of American capitalism and imperialism." "Black anti-Semitism is a tremendous disgrace to Jews; for this is not an anti-Semitism rooted in . . . hatred of the Christ-killers but rather one rooted in the concrete fact of oppression by Jews of blacks in the ghetto . . . in part an earned anti-Semitism." " . . . The synagogue as currently established will have to be smashed." "This anti-Zionism [of young Jews] is irrational in its conclusions [that Israel should be destroyed]" but "I know it to be correct in its fundamental impulses."[5] The publication of his article, which expressed views difficult to distinguish from those of non-Jewish anti-semites, led to the resignation of some of the editors of the magazine (one of whom moved to *Commentary*).

A few months later, in a February 22, 1970, interview in the *Seattle Times*, Lerner predicted that he would be fired from his academic post (as visiting assistant professor) at the University of Washington because "I dig Marx," and that "three years from now I don't expect to be alive. I'm too public a person." At least one of these predictions came true when, on

March 3, the philosophy department voted against renewing Lerner's appointment. Although many students alleged that Lerner used his classes to recruit members for his Seattle Liberation Front (which, he used to boast, was the nation's largest, most active white radical group),[6] and State Senator James Andersen (later a state supreme court justice) said the taxpayers were "fed up to their ears with paying Lerner to teach violence," the philosophy faculty insisted that Lerner was being denied reappointment solely because his qualifications did not measure up to those of other applicants for the two positions open. Lerner, however, disputed the very right of the faculty to make decisions about a Marxist like himself: "It is ludicrous for any member of this department to judge me, just as I wouldn't be qualified to judge a logician." Like his own Seattle Liberation Front, which presented the "non-negotiable" demand that a mass meeting of "the people" be summoned to vote on his reappointment, Lerner accused the faculty of usurping power: "That power has to be taken from them."[7] But neither these threats nor the Bacchanalian protests of Lerner's followers during the philosophers' deliberations (according to the *Seattle Times*, one Lerner supporter, "a small girl in jeans, bare from the waist up, ran back and forth along the table twice while the meeting went on") could save the day.[8]

Lerner promptly announced that "I can't get a job anywhere because of my political views. . . . My own case is further proof that working for change in America through the normal channels . . . is a useless strategy. The only place left for those who want social change is to be fighting in the streets."[9] Two days later Lerner helped to organize a series of demonstrations at the university which culminated on March 11 when his followers in the Seattle Liberation Front (SLF) joined with the Black Student Union to form a combined mob of 1500–2000 that invaded six university buildings and brutally beat at least fourteen instructors and students who did not heed their "strike" order. (Lerner, if we can judge from newspaper photos, remained at a safe distance, bullhorn in hand.) The issue in question, lest one forget to mention it, was indeed a momentous one: the refusal of the university to cancel an athletic competition with the Mormon Brigham Young University, which Lerner had labeled a racist institution because it did not admit blacks to its priesthood. Lerner's SLF declared that "The issue of racism . . . cannot be debated, but must be eliminated."[10] Impatience with debate had already been in evidence in early February, when Steve Weiner, editor of the *University of Washington Daily*, was roughed up for an editorial which campus radicals deemed "racist."

In spring of 1970 (June 2) Lerner sued Slade Gorton, then attorney general of Washington state (now U.S. senator) for libel, claiming two million dollars in damages. Gorton, in a May 13 speech in Walla Walla, had described Lerner's Seattle Liberation Front as "totally indistinguishable from fascism and Nazism." Lerner contended that this remark prejudiced his right to a fair trial on a conspiracy indictment stemming from a 17 February 1970 demonstration in which members of the Seattle Liberation Front had broken store windows and lobbed tear gas and paint bombs at the U.S. courthouse in downtown Seattle. In reply to Lerner's libel suit, Gorton said that "I would suggest to Professor Lerner that if he can't stand the heat of public discussion he may withdraw from the scene." At the end of June, when state attorneys were about to ask for a dismissal of Lerner's suit on grounds that it was "an infringement of free speech," Lerner (sometime leader of Berkeley's Free Speech Movement) withdrew the suit.[11]

Lerner's sayings and doings of twenty years ago would not merit more attention than we usually give to the origins of an ambitious public figure's politics—unless they served to reveal a startling continuity between the Lerner who in 1969 advocated the "smashing" of synagogues and the Lerner who now advocates the cause of the PLO, no mean hand at synagogue-smashing itself. "Our deeds still travel with us from afar," wrote George Eliot in *Middlemarch*, "And what we have been makes us what we are."

In his *Judaism* essay of 1969 Lerner had singled out the journal *Commentary* for special scorn as the instrument of the Jewish "establishment" in league with "the American ruling class," "American imperialism," and "racism" (because it had criticized black antisemitism). In 1986 he came to prominence by founding *Tikkun* as a kind of antimagazine, which took its primary meaning and purpose from the desire to pull down

Commentary (and its secondary one, as noted above, from the modest aim "to mend, repair, and transform the world"). In its first issue the egregious Anne Roiphe sounded the favorite theme of the youthful Lerner by damning contributors to *Commentary* as "Court Jews of the Right" (an epithet that may return to haunt Lerner as he stalks the corridors of the White House). At Jewish conferences young *Tikkun* hucksters peddled anti-*Commentary* t-shirts.

The zeal with which *Tikkun* argued the Palestinian cause within the Jewish community soon made Lerner a favorite display Jew of the news media: a kipah-wearing, rotund beard-plucker[12] of vaguely "rabbinic" appearance who could always be relied on to blame Israel and not the Arabs for the absence of peace, and to liken Israeli defense against Palestinian Arab violence to "medieval Christian mobs . . . organizing pogroms against the whole Jewish community."[13] His denunciatory comments on the *intifada* seemed "perfectly right" to Professor Edward Said, member of the Palestine National Council, adviser to Arafat, and ideologue of terror. (Said was a major speaker at *Tikkun*'s December 1988 conference in New York.) Since Lerner fitted perfectly into the popular journalistic conception of "prophetic" Judaism as reaching its apotheosis in St. Marx and the left wing of the Democratic party,[14] he was crowned by the *New York Times* and the television networks as philosopher king of American Jewry, the ultimate authority on the manifold misdeeds of Israel.

Once the *intifada* got under way, it was hard to watch American television or read the American press for very long without becoming aware that Michael Lerner himself had become, if not quite the Jewish establishment, then the omnipresent, gentile-appointed voice of the Jewish community. Yet his antiestablishment rhetoric remained very much what it had been in 1969–70. Thus, on February 24 of 1989 the *New York Times* afforded him space to hold forth, in a typically self-serving piece, on the way in which the voice of progressive Jews like himself, "the silenced majority" who were "appalled by Israel's brutal repression of the Palestinian uprising," had been "stifled" by the "establishment leadership." Never before had a stifled voice been heard by so many millions, or been trumpeted with such metronomic regularity. In fact, Lerner's *Times* essay was soon reprinted, with some variations, in the March 17 issue of the *Jerusalem Post*.

Now, even more absurdly than in 1969, Lerner pictured himself as both the true voice of the people and a lonely knight, a sensitive soul sallying forth to confront a mob of thick-skinned conformist louts who would eat him alive if they could. Meanwhile, this self-proclaimed dissenter consented to the prejudices of at least half the world in blaming Israel for the state of war forced upon it by the Arabs and for defending itself against the organized violence of the *intifada*. (For good measure, he characteristically suggested (*American Journal of Sociology*, November 1988) that Israel's existence and the tendency of diaspora Jews to identify with the Jewish state were creating antisemitism in the Third World.) After organizing ads in the spring of 1988 calling for Israel to "end the occupation"—typical products of those American Jews who would like to rule Israel from northern California or Manhattan— Lerner told the press that for such an enterprise "courage is necessary," and that he had received death threats in the mail.[15] (Presumably they were being filed alongside the ones he intimated receiving in 1970.) Not content to aid the Palestinian cause in the temporal realm alone, Lerner, in the fall, instructed the *Tikkun* faithful to devote Yom Kippur to contrition for Jewish mistreatment of the Palestinian Arabs— prompting long-time Labor Zionist Marie Syrkin to observe, in December 1988, two months before her death, that "the 'progressive' Jewish magazine, *Tikkun*, recently exhorted the Jewish people to observe the Day of Atonement (remember Yom Kippur, 1973?) with an orgy of confession of 'collective guilt.' What sanctimonious chutzpah if not accompanied by the breast-beatings of far greater sinners!"[16] In April of 1989, when Prime Minister Shamir visited Washington, Lerner organized an ad in the *New York Times*, diligently rounding up the Jewish petition-signers always ready to spill their ink on behalf of those who spill Jewish blood. The ad, designed to undercut Israel's bargaining position, not only ordered Shamir to negotiate with the PLO, but (with Lerner's customary modesty) told him that negotiations must be allowed to culminate in a PLO state.

The invasion of Kuwait by Iraq in 1990 seems to have caught Lerner, like the Kuwaitis, off guard. The standard anti-Israel line was "linkage," as set forth by, for example, *Tikkun* contributing editor Milton Viorst, who told the magazine's readers (January/February 1991) that "the disappearance of Kuwait would not be one of the great tragedies of history," but also that the root cause of the Gulf War as of all other Middle Eastern problems was the "atmosphere of instability" created by the ultimate villain of the region: Israel. Lerner too advocated linkage between Iraq's invasion of Israel and Israel's "occupation" of the disputed territories, but with a difference. In September (see *Washington Jewish Week*, 20 September), "after deep soul-searching," he opposed reliance on economic sanctions against the Iraqi invaders and exhorted the U.S. "to quickly escalate the struggle against Iraq." But he added that, in order to conciliate "moderate Arab allies," American military intervention should be "linked" to a promise "to put massive pressure on Israel to agree to a Palestinian state." In other words, the Arabs should receive huge bribes, paid in Israeli currency, for doing America the great favor of allowing her to defend their interests.

By January, however, Lerner—terrified to find himself dissenting from the conformity of dissent against impending war—realigned himself with the orthodox definition of linkage, opposed the war, urged reliance on economic sanctions, blamed Bush for not acceding to Saddam Hussein's demand for an international conference, and claimed that his position on the Gulf crisis had all along been as constant as the Northern Star.

About two months after the Scud missiles had stopped raining down on Israel, Michael Lerner betook himself and the *Tikkun* entourage to Israel to preside over a June conference entitled "How to End the Occupation: A Strategy for the Peace Movement." The conference manifesto displayed the openness to debate that Lerner had learned in Berkeley's Free Speech Movement and practiced at the University of Washington: "To create a safe space for this discussion, we invite you only if you already agree that Israel should enter negotiations aimed at creating a demilitarized Palestinian state. . . . "[17] The conference's overriding purpose was to recommend ways to disturb what Lerner disparaged as the "quiet daily life" of Israelis, "protected from having to confront the moral outrage of . . . Israeli oppression of Palestinians." Lerner, surveying Israeli life from the (distant) perch of his ethical superiority, had concluded that the Israelis were too much at ease in Zion. Apparently dissatisfied with the little disturbances visited upon Israelis by Iraqi missiles, bombs exploding in nurseries, school, and supermarkets, or stabbings and shootings carried out in the buses and streets, he recommended "bringing the war home" by "disrupting the daily operation of Israeli society" (*Jerusalem Post*, 13 July 1991). One of the best ways of doing this would be for Israelis to refuse to do military service if assigned to serve in the territories. Before the Israeli authorities could decide whether Lerner, a foreigner, should be prosecuted for incitement and sedition, he was back in the U.S., struggling with the unquiet daily life of a prophet (and also claiming [*Los Angeles Times*, 30 July 1991] that his remarks, intended only for "internal discussion," had been taken out of context). Although the conference brochure announced that "WE WILL BE ASKING THE TOUGH QUESTIONS," Lerner and his acolytes seem to have overlooked the distinctly *ethical* (if not very tough) question, of how an American Jew is justified in advocating, and even working to force upon Israel, concessions to Palestinian Arabs that bring risks which will be borne by Israeli Jews alone.

Not long after returning from Israel, Lerner found himself faced with intricate foreign policy decisions. Soon he would have to decide whether he could "dissent" from American policy as readily as he had just done from Israeli policy. The American administration, having failed to achieve the primary war aim of removing Hussein from power, decided to pursue, yet again, the idea of a regional peace conference. As always, George Bush and James Baker could discern but a single "obstacle to peace" in the region: Jewish settlements in Judea and Samaria. Therefore, in the summer of 1991, Bush decided to force Israel, in advance of any negotiations, to freeze settlements by reneging on his longstanding promise to recommend U.S. guarantees of a ten billion dollar bank loan for meeting the housing and employment needs of a huge immigration from the USSR. In his press conference of 12 September 1991

Bush depicted American Jews as an alien presence in the American body politic, a conglomeration of "powerful political forces," "a thousand lobbyists" besieging poor, helpless Bush, "one lonely little guy down here." The president did not hesitate to use the basest slanders of the anti-Israel propagandist's trade. This veteran backroom politician painted American Jewish "lobbyists" as a fifth column in their own country, contriving schemes to steal the Wheaties from American breakfast tables so that Israeli Jews could periodically be showered with thousand dollar bills. He suggested (in a rewriting of history worthy of the Stalinists) that American lives had been risked in the Gulf War in order to defend Israel.

The professional Jewish critics of Israel had, of course, preceded Bush in urging that aid for absorption of immigrants be made contingent on Israel's cessation of settlement activity in the territories. In the *New York Times* of 16 July 1991, for example, David Biale, Michael Lerner's loyal bulldog, recommended that America withhold aid to immigrants in order to pressure Israel to accept Arab terms for a peace settlement. If Bush's statements of September 12 had merely done precisely what Lerner and the other Jewish "dissenters" from the Jewish community had for years been urging presidents to do, their approval of his performance would hardly merit notice. But Bush had done something more than use the immigrants as hostages to force Israel to surrender Judea and Samaria prior to peace talks: he had also demonstrated a keen awareness of, and a still keener desire to exploit, the fact that antisemitism is a light sleeper.

Yet Lerner not only was unperturbed by Bush's cynical exploitation of anti-Jewish resentment; he applauded it. Back in June he had excoriated Bush for suspending the U.S. "dialogue" with the PLO merely because Arafat had been escalating his terror campaign against Jews. But now (*New York Times*, 16 September) Lerner declared his great satisfaction with Bush's action and said that the loss of the loan guarantee, the arousal of antisemitism, and the breakdown of American-Israeli relations were "the fault of Shamir, not Bush." It was, according to Lerner, tough lobbying in Washington by American Jews that threatened to stir up antisemitism. Israel, moreover, was guilty of the sin of trying "to use the Russian Jews to solve the demographic gap." At that moment it must have occurred to Lerner that, at least to unprogressive Jewish minds, serving as a haven for Jews in flight from persecution and striving for a Jewish majority in the land of Israel come close to defining the nature of Zionism and the purpose of the Jewish state. He therefore hastened to assure his interviewer that he was really "very pro-Israel." Despite this claim, he earned high marks from Patrick Buchanan two days later in a column that excoriated Israel and American Jewry in general, but made exception for two deserving Jews: the old pro-PLO warhorse Israel Shahak and Michael Lerner. Lerner's lifelong tendency to play the (fraudulent) role of "dissenter" from the Jewish community (a community that wields no power over, and therefore poses no threat to, dissenters)—had now made him a bedfellow of the Republicans. In March 1992 he was still lauding Bush for "a form of tough love that is actually in the best interests of the Jewish people," and insisting that "he needs to be congratulated and supported."[18] It is not known whether the Clintons were paying close attention to Lerner's statements at this early stage of the presidential campaign.

Although it might at first seem that the man who has now been anointed the Jewish Rasputin to Hillary Clinton bears little resemblance to the ferocious radical who in 1970 wielded a bullhorn, and posed for photographs in front of the hammer and sickle, in fact Lerner merits congratulation for the extraordinary consistency of his first principles (or primal instincts) in the quarter century of his public career. He was, for once, speaking the truth when in an interview of November 1989 (*East Bay Express*) he said: "I've been on the same path all along. I haven't shifted since I was twelve years old as far as I can see."

The mainspring of his career has been the abandonment of his own people when they are under attack, whether by antisemitic blacks or by PLO killers (and their countless apologists) or by unscrupulous and powerful politicians like George Bush; and this abandonment has always come dressed in the long robes of the prophets and "ethical idealism." Now, as in 1969, Lerner blames the Jews—this time mainly the Israeli Jews—for the murderous hostility, the "earned anti-Semitism," of their "oppressed" enemies. His methods too remain, in essentials, unchanged. In 1970, as we have noted, he tried to silence criticism of the thuggish tactics of his Seattle Liberation Front by litigation. In the spring of 1989, I submitted an essay about Lerner to several Jewish papers, including the *Jerusalem Post*. The *Post* and *Washington Jewish Week*, among others, accepted the piece yet never published it. An explanation for its mysterious fate was offered by Susan Rosenbluth, editor of the (New Jersey) *Jewish Voice*, who reported in her June 1989 issue that, in an interview with her, "Mr. Lerner said he intends to sue publications that print Dr. Alexander's piece."

"The child is father of the man," wrote Wordsworth. The 27-year-old Michael Lerner who in 1970 wore a bandana is the father of the man who 20 years later would play with his skullcap before a background of Jewish books for the TV cameras. Still sick with self-love, still dramatizing his courage as a "public person," still blaming the Jews for the aggression of their enemies, Lerner has grown fat on the *intifada* and used the constant burden of peril of the people of Israel as an opportunity for self-aggrandizement. Is it for these efforts that he has been rewarded by being elevated, to borrow a phrase from *Tikkun* magazine, to the status of Court Jew of the Left, or is the first lady really enraptured by his vapid maunderings about the politics of meaning? Let us hope that the sentimentally Christian Mrs. Clinton, whose theology tends to be formed by her politics, sees in Lerner only an exotic purveyor of Jewish-accented leftism and not a Jewish exponent of "liberation theology" who has given to it the original twist of wishing to discredit rather than liberate the community from which he comes and the homeland to which it is attached.

So far there is no evidence that Lerner poured his ideas on the world's need for a PLO state into Mrs. Clinton's ear during their White House meeting of 26 April 1993. But wait— Lerner recalls telling her: "Gee, I have so many things that we ought to discuss." And she replied, "Well, we don't have to do it all today; this is just the first of several meetings."[19]

CHAPTER 16

Noam Chomsky and Holocaust Denial

PART ONE: *The Neo-Nazis and Their Apologists**

Among the various forms of travesty and exploitation of the
Holocaust—relativization, mitigation, appropriation—the crud-
est but also most highly publicized is the outright denial that
the destruction of European Jewry ever took place at all. It
used to be said that Stalinism was a more sophisticated totalitarianism than Hitlerism because whereas Hitler ordered books
to be burnt, Stalin had them rewritten. The Holocaust deniers
are mainly followers, latter-day disciples, and adulators of Adolf
Hitler rather than of Stalin. But since the documents bearing
witness to the systematic destruction of European Jewry at the
hands of National Socialism by now mount into the thousands,
burning them would be a formidable task indeed; and so these
"neo-Nazis" (as the deniers are usually called) have had to
resort to some of the methods of their erstwhile rivals in mass
murder, the Stalinists, in order to clear their political ideal of
the taint of genocide.

Deborah Lipstadt's book, *Denying the Holocaust*, provides
a detailed and incisive account of the antecedents, origins, and
development of Holocaust denial, starting with "revisionist"
polemics against American involvement in World War I and
proceeding through the initial steps taken in France by Maurice
Bardeche and Paul Rassinier and in America by a variety of
Nazi sympathizers starting with Austin J. App. It is to App,

---

*Reprinted from Commentary, November 1993, by permission; all
rights reserved.*

a professor of English at the University of Scranton and La Salle College (Philadelphia) that Lipstadt assigns the dubious credit for enumerating the eight assertions that would form the credo of all subsequent deniers. These "principles," which keep turning up as recycled and repackaged trash in what the poverty of the English language compels one to call the "ideas" of those who engage Lipstadt's attention in the central chapters of her book—Arthur Butz, Ernst Zundel, Robert Faurisson, Fred Leuchter, and David Irving—are as follows: 1) The Reich plan for the Jews was never annihilation, only emigration. 2) The gas chambers never existed. 3) Most Jews who disappeared were under Soviet, not German, control. 4) Those Jews who did die in German hands deserved what they got because they were spies, saboteurs, criminals. 5) If the Nazis really had murdered six million Jews, then "World Jewry" would demand subsidies to conduct research on the subject and Israel would open its archives to historians. (The fact that Israel has, of course, opened its archives is not the kind of evidence likely to interfere with the lucubrations of the deniers.) 6) The Jews who exploit the six million figure have never supplied a shred of evidence to prove it. 7) The "Talmudists" and "Bolsheviks" have so bullied the helpless Germans that they pay billions in reparations without even demanding proof of the allegations against them. 8) The fact that Jewish scholars themselves do not agree in their calculations of the exact number of victims constitutes irrefutable evidence that they lack scientific proof of the occurrence of the Holocaust.[1] Few things better illustrate the fumbling logic of the deniers than this last "principle" of theirs, since it invites the obvious retort: If world Jewry is indeed all-powerful, why didn't it require its paid scholars to be in perfect agreement on their findings? For that matter, as Lipstadt observes in one of her few impassioned moments, the omnipotent Jews who have allegedly forced Washington to cooperate in the Holocaust "hoax" are the very same Jews "who were unable to convince [Washington] during the prewar and war years to liberalize the immigration system, open its doors to the nine hundred Jews on the *St. Louis*, admit German Jewish refugee children, transport refugees on empty transport ships returning from Europe, or permit any more than one thousand Jews to enter the United States during the war itself" (127).

The Holocaust deniers may be devilish, but they have little of the devil's traditional guile or subtlety in promoting their grotesque absurdities. Their iron law—denial of all evidence attesting to the Holocaust—gives rise to methods of "argument" that have been briskly summarized by the French writer Nadine Fresco:

> The basic rule of revisionist argumentation is that all evidence of extermination is by definition inadmissible. A document dating from the war is inadmissible because it dates from those years. The deposition of a Nazi at his trial is inadmissible because it is a deposition from a trial. This is applicable to all the Nazis who were tried. If, as is the case, not one of them denied the existence of gas chambers, it is not because the gas chambers existed ... but because the witnesses believed that if they assisted the victors, the judges would reward them with clemency. As for the testimonies and depositions of some hundreds of Jews who pretended to be survivors of the genocide, they are inadmissible because given by people who could only be instigators or, at best, accomplices in the rumor that led to the swindle from which they benefited.[2]

Lipstadt adopts a similar tone in describing the quaint logic of Northwestern University's Arthur Butz (a professor of electrical engineering). Butz alleged that "the myth of the six million" was based upon the Jews' mass forgery, after the war, of thousands of documents designed to prove that the Nazis intended to murder the Jews, whose diabolical cleverness included the ability to convince "the very people they accused of perpetrating the hoax that it had actually happened" and in "winning the defendants' cooperation in their *own* incrimination!" (131).

So far from being elusive, amorphous, ill-defined, the Holocaust is by now one of the most fully documented events in all history. It would therefore seem virtually impossible for any reputable historian to deny that it happened at all. And indeed no reputable historian has done so. The deniers are a collection of antisemitic cranks, compared with whom the devotees of the flat-earth theory are sober and disinterested scholars. Their ranks include veterans of fascist and Nazi organizations, convicted frauds and libelers, peddlers of electric chairs, pornographers, and similar worthies. How then, given the level of discourse at which they operate and the frequency with which they have been discredited in the courts, do they continue to flourish?

One reason is that the media entrepreneurs and professional communicators are endlessly fascinated by them. In one particularly telling example, Lipstadt recounts the apparent indestructibility of Fred Leuchter, the self-proclaimed [but degreeless] "engineer" and electric-chair huckster who specializes in denying that Jews were murdered in gas chambers. After being unmasked as a charlatan and liar in the Ernst Zundel trial, and declared a fraud by the Commonwealth of Massachusetts, he was depicted by one Susan Lehman in an article on "engineering and capital punishment" in the *Atlantic Monthly* (February 1990) as a great expert on this country's execution equipment. When deluged by protests, the magazine pleaded ignorance of Leuchter's sordid past and protested that its researchers could hardly be expected to know about his peculiar "hobby." Three months later the ABC program "Prime Time Live" devoted a segment to "Dr. Death" (Leuchter, not Kevorkian), despite being informed in advance by Beate Klarsfeld and others of his record of fraud and Nazism and being warned (by Lipstadt and others) that airing the segment would enhance the reputation of this discredited man and Holocaust denial in general. The profile of Leuchter not only was aired, but studiously eliminated all reference to his Holocaust denial activity.

Lipstadt returns frequently to the subject of the eagerness of journalists and especially of TV and radio talk show hosts to give legitimacy to the Holocaust deniers, a subject that, she alleges, ought to concern us as much as the activities of the deniers themselves. She sees this compulsive desire to stage "debates" between Holocaust deniers and genuine historians or survivors as arising not only from the spirit of show business but as part of what she calls "an absolutist commitment to the liberal idea of dialogue" (25). It is this absolutization of procedures (by the very people who sneer at the notion of absolute values) that links the professional communicators to their liberal brethren at the universities, who (inappropriately) invoke the First Amendment to protect the allegedly inalienable right of Nazi Holocaust deniers to run their paid ads or receive free op-ed space in university newspapers. (Lipstadt does, however, note that the dogged devotion of editorial boards of college papers to "free speech" when Holocaust deniers come knocking at their doors flags considerably when they are offered ads for cigarettes or *Playboy Magazine* and disappears altogether when they are censoring the ever-widening range of opinions that have been deemed politically incorrect. One may also venture to guess that a movement claiming that black slavery never existed in this country, or that World War II never happened would encounter some difficulty in placing its ads and expressing its "opinions.")

The reluctance of many in the academic community, worm-eaten with deconstructionist relativism, to reject anything as untruth, or even to acknowledge that truth exists and can be known, is probably a sufficient explanation of the ability of the Holocaust deniers to make their way into the universities (whose manifold imbecilities in dealing with this problem are discussed at excessive length in the book's penultimate chapter). But Lipstadt proposes that it is mainly Noam Chomsky's argument from "civil rights and freedom" that has been echoed by students, professors, and (the sorriest performers of all) university presidents in defending the deniers. Prior to his emergence as an apologist for Holocaust deniers, Chomsky's main contribution to the discussion of Nazism had been his urgent insistence that "what is needed [in the United States] is a kind of denazification";[3] he has also succeeded in producing a book (*The Fateful Triangle*, 1983) in which, as Werner Cohn (whose excellent study of Chomsky and the Nazis[4] Lipstadt seems to have overlooked) pointed out, all references to Hitler are references to *Jewish* actions.

But in 1980 Chomsky discovered Robert Faurisson. Faurisson is a right-wing antisemite and onetime lecturer in literature at the University of Lyon-2, whose catalog of 1978 described him (with comic solemnity) as specializing in "investigation of meaning and counter-meaning, of the true and the false." His guiding dogma is that "Hitler never ordered (nor permitted) that someone be killed because of race or religion." If the

Nazis built gas chambers, it was for gassing lice. After all, did not Himmler himself say that "it is the same with antisemitism as with delousing"? One of his central premises is that the only witnesses to the Holocaust are Jews, and that Jewish witnesses are liars—because they are Jews.[5] This opinion did not prevent him from being adorned by a faction of the French ultra-left with the title of "the Jew," that is, "a man alone" (Fresco, 469), a label that fits him almost as well as "a sort of apolitical liberal," which is the sage Chomsky's description of this antisemite.[6] The lie and "swindle" about gas chambers and genocide, Faurisson alleged, originate with the "Zionists" and victimize primarily "the Germans and Palestinians" (*Vérité*, 89).

Faurisson has vaulted to fame not so much through his jejune publications, as through his good fortune in finding a powerful friend to defend him from his persecutors, that other great ally of the "Palestinians," Noam Chomsky, who came to the defense of Faurisson after his university classes had been suspended[7] and he had been brought into court in June 1981 for defamations of Holocaust witnesses and scholars of the Holocaust. Chomsky promoted and placed his name at the head of a petition supporting Faurisson's "just right of academic freedom" and worshipfully identifying him as someone who had been "conducting extensive historical research into the 'Holocaust' question" and was harassed as soon as "he began making his *findings* public"[8] (emphasis added). As Pierre Vidal-Naquet has remarked, "what is scandalous about the petition is that it never raises the question of whether what Faurisson is saying is true or false, that it even presents his conclusions or 'findings' as the result of a historical investigation, one, that is, in quest of the truth. To be sure, it may be argued that every man has a right to lies and falsehood. . . . But the right that the forger demands should not be conceded to him in the name of truth."[9]

Although Lipstadt assigns considerable blame to Chomsky's "Voltairean" defense of the Nazis' free speech for their ability to penetrate the campuses, she pays insufficient attention to its still darker implications. These were captured succinctly by the aforementioned Nadine Fresco when she commented on the pregnancy of the fact that Chomsky selects as his model the Enlightenment bigot who in 1745 said of the Jews: "You will not find in them anything but an ignorant and barbarous people who have for a long time combined the most sordid avarice with the most detestable superstition," and then added the paradoxical coda: "One should not, however, burn them."[10] Neither has Lipstadt (perhaps because she lacks training in abnormal psychology) tried to track Chomsky down the winding path whereby he moved deeper and deeper into the revisionist morass, arguing, first, that denial of the Holocaust is no evidence of antisemitism; second, that anti-Zionism, too, implies no presumption of antisemitism; and third, in a truly spectacular example of *tu quoque* that he concocted in 1991, that anyone who says that the Jews alone were singled out by Hitler for total annihilation is involved in "pro-Nazi apologetics" (presumably because a genuine anti-Nazi would insist— erroneously—that Hitler wanted to annihilate *all* identifiable groups except ethnic Germans).[11]

At times Chomsky has given the impression that immaculate agnosticism moves him to defend the deniers. In *Liberation* (23 December 1980) he wrote that "I don't know enough about [Faurisson's] work to determine if what he is claiming is accurate or not." In *Le Matin* (19 January 1981) the newly tolerant linguist wrote that "we don't want people to have religious or dogmatic beliefs about the existence of the Holocaust." But we may conjecture that even though he does not directly endorse the claims of Faurisson and the other cranks, he wishes them well in their endeavor; for he believes that to undermine belief in the Holocaust is to undermine belief in the legitimacy of the State of Israel, which many people suppose (albeit mistakenly) to have come into existence because of Western bad conscience over what was done to the Jews in World War II. Chomsky would feel no compunction about joining "right-wing" forces to achieve the great desideratum of delegitimizing the Jewish state.

Chomsky surely recognizes that the underlying motive of the Holocaust deniers, like that of much of his own political labor, is hatred of the state of Israel. Indeed, the crucial place of Israel in the demonology of the deniers is the most relentlessly pursued theme of Lipstadt's book.[12] Almost without exception they claim that the Jews invented the "legend" of the Holocaust because they wanted license from the world to "displace" the poor Palestinians and establish the Jewish state; and they wanted the helpless, defeated Germans to finance the operation. Of course, the neo-Nazis ignore the fact that most reparations money was paid to individuals, and constantly accuse Israel of exaggerating the number of Jews killed so it could receive more German money. In fact, as Lipstadt remarks, since the money Israel did receive was based on the cost of resettling *survivors*, it would have been in Israel's interest to claim that fewer than six million had been killed and that more had managed to reach Israel. App accused the "Talmudists" of using "the six million swindle to blackmail West Germany into 'atoning' with the twenty billion dollars of indemnities to Israel" (95). (The sum Germany paid to the State of Israel was $110 million.)

Denying the Holocaust is a book that was undertaken with great reluctance, for its author was keenly aware that for the deniers there is no such thing as unfavorable publicity. (One of them, Ernst Zundel, said of his conviction by a Canadian court of promoting racial hatred that "it cost me $40,000 . . . but I got a million dollars worth of publicity for my cause.")[13] She began as "an ardent advocate of ignoring them" but after examining their activities closely decided that they will not retreat unless aggressively beaten back. Without according them legitimacy by "debating" them, either in the TV talk shows that have incessantly invited her to do so or in the book itself, Lipstadt has, in her scholarly and dispassionate expose of the deniers' political program, fake scholarship, and fraudulent methods, exploded every one of their claims. Whether her tenacious effort will explode the movement itself remains to be seen. "The wicked," says Isaiah (57:20), "are like the troubled sea;/ For it cannot rest,/And its waters cast up mire and dirt."

PART TWO: *Edward Alexander Replies to His Critics**

The passage of time has done nothing to diminish those qualities of mind and character, that unique blend of propa-

---

Reprinted from Commentary, *February 1994, by permission; all rights reserved.*

gandist's tricks and low cunning, which led Arthur Schlesinger, in the March 1969 issue of *Commentary*, to label Noam Chomsky (who had been forced to confess faking "quotations" from Harry Truman) "an intellectual crook." Only the third sentence of Chomsky's lengthy letter refers to anything I wrote in my review of Deborah Lipstadt's book; but I can readily understand his eagerness to avoid the subject of his prolonged collaboration with the neo-Nazis by ponderous ironies about my alleged campaign against Gypsies, American Indians, and black slaves.

The mind of the propagandist is very much like the spider in Swift's fable (in *Battle of the Books*) "which by a lazy contemplation of four inches round, by an overweening pride, feeding and engendering on itself, turns all into excrement and venom, producing nothing at all but flyband and cobweb." Those who are morbidly curious about how Chomsky weaves his cobweb may wish to contemplate the following. In the May/June 1990 issue of *Congress Monthly* I referred, in the midst of a literary review and with no further elaboration, to "every exploded fiction about the Holocaust—ranging from the notion that not only Jews but also Poles, Gypsies, Communists, and homsexuals were chosen by the Nazis for annihilation." Here, thought Chomsky, was solid meat and drink to batten on at last—the opportunity to project one's own intentions upon the enemy and to claim, as he has done repeatedly since then, that I am the author of "pro-Nazi apologetics." For the benefit of readers who may find Chomsky's vatic insights here a bit murky, I will volunteer my services as logician-in-ordinary to the sage of MIT, who appears to be saying this: "you people who claim that the Jews alone were singled out by the Nazis for total destruction are the true Nazi apologists because a genuine anti-Nazi would insist [erroneously, of course] that Hitler planned to annihilate all identifiable groups except ethnic Germans." There is a kind of logic here, but it is of the sort that Pierre Vidal-Naquet imputes to Chomsky: "When logic has no other end than self-defense, it goes mad" (73).

Chomsky, of course, does not value truth for its own sake, but has now become a champion of the Gypsies in order, so he thinks, (to) *épater les Juifs* by making Hitler into an equal-opportunity destroyer. Neither in the essay mentioned above nor anywhere else have I denied Nazi persecution, sometimes extending to murder, of Gypsies (as well as of Poles and homosexuals). In the case of the Gypsies (Romani), the word "genocide," in the sense defined by Raphael Lemkin in 1943—humiliation, dehumanization, forcible, even murderous denationalization of a group—may be appropriate. But since some Gypsy tribes were protected, since individual Gypsies living among the rest of the population were not hunted down, since Himmler's order of 15 November 1943 stipulated that "sedentary Gypsies and part-Gypsies are to be treated as citizens of the country," and since the Germans used Gypsy manpower for military means, most scholars have distinguished between the Nazi campaign against the Gypsies and the Holocaust, the campaign to murder every single Jewish person. The scholarly journal published by Oxford University Press—*Holocaust and Genocide Studies*—recognizes this distinction.

But distinctions are not the business of propagandists like Noam Chomsky. For him everything must be reduced to pellets of ideology small enough to be ingested by—if I may be allowed to change the metaphor I used above—a discursive mouse. One may see this process at work in his construal of a passage in another essay of mine which has set his febrile imagination ablaze. The passage, as any ordinarily attentive sixth-grader would have recognized, was a paraphrase of a statement by Professor Ali Mazrui of SUNY, and read as follows: "He [Mazrui] argues that the term 'holocaust' should not be reserved to describe the Nazi murder of European Jewry but should 'remain a general metaphor' embracing the oppression of American Indians and black slaves as well." From this Chomsky infers (or pretends to) that by repeating the word "oppression" (from the *New York Times* 21 June 1991 account of Mazrui's statement, I should add) I was somehow denying the existence of black slavery and the persecution of American Indians. One might be tempted to say of this "interpretation" that no human being ever went lower for a proof, but in fact Chomsky's crony Alexander Cockburn, in the 17/24 August 1992 issue of the *Nation*, expressed the identical outrage at my use of the word "oppressed." Whether Chomsky is indebted to Cockburn or Cockburn to Chomsky for this contemptible piece of flummery, I cannot say; but the two working in concert do remind me of nothing so much as the Yiddish expression—*tsvey meysim geyn tantsn* (two corpses go dancing)—to describe two persons of equal incompetence joining their talents. (I did suggest to Cockburn, in a letter that the *Nation* printed after six months of resistance, that he take up—and this as soon as possible—his complaint about my [and Mazrui's and the *New York Times'*] use of the word "oppression" with the authors of the old Negro spiritual that epitomizes the experience of slavery in the words "oppressed so hard they could not stand.")

I am greatly relieved that Michael McClain, after mental struggle, has concluded that he could not "honestly say that the . . . Holocaust never occurred." If he "seriously doubts" that Holocaust denial appears in PLO publications, let him consider the following: In 1990, the PLO weekly, *El Istiqlal*, published a series of articles denying the Holocaust. One declared that "the burning of the Jews in the Nazi chambers is the lie of the 20th century . . . the gas chambers would have had to operate for 1300 years in order to burn six million Jews." In the same year, *Balsam*, the publication of the PLO-affiliated Palestinian Red Crescent, called the existence of Nazi gas chambers "a Jewish hoax to bilk money for Israel from Germany." I leave it to Mr. McClain to decide whether the Palestinian cause has now been tainted by "liars and wilfully blind idiots." Since the Palestinian Arabs have long aspired to usurp the role of Jews and to appropriate Jewish symbols and Jewish history—"the Arab diaspora," the PLO "covenant," the Arab *Exodus* ship, the United Palestine Appeal—how could they possibly do without a Holocaust, even a second-class one, involving refugee status, not death? McClain may want to suggest to the conjectural scholar who writes *Denying the Nakba* that he ask the Arab nations who brought about the Palestinian Arab catastrophe of 1948 to underwrite his research as a small act of contrition.

Like his hero Chomsky, Patrick O'Hayer prefers to deal with a nonissue—Deborah Lipstadt does not ever say that Chomsky supports Holocaust denial "as a fact"—rather than with the scandal of his promotion of a petition riddled with falsehoods and his collaboration with Robert Faurisson and other antisemites and Nazis. When Vidal-Naquet learned, in 1979, that Chomsky was writing a preface to Faurisson's *Mémoire en Defense*, he warned his fellow-leftist that Faurisson was a long-time, well-known antisemite. This did not prevent Chomsky from going ahead with his preface or from affixing to Faurisson the inane label: "a sort of apolitical liberal." When he was taken to task for referring in the petition to the "findings" that resulted from Faurisson's "historical research," Chomsky had the gall to claim that Frenchmen with imperfect English did not understand that "findings" means "conclusions" rather than "discoveries." As I remarked in my review, Faurisson's right to teach was not withdrawn; neither was he, as the petition falsely claimed, denied access to public libraries and archives. The only important sense in which Chomsky's involvement with the Nazis concerns free speech is that, as everybody knows, Chomsky has a nasty habit of labeling all who disagree with him as enemies of freedom or (in my case) "some Mullah of Qom." Vidal-Naquet suggests in his book that Chomsky's zeal on behalf of Faurisson is unlikely to cool until the French republic passes a law requiring that his works be read in public schools and advertised and sold at the entrance to synagogues.

John Zimmerman's letter about the similarity between Chomsky's apologetics for the Khmer Rouge and the methods of the Holocaust deniers may remind us of a controversy of 1984 that shed light on Chomsky's idiosyncratic idea of free speech. In an article in *New Criterion* (October 1984) called "Censoring 20th-Century Culture: The Case of Noam Chomsky," the British linguist Geoffrey Sampson recounted what happened after he had written in the English *Biographical Companion to Modern Thought* that "Chomsky forfeited authority as a political commentator by . . . repeated polemics minimizing the Khmer Rouge atrocities in Cambodia and endorsement of a book that denied the Holocaust." Chomsky, displeased, prevailed upon the American publisher to expunge Sampson's remarks from the American (Harpers) edition of the work. By way of explaining how this act of censorship comported with his passionate devotion to the free speech of Nazis, Chomsky averred that "With regard to a book, readers can form their own conclusions. But an entry in a reference work is something quite different" (letter to *New Criterion*, January 1985). As Werner Cohn acidly remarks: "Chomsky does not revoke his principle of absolute freedom of expression for everyone. It's just a matter of a little exception that he finds necessary . . . " (16)—the little exception, of course, being the truth about himself.

CHAPTER 17

Israel's Embrace of the PLO: The Beginning of the End?

> We are at the beginning of the end. . . .
> —Shimon Peres, 21 April 1994

On 9 September 1993 Yasser Arafat sent a letter to Yitzhak Rabin in which he promised (precisely as he had done in a Geneva press conference in 1988) to renounce terror ("assuming responsibility over all PLO elements and personnel in order to assure their compliance") and to recognize Israel's right "to exist in peace and security."[1] This brief letter constitutes the entire basis upon which Israel declared that there is a new PLO. The text of the lengthy "Declaration of Principles," as numerous commentators have stressed, consists only of *Israeli* commitments to satisfy PLO demands: there is no mention of the PLO eliminating its Covenant or its "phased plan" for Israel's destruction, or halting the intifada. In the Declaration, Israel agrees that elections in the West Bank and Gaza Strip will "constitute a significant interim preparatory step toward the realization of the legitimate rights of the Palestinian people and their just requirements."[2] On the very same day that he signed the Declaration in Washington, Arafat told Jordanian TV (as he had already told students at Nablus's Najah University on September 1) that he was now implementing the "phased plan." By contrast, Yitzhak Rabin, about a month later, admitted that "When we signed the agreement with the PLO . . . I never thought there would be so many problems," an admission which prompted Hillel Halkin to write: "Oslo was a mistake because it violated a simple axiom of doing business that no first-year lawyer would dream of ignoring, namely: Never put your name on a contract that does not spell out the details of the deal, because once you sign it, it is too late to back out."[3]

Why did the Labor government that was elected in 1992 decide to enter into an agreement with the PLO and Yasser Arafat that would surrender to the world's leading Jew-killing organization control of the disputed territories of Judea and Samaria, control that will almost certainly lead to an independent PLO state there? Why did it agree to a preamble to the Declaration of Principles which speaks of the "mutual legitimate and political rights" of the two sides, thus putting Israel and the PLO on equal footing and sending a message to the world that terrorism does indeed pay and that war criminals need not be brought to justice if it seems politically inexpedient to do so?[4] Why did Rabin sign an agreement which will add, before the interim period concludes, close to half a million refugees from the 1967 war to the two million people who already inhabit the territories that will become the new state of Palestine and very likely another million from the "refugee camps" in Lebanon, Jordan, and Syria after that? Why does the agreement include Jerusalem as an issue to be raised at the permanent-status negotiations due to start "as soon as possible, but not later than the beginning of the third year of the interim period"? Why did the Israeli government choose retroactively to condone the hundreds of acts of unspeakable terror against Jews, not only in every part of Israel—have we already forgotten the schoolchildren of Ma'alot, the mothers and babies of Kiryat Shemona, the women of Kibbutz Shamir?—but all over the world, in synagogues in Istanbul, Paris, Vienna, Antwerp, Copenhagen, and Rome, at the Munich Olympics, at restaurants in Paris, airports in Germany and Italy, airplanes everywhere? Did Rabin and his colleagues weigh the loss to Israel's moral character of its hard-won reputation as the one nation in the world that would not cave in to terrorism?[5] Why, during the Oslo talks, was there a total absence of any consultation between Israel's negotiators and the Israeli military? As Yigal Carmon, the reserve colonel who served as Adviser on Countering Terrorism to both Prime Minister Shamir and

Prime Minister Rabin, observed in *Commentary* (March 1994), "The Israelis were there for one of the most momentous diplomatic moves in the history of their country without having consulted a single military authority, a single intelligence officer, or a single expert on Arab affairs."

Yitzhak Rabin had campaigned in 1992 on a platform of uncompromising national strength, and (paradoxically) much of his support among the electorate derived from the fact that Shamir had chosen him as the person best suited to control the *intifada* with a firm hand. In his campaign, Rabin promised that there would be no negotiations with the PLO,[6] no Palestinian state, no concessions on the Golan Heights; he also promised to preserve a united Jerusalem under Israeli sovereignty as Israel's capital, and to protect the 136,000 residents of the Jewish cities, towns, and villages in the territories of Judea, Samaria, and Gaza. It is now evident to everyone that these promises were utterly cynical campaign ploys, designed to build on Rabin's reputation as the 1967 liberator of Jerusalem, which according to his stream of the Labor party as well as to their Likud opponents, was to remain unified as the capital of Israel for all time. The organizers of the Labor party's electoral campaign did their best to keep Shimon Peres, the party's most prominent dove, well out of view. It is unlikely that more than a tiny portion of Israelis who voted for Labor anticipated that after the election Rabin would, under the influence of Peres (his longtime rival), renege on every one of his promises and even adopt a rhetorical style which made it hard to distinguish his utterances from those of the extreme, even anti-Zionist, left in Israeli politics.[7]

Rabin would later fail to make good on several other commitments of a different, far less public sort: One was that the peace agreement with the Palestinian Arabs would be signed by the official delegations to the peace talks in Washington, which of course did not formally include the PLO. As late as 15 August 15, five days before the Declaration of Principles was initialed in Oslo, Rabin said that he hoped the Israeli leftists in his cabinet would not undermine Washington's policy of not dealing with the PLO. But the head of the Palestinian delegation in D.C., Haidar Abdel Shafi, acting under PLO orders, refused to sign. Rabin succumbed, for otherwise (as

Carmon has pointed out) he would have faced political disaster in Israel for violating his vow (to say nothing of Israeli law) by dealing with PLO-Tunis and having nothing to show for it. Now that the PLO was officially involved, the plan was to have the agreement signed by the PLO's Abu Mazen and Peres at the State Department in Washington. But Arafat decided that he must appear at the White House, and Clinton thought this a wonderful idea. Although Rabin had insisted that he would not fly to Washington to put himself on an equal level with Arafat in the signing ceremony, Christopher had only to phone him at six on a Saturday morning, and he succumbed at once. Then, having consented to come to Washington, Rabin determined not to shake hands with the world's leading terrorist, but Arafat decided that handshaking was mandatory, informed Clinton of this, and so the deed was done. As a consolation, Israel was promised that Arafat would not wear his military uniform at the signing. He did, but the Israelis decided to refer to it in their communiqués as "a green suit." All of these incidents were symbolic expressions of the fact that, as the political analyst Dore Gold has pointed out, the PLO knows where it is going, and Israel does not. The dovish Israeli journalist Hirsh Goodman, who supports the pact with Arafat, reported his astonishment after a conversation with the "four architects" of the plan that took place a week before the scheduled (and then postponed) pullout from Jericho and Gaza. The plan's architects, he said, "do not have the slightest idea of where we are heading or why." He left the meeting "utterly confused and dejected, fearful that we are marching along an unplanned, ill-conceived path that will only exacerbate the status quo."[8]

The PLO knows that it will have a state in Judea, Samaria, and Gaza well before the end of the interim period and that, somewhat later, it will control the eastern part of Jerusalem. Israel either does not know this, or pretends not to know it—even though the more candid members of the Cabinet or the secretary general of the Labor Party Nissim Zvilli openly declare, from time to time, that—as Zvilli said on 13 February 1994—the Palestinians will have their own state by the end of the decade (and Syria will be given sovereignty over the entire Golan Heights). Moreover, the Meretz faction of the government coalition, one of whose members, Environment Minister Sarid, is a senior negotiator, is openly in favor of a PLO state; and the irrepressible Deputy Foreign Minister Beilin has already proposed giving the PLO authority over parts of East Jerusalem, even as Rabin insists the city will not be divided. How sovereignty can be shared without dividing the city, or how the establishment of a Palestinian capital in Jerusalem can fail to convince the Arabs that their state of Palestine will eventually subsume the state of Israel has yet to be explained.

Peres himself, on the day the "mutual recognition" was announced, declared the Government of Israel had not changed its position at all: "We haven't changed—it changed," he insisted, referring to the PLO. "Arafat is announcing that he opposes terrorism and will fight the terrorists. He recognizes Israel and its right to exist in peace."[9] Apparently, Peres had never noticed that Arafat had already undergone this change several times, ever since he learned, with the help of various self-appointed American emissaries, to read George Shultz's lips in Geneva in 1988. Nevertheless terrorism had continued unabated, with the great majority of terrorist acts—right up to the time of Oslo—being committed by the PLO itself; indeed, it will be recalled that the American government had been forced to break off its talks with the PLO when it became clear that Arafat's organization continued to support and carry out terrorist attacks. Not the least important result of the Israel-PLO handshake is that it has forced the American government to give up any serious attempt at curbing Arab terrorism.[10]

Of all the respects in which the current Israeli government's "peace process" has been likened to the mental operations of the inhabitants of that fictional capital of Jewish folly named Chelm, none is more startling than its policy of concocting apologias for the continued terrorism of Arafat's PLO and its allies. True, Rabin did (early in February 1994) reluctantly admit that the Fatah Hawks—the military arm of Arafat's own organization—had "returned" to full-scale activities against Israeli targets, but insisted that this was not Arafat's fault or responsibility because these Hawks do not cooperate with their leaders. But all the evidence points to collusion between PLO leaders and their followers, as between the PLO and Hamas. In any case, these leaders have openly called for continuation of the *intifada*, and blamed all acts of terrorism on Israeli actions against wanted terrorists. Nor has a single Fatah leader, from Arafat down, condemned in a public appearance the actions of Fatah Hawks, or any other terrorists, against Israelis and fellow Arabs. Israel has been willing not only to ignore PLO violations of written and unwritten commitments, but to justify them. David Bar-Illan has maintained that it is as if the government's stake in the public relations success of the agreement makes keeping its provisions a minor consideration: indeed, one wonders if there is anything at all which Rabin and Peres expect of the PLO. Peres declared in late May 1994 that "I don't think we should judge the process by the performance of Yasir Arafat. We're not negotiating with Yasir Arafat. We're negotiating with ourselves—about what sort of people we want to become."[11] After investing much rhetorical energy in persuading the Israeli public that a deal with the PLO was the only way to defeat Hamas, Rabin, faced by indisputable evidence of collusion and division of labor between the PLO and Hamas,[12] decided to support the PLO's efforts to cooperate with the allegedly intransigent fundamentalists.

One widely cited reason for Israel's embrace of the PLO in the Oslo agreement that produced the Declaration of Principles was that the Madrid negotiations were going nowhere, and that—as many Israelis who are very far from being leftists are wont to say—"we had to do something, there was no alternative. We could not go on in this way." Such an explanation virtually admits exhaustion as a motive for the agreement, and none of us who live outside of Israel should underestimate the force of this exhaustion. Israel has lived in a permanent siege since its beginnings in 1948. A constant burden of peril, the unrelenting hatred of their neighbors (and of many of the Arabs within the borders of the state itself), the crushing burden of military service (until age 55), the ever-enlarging military cemeteries: who can doubt that the citizens of Israel are tired? But is it really true that the solution chosen in Oslo—that is to say, acceptance of a Palestinian state on the 1949 armistice lines (with minor adjustments) and the resultant uninterrupted, radical, Arab-Muslim mass from Pakistan to the outskirts of Tel Aviv, and surrender of the natural barriers of the Golan Heights and the Judea-Samaria Mountains—was the only alternative to the Madrid-formula negotiations? Or is it in fact the worst alternative of all? Oslo is a distinct departure from the Camp David accords, not a broadening of them. Camp David had no territorial jurisdiction attached to the autonomous council envisioned for Palestinian Arabs; Camp David did not, like Oslo, specify all the standard features of a government—legislative, executive, and judicial; Camp David did not, like Oslo, require return to the 1949 armistice boundaries; Camp David did not, like Oslo, bring up the question of Jerusalem. Whatever the Oslo Declaration of Principles is, it is not an extension of Camp David.

David Bar-Illan, writing in *Commentary* in February 1994 (Letters) pointed out that the Madrid-formula negotiations between Israel and its neighbors had not broken down, even though they were not speeding along to easy success. The Shamir government had, however, achieved something that had been considered both highy desirable and virtually impossible since the founding of the state: direct, bilateral talks with Syria, Lebanon, and Jordan, and with a Palestinian delegation representing only the Arab inhabitants of Judea, Samaria, and Gaza. Neither the Jerusalem Arabs nor the Palestinian exile groups—such as the PLO in Tunis—were represented. This meant that both the Arabs of Palestine and the Arab regimes were agreeing to negotiate without the PLO, which stands for Palestinian statehood and the "right of return" for Palestinian refugees, both of them formulas long assumed, by Labor as well as Likud, to be code words for the end of Israel.

Of course the Arabs constantly created impasses in the Madrid negotiations, knowing as they do that they could always count on international pressure to be mobilized against Israel, as well as on the support of world opinion, to say nothing of free-lance spokesmen of the Israeli left, ever eager to offer "concessions." (It does not require keen powers of observation to notice that the PLO has constantly created impasses even in the many months of discussion that have followed the handshake of September 1993.) Shamir's government could have hastened the negotiating process by making concessions that all Israeli governments until the present one considered suicidal, but it did not. That exclusion of Arafat from negotiations reduced his support in the administered territories. Indeed, Arafat and his organization were nearly finished off—partly as a result of his support of Saddam Hussein in the Gulf War—when they were rescued by Rabin and Peres. Had the Madrid negotiations been allowed to take their natural course, the PLO would have become irrelevant and talks with representatives of the local Arab population in the territories *might* have proved fruitful. (Indeed, Rabin himself had long taken the position that Israel could and should reach an understanding only with the local inhabitants, not with the PLO.) Of course such negotiations would have dragged on, but if, as Bar-Illan says, the U.S. could take fourteen years to settle the dispute over the Panama Canal, surely Israel might have been allowed fourteen months to secure the future of its people. True, the talks might have failed and left Israel to live with the status quo. But in the months that have elapsed since the Arafat-Rabin handshake, months of increased bloodshed, Arafat has made good neither on his promise to control his terrorist bands nor on his central commitment to alter the PLO covenant. According to Shimon Peres, in his book *The New Middle East*, Israel's most important condition for recognition of the PLO was "that the PLO nullify the 33 articles of the Palestinian covenant, which call for, directly (twenty-eight) or by implication (five), the destruction of Israel."[13] It is, then, only too clear that the claim that nothing could be worse than the status quo is absurd.

We also now have a situation unprecedented in Zionist history. The Jewish national anthem is "Hatikvah"—hope; and Jews have long been the people of hope, but of hope in their own capabilities. Now, as Ruth Wisse has aptly put it, for the first time, Jews are asked to place their hope and trust in others, and most especially in Yasser Arafat, who during the Gulf War had sent his followers marching through the streets of the territories to chant: "Saddam, you hero, incinerate Israel with poison gas!" and who in a Johannesburg mosque in May 1994 called for a *jihad* (holy war) to liberate Jerusalem from the Jews, a call quickly interpreted by the ever-nimble Peres as a call for a peaceful, "friendly" *jihad*.[14] Beyond that, Israelis are asked to place their hope—though one wonders why, if Rabin and Peres really believe that their enemy has "changed" overnight—in American troops on the new borders.

Although the political forces, psychological pressures, and historical circumstances that drove Israel to embrace the PLO in 1993 cannot be reduced to the psychology of two men, neither can that fateful decision be understood without examining the guiding ideas of the two chief designers of what has come to be called the peace process: foreign minister Shimon Peres and his deputy Yossi Beilin.

One wonders whether, in the history of diplomacy, there has ever been a phenomenon comparable to Shimon Peres (who himself boasts that "the peace process is unprecedented, unlike anything else in the world"). Officially and ostensibly the foreign minister of Israel, he generally speaks as if he were actually the foreign minister of his region or even of the Arab countries in particular, or perhaps the hired defense attorney for Yasser Arafat, protecting him against accusations of murder and treachery hurled by the benighted citizens of Peres' own country. In public forums he stresses the need to "close the income gap" between Israel and the Arab nations (which include several with the highest per capita income in the world), and avidly appeals for cash for the PLO and its burgeoning army (euphemistically called "Palestinian police"). All evidence that Arafat pays not the slightest attention to any of the (meager) obligations he accepted is greeted by Peres with the rote response that words are unimportant, that pursuing the peace talks is the paramount issue, that "all the rest does not count."[15]

Included in "all the rest" for Peres is any semblance of probity in dealing with his own countrymen. For many months following the Washington handshake, the opposition parties in Israel asserted that there were secret documents in which the Israeli government had given the PLO certain assurances about its institutions and rights in Jerusalem. Peres and Rabin steadfastly and stridently rejected all such allegations. But suddenly, in June 1994, after Arafat himself had boasted such a letter existed, the government was forced to acknowledge that Peres had in fact written the letter in October 1993 to prevent negotiations with the PLO from breaking down. Nothing daunted by the revelation that he had written a letter referring to "East Jerusalem" as a separate entity even as he (and Rabin) were proclaiming their intention to keep Jerusalem united under Israeli sovereignty, Peres said he had not really lied about the letter, since it was not written directly to Arafat but sent to the late John Jorgen Holst, then Norwegian foreign minister who had helped arrange the 1993 Israeli-PLO agreement.[16]

When, early in 1994, President Clinton nominated Strobe Talbott, former *Time* magazine writer and longtime warrior against the state of Israel, to be deputy secretary of state, it was not Peres and the Israeli foreign office that opposed his nomnination, but numerous U.S. senators long friendly to Israel, the Zionist Organization of America, and the National Jewish Coalition. Senators Mack of Florida and D'Amato of New York pointed out (what everybody familiar with Talbott's record knew very well) that his writings "go beyond common criticisms to a systematic attack upon the foundations of America's close relationship with Israel." Senator Biden also recalled Talbott's more conventionally antisemitic remarks about how American Jews had power in their country far out of proportion to their numbers. But none of this troubled Peres or his lieutenants in the least. They indicated that they had no objection to Talbott, and his nomination was approved, putting him in line to succeed Warren Christopher as secretary of state. Something very similar happened when the UN was considering a condemnation of the Hebron massacre which would include a reference to East Jerusalem as part of the "occupied territories." The U.S. Senate unanimously passed a call urging a veto of the resolution, but Peres and his government preferred to collude in their own condemnation by the UN and opposed a veto, claiming—as always—that the delicate, exotic plant known as the peace process would be endangered by a veto. Little wonder, then, that on May 24, in the Presidential Ballroom of the Capital Hilton, a dinner sponsored by a kind of Who's Who of Israel's longtime enemies in the United States (Council for the National Interest; Arab-American Institute; American Near East Refugee Aid; National Association of Arab-Americans; Institute for Policy Studies) presented its Pax World Peace Award to none other than Shimon Peres.

Although Peres' actions seem inconsistent with his official position, they follow logically from his words, a superabundant cornucopia of folly and ignorance. He has repeatedly declared that in Israeli negotiations with the PLO "there is nothing the Palestinians could give us. We just have to decide what we want to give them"; he has insisted, most notably during the Cairo negotiations of February 1994, that Israel must not press its claims so forcefully as to "embarrrass" Arafat; in the same month he averred that cable television is a much greater threat to Israeli youth than the surrounding Arab armies or local terrorists—a claim that sounds almost ghoulish in light of the enormous upsurge in terrorist killings of Israelis since "peace" was made with the PLO.[17] In a display before Barbara Walters, early in February 1994, he said: "If I were in Arafat's party, I would not vote for him. He is a leader who belongs to the past. He believes in nationalism, not in economics."[18] Thus, about a quarter of a century after it became obvious that Arafat was a fanatically devoted nationalist, not a devotee of Adam Smith and the free market, Shimon Peres announced a revelation. And if he had had this revelation six months earlier, would he not have gone ahead with the handshake and the Declaration of Principles? Even now, to talk of "voting" in the context of "Arafat's Party" suggests a naivete about the political character of the PLO—does anybody other than Peres really believe it is a democratic body?—that should strike fear into anyone with Israel's well-being at heart. The remark reveals not only ignorance, however, but also arrogance—let us call it, perhaps, the arrogance of ignorance. By projecting his vision of "economic Zionism" onto the PLO, he seems to be convinced that all that is needed to eradicate fundamentalist fanaticism, nationalist extremism, and the endemic terrorism of the Palestinian Arabs is the promise of Volvos, villas, and VCR's. Alas, one of the elementary facts of Jewish history is that economic relations are not equivalent to political recognition. (But who expects knowledge of Jewish or any other history from a man who could tell the UN in May 1994 that the Nazi Holocaust and the American dropping of atomic bombs on Japan were "twin Holocausts," morally equivalent, because "nuclear bombs are like flying holocausts"?[19]

Peres's recent book shows his inability to imagine that the Arabs are motivated by anything apart from improving their economic condition. He imputes Arab fundamentalism to poverty—"In frustration . . . these people have turned to mysticism and otherworldliness" (38)—and the Arab-Israel conflict, even though any reader of newspapers knows that Hamas fundamentalist leaders are overwhelmingly members of the professional classes, doctors, lawyers, teachers; moreover, the greatest success of fundamentalism has been in Iran, relatively wealthy and very distant from the conflict. Peres' belief in the benign effects of Western investment in the Middle East is a superstition based on no evidence at all. The U.S., as Rael Isaac has pointed out,[20] has put $20 billion into Egypt since its treaty with Israel, with no visible effect either on that country's poverty or its fundamentalism. Besides, even though we can readily admit that some Arabs prefer economic well-being to hating and killing Jews, the political culture of the Arab countries does not favor such moderates, who are more numerous in cemeteries than in Arab government ministries. Peres has not yet drawn back from his delusion about the Syrian desire for peace and prosperity: "Syrian youth," he said not long ago, "are becoming democratic. Soon they will not tolerate a dictatorial government." If Peres really believes this, then he must also believe that Syria, once it has regained the Golan, will start to disarm, will throw out the Palestinian terrorist bands, will disband Hizbullah, will end its ideological subservience to Iran, and will give up its central doctrine of manifest destiny to regain Greater Syria (which includes Israel). If, however, Peres really does believe all this, one would very much like to meet him and see if he is interested in some choice real estate in downtown Sarajevo.

Peres also, immediately after concluding the Cairo talks with PLO leaders on security arrangements for Israeli settlers in the Gaza Strip, questioned whether small, isolated settlements (like Netzarim) in Gaza should exist at all. He put the question in such a way as to make the Jews in those areas wonder just how supportive of their security and rights Peres could have been in his discussions. "What is the point," he asked, "of maintaining a settlement with 28 families that needs workers from Thailand, that needs an army platoon to guard them, to have their road guarded by patrols? Where is the logic? What is the point?"[21] By extrapolation, of course, one might ask what is the point of the entire Zionist undertaking? To defend it, Israel has had to build, with gigantic effort and expense, an army, a navy, an air force, a police force. If there is a single town or village in Israel that does not live with the problem of securing itself against Arab terror, no one knows its location.

Peres' book, though it displays a poverty of mind truly terrifying in a man responsible for formulating his country's foreign policy at a crucial moment in its history, is essential reading for anyone who wants a full look at the abyss into which Israel may be sinking. The book accepts virtually all of the premises, many of them examined earlier in this book, that have fueled Arab propaganda against Israel for nearly half a century. "At the heart of this . . . hundred-year-old conflict . . . stood the Palestinian issue." "Egypt, Syria, Lebanon, and Jordan—and even Iraq, which has no common border with Israel— declared war on us because of the Palestinian issue." (Elsewhere in the book, incomprehensibly, he points out that Palestinian identity dates back no further than 1967.) "Israeli leaders have described [leaders of Syria and the PLO] as the devil incarnate because of their *alleged* desire to push us into the sea" [emphasis added]. The book shows a nearly total inability to distinguish between wishful thinking about the future and the actualities of the present. "Fate," he writes, "has now brought us from a world of territorial conflict to one of economic challenges. . . . The Middle East is now a winner. The ball is in our court." "The transition from the economy of strife to an economy of peace has set the stage for the Middle East." "At this stage of the game, objects that may be subject to a military takeover are no longer of value." He advocates abandoning Israel's traditional strategy of deterrence in favor of his dream of regional cooperation, and a new policy, based on "fewer weapons and more faith"—not faith in the Jewish people or the Jewish religion, but (and to this we always return) Yasser Arafat.[22]

The extent of Peres' faith in, even infatuation with, Arafat would defy belief if we came upon it in a work of fictional fantasy. Day in and day out, he lectures the Israeli people on the need to "help this partner" and "listen to [his] needs" and recalls the days and nights he has spent looking into Arafat's eyes and finding there the deep longing for peace of a man who has "decided to end the killing."[23] As Ruth Wisse has said, Arafat's most potent secret weapon is Israel's "desperate, self-destructive hunger for peace."[24]

Peres has always defended his "Land for Peace" policy (even now that it has obviously become a "Land for No Peace" policy)[25] by alleging that land is both unimportant in modern warfare and irrelevant to Judaism itself. Peres has never been known as a military strategist, and so he may be forgiven for having so quickly forgotten that the Iraqis could not be defeated in the Gulf War by the combined air forces of America, Britain, and France until their territory was invaded, and that the Syrians have not fired on Israel since 1974 because Israeli forces are on the Golan. But his repeated allegation that land plays no part in Judaism itself or in a Jewish political philosophy that names itself after a specfic mountain (Zion) leads to the suspicion that those French sociologists who used to seem so extravagant in predicting that Israel would eventually be governed, politically as well as intellectually, by Hebrew-speaking Gentiles may have been correct. A few of Peres' utterances on this topic are sufficient to reveal the drift of his thought. In the month that the "Gaza-Jericho first" agreement was announced, he declared, in a Manhattan synagogue (26 September 1993) that "Anyone who says Gaza is ours isn't a Jew" and that Orthodox Jews should be happy to let the PLO have Jericho, in view of Joshua's curse on the city. (In fact, Joshua did no such thing, but cursed anyone who rebuilt the city; once it was rebuilt, there was no ban on Jews' living there, which they did in biblical and post-biblical times.) He later added that "the religious have no permission from God to give territories preference over spirit . . . " and accused segments of Israel's religious Jews of having "turned Judaism into a territorial matter." "Judaism," he declared, "is ethical/moral and spiritual, and not an idolatry of soil-worship."[26] One is almost embarrassed to have to remind the foreign minister of the Jewish state (or is it only the state of the Jews?) that ethics and devotion to the Land are interwoven entities in Judaism. The idea of segregating them would have seemed strange to the authors of the Jewish text known as the Bible, or for that matter to anybody with the slightest information about the Jewish religion. Unless Shimon Peres is the bearer of a new revelation from Sinai, the central conception of Judaism remains the chosenness of Israel, its separation from the nations, its unique covenant at Sinai, and its destiny to occupy a special land ordained by the deity.

Standing, at least for the present, in the shadow of Peres is Yossi Beilin. In mid-January of 1994, the deputy foreign minister of Israel and chief designer of the peace agreement—or rather "Declaration of Principles"—between Israel and the PLO, made a series of statements that brought him an avalanche of publicity. Since Beilin had long been one of the Israeli left's most flamboyant and reckless sloganeers and posturers, a certified "extremist," many fail to grasp the fact that he, like Yossi Sarid or Dedi Zucker, is now a certified spokesman for the Israeli government. Unless one of his statements is directly and promptly repudiated by Peres and Rabin, it must therefore be taken very seriously, even if its intrinsic absurdity or shallowness or raw cynicism invites peremptory dismissal. Revealing his government's true intention with respect to the Golan, he suggested that the Israeli "settlers" living there should in future live under Syrian sovereignty. For decades the Israeli government used all of its diplomatic, political, and moral resources, plus whatever assistance it could get from the United States, to compel the Syrian dictator Assad to release the 2000–3000 Jews of Syria from his oppressive rule. Now the government of Israel, speaking through Yossi Beilin, was proposing, in order to remove what it takes to be a major obstacle to peace with Syria, that another 10,000 Jews should be added to those living under Assad's dictatorship. Those critics of the current Israeli policy who have alleged that the government's readiness to abandon the Jewish residents of Judea and Samaria is partly explainable by the intense hatred of the Israeli left for religious Jews would seem, therefore, to be wrong. The residents of the Golan are for the most part the Labor party's own people and loyal supporters; nevertheless, they too may be offered up as proof that Israel's readiness to leave territories it acquired in 1967 will not be impeded by concern for Jewish residents any more than for national security.

Beilin's superior, Peres, it should be recalled, is known to have favored the stationing of foreign troops in the Golan as far back as the 1970s. Beilin is now the leading advocate of stationing foreign, especially American, troops not only in the Golan, but on the borders of the Palestinian state he looks forward to in Judea, Samaria, and Gaza. Such a scheme not only endangers Israel's security and its good relations with

America, but contradicts all that Zionism ever stood for and makes a travesty of the idea of Jewish independence. The pattern, as always, is the same: placing hope for the future not in Israelis themselves, but in the troops of the U.S. Army and the "police force" of Yasser Arafat, which has made Gaza into another southern Lebanon, a safe haven and training base for terrorists.

For Peres and Beilin and Rabin and the Israeli leftist intellectuals who set both tone and policy for the current government, Zionism is merely the Jewish variant of the modern secular religion of nationalism. Contemptuous of the notion that modern Zionism is a continuator of the ancient Zionism of the Bible, they see no reason for staking any claim to the biblical heartland of Eretz Yisrael. But they have yet to face the question of whether the State of Israel can casually abandon that claim and nevertheless insist that it is in Tel Aviv or the land of the Philistines by right. If Jews have no claim to the highlands of ancient Israel, to Hebron, Shiloh, and the Old City of Jerusalem, why should they claim the Philistine coast? By what right? Anyone who doubts that the Arabs, once they have gained control of Judea, Samaria, Gaza by the easy path of negotiation with an endlessly concessive government rather than the arduous one of war, will press this question cannot have paid much attention to the war of ideas that the Arabs have waged, so successfully, against the Jews since 1967. The Arabs have always argued from right, almost never from "security" (with the notable exception of the days following the Hebron massacre at the end of February 1994).

To gain some perspective on this question, we need to stand back from the contemporary for a moment. Why, one wonders, did so politically astute a figure as Winston Churchill say that the creation of the State of Israel would in time be considered the major historical event of the twentieth century? His own country, to be sure, played a large role in the establishment of that state through the Balfour Declaration of 1917 and the formal mandate of the League of Nations which in 1922 charged Great Britain with the task of developing a National Home in Palestine for the Jewish People. Churchill no doubt respected the fact that virtually no nation-state anywhere in the world was more solemnly founded in international con-

sent than Israel. Yet his words strongly suggest that the significance of the State is rooted in more deep and ancient foundations than these modern covenants or the modern Zionist
movement: "The coming into being of a Jewish state . . . is,"
said Churchill, "an event in world history to be viewed in the
perspective not of a generation or a century, but in the perspective of a thousand, two thousand or even three thousand
years."[27] Three thousand years was Churchill's shorthand way
of referring to the biblical account of how, three thousand
years ago, the Jews' entry into their appointed land took place
with consciousness of a mission from above to set up a just
way of life that could not be realized by individuals in their
private existence, but only by a nation. For him, Zionism was
not simply the Jewish variant of modern nationalism but the
realization of the ancient Hebrew idea of the Jews' relationship
to the Land of Israel, metaphorically embodied in the mountain called Zion.

But the current leaders of Israel have lost interest in the
Zionism that links Jewish settlement in Palestine and the establishment of the state of Israel to 3,000 years of Jewish history.
They, like many ordinary Israelis, are not merely "post-Zionist"
but perhaps also "post-Jewish" in their preference of happiness
and "normalization" to the obligations of Jewishness. "Nor-
malcy," the Israeli sociologist Daniel Elazar has written, "may
be good for Jews but, left alone to unfold, will end the Jewish
state as such."[28] Although I have indicated some of the chi-
canery and double-dealing by which the Labor party came to
power, concocting an electoral platform that concealed virtually
all of its true sentiments, it must also be admitted that it could
never have remained in power after the deal with the PLO
unless a substantial portion of the Israeli population was also
ready to forsake the old and apparently sacrosanct national con-
sensus against returning to the 1949 boundaries.

At the outset of this book I quoted John Stuart Mill's
statement that speculative ideas, "which to the superficial [ap-
pear] a thing so remote from the business of life and the outward
interests of men, is in reality the thing on earth which most
influences them." In June of 1994, the Israeli novelist Aharon
Megged, himself a longtime supporter of the Labor Party,
wrote an explosive article in *Ha'aretz* on "The Israeli Suicide

Drive" in which he connected the Rabin government's record
of endless unreciprocated concessions to a PLO that had not
even canceled its Charter calling for Israel's destruction, to the
self-destructiveness that had infected Israel's intellectual classes.
"Since the Six Day War," Megged wrote, "and at an increasing
pace, we have witnessed a phenomenon which probably has no
parallel in history: an emotional and moral identification by
the majority of Israel's intelligentsia with people openly committed to our annihilation." He argued that "since the Six Day
War, and at an increasing pace, we have witnessed . . . a [grow-
ing tendency on the part of Israeli intellectuals to] regard religious, cultural, and emotional affinity to the land . . . with
sheer contempt"; and he noted that the equation of Israelis
with Nazis (often commented on in this book) had become
an article of faith and the central idea of "thousands of articles
and reports in the press, hundreds of poems, . . . dozens of
documentary and feature films, exhibitions and paintings and
photos."[29] The minds of the majority of those who today
carry on the "peace process" of the Israeli government were
formed by the writers, artists, publicists whom Megged excoriated. Although they tirelessly repeat the slogan that "you make
peace with your enemies," it is clear that, as Jerold Auerbach
has remarked, they can far sooner make peace with enemies
wearing keffiyehs than with enemies wearing yarmulkes and
tefillin.

Just how this suicidal drive is likely to play itself out if
it is not reversed has been best described by Israel's most nimble
advocate of Zionism, Hillel Halkin, in an essay entitled "Israel
Against Itself." He concludes by expressing the hope that it
will not prove necessary to read, in some history book of the
future, the following:

As the 20th century neared its end and the Arab world
began grudgingly to accept Israel's existence and to seek
to make peace with it, Israel found itself in an internal
conflict between its traditional Zionist determination to
secure a Jewish state within militarily and historically
meaningful borders and its post-Zionist desire for a normalization of life on the American and West European
model. Given the steady attrition of the first state of mind

and the steady strengthening of the second, the eventual outcome of the conflict was inevitable. But unfortunately for the country, this outcome was unnecessarily accelerated by the beliefs and actions of its leaders, who thus seriously undermined their own bargaining position in the negotiations then in progress with the Arab states.

In consequence, in return for the diplomatic recognition of its neighbors and certain security arrangements on their part, Israel agreed to return to its 1967 borders on all fronts, acquiesce in the establishment of a Palestinian state with the eastern half of Jerusalem as its capital, and remove all Jewish settlers from the Golan Heights, the West Bank, and the Gaza Strip.

Deprived of the military advantages of the Golan and the Jordan Valley with its controlling hills, and expelled from the biblical heartland of Judea and Samaria, the country, its overcrowded population concentrated in the narrow coastal strip between the state of Palestine and the sea, experienced not a sense of well-being after peace was concluded but a profound moral and psychological malaise. Thus, it was ill-prepared to resist demands presented to it at a later date that it cede the heavily Arab-populated Galilee to Palestine and the southern Negev to Egypt, in order to create a land bridge between the eastern and western halves of the Arab world. The results can be seen in the maps on the following page. . . . [30]

NOTES
INDEX

NOTES

INTRODUCTION

1. *The Origins of Totalitarianism*, 3 vols. (New York: Harcourt, Brace, 1951), I, x.

2. *Mill on Bentham and Coleridge*, ed. F. R. Leavis (London: Chatto & Windus, 1959), 39.

3. See *Cross Roads to Israel* (London: Collins, 1965).

CHAPTER 1. *Making Arabs into Jews: David Grossman's* The Yellow Wind

1. *The Yellow Wind*, trans. Haim Watzman (New York: Farrar, Straus & Giroux, 1988), 212. Subsequent references to this work will be cited in text.

CHAPTER 2. *To Mend the Universe or Mind the Vineyard?*

1. *Where Are We? The Inner Life of America's Jews* (New York: Harper & Row, 1988), 108. Subsequent references to this work will be cited in text.

2. The sexual boundary is particularly galling to Fein, who has tried to placate Big Sister by writing his book in Feminese. Not only does he strive for equal-opportunity pronouns—"his/her," "he/she"—in dealing with mere mortals; he even urges us "to love God whether or not He (or She, or It) exists" (28).

3. "Prior to the time of [Moses] Mendelssohn . . . I challenge you to produce a single Jewish text . . . in which the idea of a state of universal social justice is more than a marginal concern or messianic afterthought; and I challenge you to find *anywhere* the concept of a Jewish mission to help bring about such a state. Nothing in fact could be further from the traditional Jewish mentality, which has always looked upon the Gentile world as an arena of blindly chaotic and idolatrous forces. . . . One might as well seek to pacify earthquakes and floods. In such a view . . . social justice in the world is anything but the proper worry of a Jew."—Hillel Halkin, *Letters to an American Jewish Friend* (Philadelphia: Jewish Publication Society, 1977), 88.

4. *To Mend the World* (New York: Schocken Books, 1982), 312–13.

5. *Jews in Unsecular America,* ed. Richard John Neuhaus and Ronald Sobel (Grand Rapids: Eerdmans, 1987), vii. Subsequent references to this work will be cited in text.

6. *The Writings of Martin Buber,* ed. Will Herberg (New York: Meridian, 1956), 281.

CHAPTER 3. *Antisemitism, Israeli-Style*

1. All of these examples of Jewish antisemitism are discussed in Sander L. Gilman, *Jewish Self-Hatred* (Baltimore: Johns Hopkins University Press, 1986).

2. *Table Talk,* 14 August 1833.

3. Quoted in Arnold Ages, "Jewish Nativism," *Congress Monthly* 55 (January 1988): 22, a review of James S. Diamond, *Homeland or Holy Land? The "Canaanite" Critique of Israel.* See also Rael Jean Isaac, *Israel Divided* (Baltimore: Johns Hopkins University Press, 1976).

4. Hillel Halkin, *Letters to an American Jewish Friend,* 180.

5. *Jerusalem Post,* 19 April 1987.

6. *Ma'ariv International Edition,* 21 August 1987 (Magazine).

7. *Ma'ariv International Edition,* 21 August 1987.

8. These "implications" are explored, idiosyncratically but suggestively, in Philip Roth's *The Counterlife* (1986).

9. *The Siege: The Saga of Israel and Zionism* (New York: Simon and Schuster, 1986), 258.

10. *Jerusalem Post,* 6 July 1982.

11. *Counterpoint,* September 1987, 7.

12. *Le Racisme de l'Etat d'Israel* (Paris, 1975), 267.

13. *Jerusalem Post,* 2 May 1982.

14. In Seattle, Yermiya petulantly attacked Jews who consider the Holocaust "a private asset . . . which must not be mentioned in the same breath as their own actions." *University of Washington Daily,* 2 May 1981.

15. David K. Shipler, *Arab and Jew* (New York: Times Books, 1986), 348, 340.

16. Norma Rosen, "The Second Life of Holocaust Imagery," *Midstream,* 33 (April 1987): 56–59.

17. See Ya'acov Friedler, "Jewish anti-Semitism," *Jerusalem Post,* 27 March 1985.

18. Harold Fisch, "Art and Statism: The Question of Funding the Arts," in *The Israeli Fate of Jewish Liberalism,* ed. Robert J.

Loewenberg and Edward Alexander (Lanham, Maryland, New York, and London: University Press of America, 1988), 66.

19. See Marsha Pomerantz, "Storm Over Play," *Jerusalem Post*, 6 November 1982.

20. *Mill on Bentham and Coleridge*, 122.

21. Ever since Hannah Arendt's spiteful and ill-considered remarks about Eichmann's "Zionism" in her book on his Jerusalem trial, it has been a commonplace among anti-Zionist propagandists that the Nazis were devoted Zionists.

22. Henryk M. Broder, "Sobol: Making a Scene," *Jerusalem Post Magazine*, 6 February 1987.

23. Ibid.

24. *Jerusalem Post Magazine*, 8 May 1987.

25. *Jerusalem Post*, 26 March 1989.

26. *Jerusalem Post*, 3 May 1989.

CHAPTER 4. *Professor of Terror*

1. "An Exchange on Edward Said and Difference," *Critical Inquiry*, 15 (Spring 1989): 645–46. Subsequent references to this work will be cited in text.

2. *The Question of Palestine* (New York: Times Books, 1979).

3. *New Leader*, 11 August 1980.

4. *Interview* [Tunis], December 1988.

CHAPTER 5. *The Wit and Wisdom of Alexander Cockburn*

1. See Henry Fairlie, "The Fifth Columnist," *New Republic*, 28 December 1987, 27.

CHAPTER 6. *Praying for Nazis, Scolding Their Victims: Archbishop Tutu's Christmas Message to Israel*

1. Gideon Shimoni, "South African Jews and Apartheid,"*American Jewish Year Book* (New York: American Jewish Committee, 1988), 51. Subsequent references to this work will be cited in text.

2. Eric Breindel, "The Tel Aviv–Pretoria Myth," *New York Post*, 9 February 1989.

CHAPTER 7. *The Holocaust . . . and Me*

 1. *Testimony: Contemporary Writers Make the Holocaust Personal* (New York: Random House, 1989). Subsequent references to this work will be cited in text.

 2. In fairness, it should be noted that, in one particular, the book's final version is an improvement on the bound proofs. The latter contain Phillip Lopate's most memorable words about the Holocaust: "I am deeply sorry it happened." Although this classic utterance would have given new meaning to the idea of the banality of evil, Rosenberg and Lopate chose to sacrifice it in the final version of the book.

 3. Emil L. Fackenheim, *The Jewish Return into History* (New York: Schocken Books, 1978), 54.

CHAPTER 8. *Nelson Mandela and the Jews: The Dickens-Fagin Pattern*

 1. Don Caldwell, "The Underside of the A. N. C.," *New Republic*, 9 & 16 July 1990, 16.

CHAPTER 9. *The Last Refuge of a Scoundrel: Patrick Buchanan's Anti-Jewish Patriotism*

 1. See Alan Dershowitz, "Is Pat Buchanan Getting Ready to Claim the Holocaust Never Happened?" *New York Post*, 20 March 1990.

 2. Jacob Weisberg, "The Heresies of Pat Buchanan," *New Republic*, 22 October 1990, 26. The most thorough discussion of Buchanan's antisemitism is Joshua Muravchik, "Patrick J. Buchanan and the Jews," *Commentary*, 91 (January 1991): 29–37.

 3. See also *New Republic*, 16 & 23 September 1991, 10.

CHAPTER 10. *Why Jews Must Behave Better than Everybody Else: The Theory and Practice of the Double Standard*

 1. David Bar-Illan, "Milton Viorst: Master of the Double Standard," in *With Friends Like These: The Jewish Critics of Israel*, ed. Edward Alexander (New York: SPI Books, 1993), 77–83.

 2. *New York Times*, 28 July 1982. See also Jacob Heilbrunn, "Spurious George," *New Republic*, 4 July 1994.

 3. *Ma'ariv*, 10 January 1985.

4. "Judging Israel," *Time*, 26 February 1990.
5. See Ruth R. Wisse, "The Deligitimation of Israel," *Commentary*, 74 (July 1982): 29–36.
6. Evidence Submitted to the Palestine Royal Commission (1937), quoted in *The Zionist Idea*, ed. Arthur Hertzberg (New York: Atheneum, 1975), 559–70.
7. Thomas Friedman, *From Beirut to Jerusalem* (New York: Farrar, Straus & Giroux, 1989). See review by Martin Peretz in *New Republic*, 4 September 1989.

CHAPTER 11. *Multiculturalism's Jewish Problem*

1. Quoted in *New Republic*, 15 & 22 July 1991, 6.
2. *New York Times*, 21 June 1991.
3. *New York Times*, 20 April 1990.
4. *New York Times*, 7 August 1991.
5. Nat Hentoff, "Strange Speech on Campus," *Washington Post*, 21 May 1991.
6. "Racism 101," *New Republic*, 26 November 1990, 18–21.
7. *Jewish Journal* (Los Angeles), 7–13 June 1991.
8. Ibid.
9. Nat Hentoff, "Why Do They Hate Us?" *Village Voice*, 28 May 1991.
10. *If I Am Not for Myself . . . The Liberal Betrayal of the Jews* (New York: Free Press, 1992), 47.

CHAPTER 12. *Some of My Best Friends Are Antisemites: William F. Buckley's Dilemma*

1. "In Search of Anti-Semitism," *National Review*, 30 December 1991. Subsequent references to this work will be cited in text.
2. Quoted from interview in *London Sunday Telegraph* in *New Republic*, 27 January 1992, 6.
3. See, on this topic, note 9 in the concluding chapter of this book.

CHAPTER 13. *What the Holocaust Does Not Teach*

1. Lewis chose not to mention that, long before she wrote her article, Israel had already given haven to Muslim refugees, especially

children, from "ethnic cleansing" in Bosnia. When Israel admitted 101 Bosnian Muslim refugees in February 1993, the country's Arab community stridently protested. Arab leaders traditionally do not recognize refugees, Arab or Muslim or both, as anything other than political instruments.

2. *The Messianic Idea in Judaism* (New York: Schocken Books, 1971), 281.

3. "Reflections on the Possibility of Jewish Mysticism in Our Time," *Ariel*, 26 (Spring 1970): 46.

4. *What is the Use of Jewish History?* ed. Neal Kozodoy (New York: Schocken Books, 1992), 70–73. Subsequent references to this work will be cited in text.

5. *Ordinary Men: Reserve Police Battalion 101 and the Final Solution in Poland.* (New York: Aaron Asher Books, 1992), 170. Subsequent references to this work will be cited in text.

6. Lionel Trilling, *The Liberal Imagination* (New York: Viking, 1950), 264–65.

7. Primo Levi, *The Drowned and the Saved* (New York: Vintage, 1949), 48.

8. Ibid., 58–60.

9. Raul Hilberg, *The Destruction of the European Jews* (Chicago: Quadrangle Books, 1961), 3.

10. *Perpetrators Victims Bystanders: The Jewish Catastrophe, 1933–1945* (New York: Aaron Asher Books, 1992). Subsequent references to this work will be cited in text.

11. Hans Globke, the "names expert" of the Interior Ministry, Hilberg remarks, "was promoted after the war to the Federal Chancellor's Office, which he headed until 1963, and from which he was retired with honors to pursue his hobby of numismatics, particularly the collection of the coins of Axium and Armenia" (25).

12. Hilberg, it should be noted, has entered this combat by serving as a leading prosecution expert at the 1985 and 1988 trials of Ernst Zundel, the Canadian publisher and Hitler idolator.

CHAPTER 14. *The Nerve of Ruth Wisse*

1. *If I Am Not for Myself . . . The Liberal Betrayal of the Jews* (New York: Free Press, 1992), 42. Subsequent references to this work will be cited in text.

2. George Eliot, "The Modern Hep! Hep! Hep!" *Essays of George Eliot* (New York: Doubleday, 1901), 413, 422.

3. A letter that Alter and some colleagues sent to local book-

stores criticizing their sponsorship of one of Chomsky's PLO front groups provoked an avalanche of hate mail, attempts to get them "censured" by the university and the local PEN chapter, and allegations in the "alternative" press that they were linked with the CIA.

4. "Enemies, a Love Story," *New Republic*, 30 November 1992, 28–33. Subsequent references to this work will be cited in text. Wisse's book is paired, apparently for polemical purposes, with Anita Shapira's *Land and Power: The Zionist Resort to Force, 1881–1948* (New York: Oxford, 1992).

5. "The Masada Complex," *Commentary*, 56 (July 1973): 19–24. Subsequent references to this work will be cited in text.

6. *Matthew Arnold* (New York: Meridian, 1955), 233.

7. This view is an article of fundamentalist faith among Israeli leftists and their American supporters. It is as impervious to all empirical evidence as any myth ever devised. They have for decades argued that Israel can "take risks for peace" because she is fully capable of defeating with ease any combination of Arab countries. Yet in 1991 a 28-nation alliance headed by the greatest power in world history and flying 2,000 to 3,000 bombing sorties a day required two months to defeat the single Arab nation of Iraq. Israel has half the combat aircraft of the allied forces. She has no strategic bombers, no AWACS planes, no aircraft carriers, no nuclear submarines, no M-1 tanks—and, of course, no allies in the region.

8. Or, for that matter, with the three "noes" of Khartoum, August 1967: *No* peace with Israel, *no* negotiations with Israel, *no* recognition of Israel.

9. "From Myth to Murder," *New Republic*, 20 May 1991, 36.

10. See *New Republic*, 15 March 1993, for Wisse's lengthy reply to Alter and his shorter, but equally acrimonious, response. She says there that "I differ from [Alter] in *not* entertaining a frozen view of history, in wanting, rather, to change its course. . . . I think that liberals should break with their past, and express their faith in the potential transformation of Arab society by insisting that the Arabs turn their attention away from the Jews toward their own self-improvement."

11. S. Ansky, "The Destruction of Galicia," in *The Dybbuk and Other Writings*, ed. D. G. Roskies (New York: Schocken Books, 1992), 195.

12. *Northern California Jewish Bulletin*, 17 April 1992; *Jerusalem Post International Edition*, 7 November 1992.

13. Dan V. Segre, "Is Anti-Zionism a New Form of Antisemitism?" *Antisemitism in the Contemporary World*, ed. Michael Curtis (Boulder and London: Westview Press, 1986), 153.

14. *Jerusalem Post Magazine*, 20 March 1987.

CHAPTER 15. *Michael Lerner: The Clintons' Jewish Rasputin*

1. Michael Kelly, "Saint Hillary," *New York Times Magazine*, 23 May 1993, 63.

2. Edward Rothstein, "Broken Vessel," *New Republic*, 6 March 1989, 19.

3. Henry Allen, "A New Phrase at the White House," *Washington Post*, 9 June 1993.

4. Thomas Fields-Meyer, "This Year's Prophet," *New York Times Magazine*, 27 June 1993, 28.

5. Michael P. Lerner, "Jewish New Leftism at Berkeley," *Judaism*, 18 (Fall 1969): 474–76.

6. *New York Times*, 26 April 1970.

7. *Seattle Times*, 4 March 1970. After his arrival at the White House, Lerner told Anne Gowen of the *Washington Times* (7 June 1993) that "I am not now, nor ever have been, a Marxist."

8. As recently as 1991, Lerner sent a barrage of letters to university administrators, Seattle city officials, and Seattle newspaper editors urging that the University of Washington repent for its transgression of 1970 by rehiring him—*Seattle Times*, 6 February 1991.

9. *Seattle Times*, 4 March 1970.

10. *Seattle Times*, 6 March 1970; *University of Washington Daily*, 9 March 1970.

11. *Seattle Post-Intelligencer*, 18 February, 3 June, and 30 June 1970. Lerner and seven others were charged with conspiring to damage federal property. They were tried in Tacoma in November 1970. Deciding to put the court on trial, Lerner and the other defendants constantly disrupted proceedings, and even draped a swastika over Judge George Boldt's bench and shouted: "Heil Hitler!" They refused to return to court when ordered, causing a mistrial to be declared—followed by a riot between some defendants and marshals. Lerner spent ten weeks at California's Terminal Island federal penitentiary for contempt of court. The original charges were never refiled.

12. Not long after this article appeared in an earlier version in 1988, Lerner shaved his beard.

13. *Moment*, June 1990, 33.

14. The late Irving Howe caused consternation at one *Tikkun* conference (December 1988) by stating the obvious: there is no sanction in Jewish religion for liberal politics. "To claim there is a connection," said Howe, "can lead to parochial sentimentalism or ethnic vanity." See Rothstein, "Broken Vessel," 19.

15. *Jerusalem Post*, 26 April 1988.

16. *Midstream*, 34 (December 1988): 31.

17. See Ze'ev Chafets, "Why I'm Not Going to *Tikkun* Conference in Israel," *Northern California Jewish Bulletin*, 21 June 1991. This declaration would seem to demonstrate a shockingly un-Lernerian inhospitability to Arabs, since every Palestinian spokesman, "moderates" included, fiercely rejects demilitarization.

18. *New York Times*, 19 March 1992.

19. *Washington Times*, 7 June 1993.

CHAPTER 16.   *Noam Chomsky and Holocaust Denial*

1. *Denying the Holocaust: The Growing Assault on Truth and Memory*. (New York: The Free Press, 1993), 99–100. Subsequent references to this work will be cited in text.

2. Nadine Fresco, "The Denial of the Dead: The Faurisson Affair—and Noam Chomsky," *Dissent*, 28 (Fall 1981): 477. Subsequent references to this work will be cited in text.

3. Noam Chomsky, *American Power and the New Mandarins* (New York: Pantheon, 1969), 16.

4. Werner Cohn, *The Hidden Alliances of Noam Chomsky* (New York: Americans for a Safe Israel, 1988). Subsequent references to this work will be cited in text.

5. Serge Thion, *Vérité historique ou vérité politique? Le dossier de l'affaire Faurisson: La question des chambres à gaz* (Paris: La Vieille Taupe, 1980), 89; Robert Faurisson, "How the British Obtained the Confessions of Rudolf Hoss," *Journal of Historical Review* 7 (1986–87): 389–403. Subsequent references to Thion's *Vérité* will be cited in text.

6. Preface to Robert Faurisson, *Mémoire en Défense contre ceux qui m'accusent de falsifier l'histoire/La question des chambres à gaz* (Paris: La Vieille Taupe, 1980), xiv–xv.

7. Faurisson's right to teach was not withdrawn, and his request of a transfer to teaching correspondence courses was approved.

8. The petition is quoted in full in Cohn, *Hidden Alliances*, 6.

9. Pierre Vidal-Naquet, *Assassins of Memory* (New York: Columbia University Press, 1992), 58. Subsequent references to this work will be cited in text.

10. See the entry "Juif" in Voltaire's *Dictionnaire Philosophique*.

11. Electronic mail USENET network ("soc.culture.Jewish" newsgroup), 19 August and 12 September 1991.

12. It is worth noting, even at the risk of offending the current Israeli government, that articles denying the Holocaust have long been a staple of publications of the PLO.

13. "Holocaust 'Revisionism': A Denial of History," *ADL Facts*, 31 (Winter 1986): 6.

CHAPTER 17.   *Israel's Embrace of the PLO: The Beginning of the End?*

1. *New York Times*, 10 September 1993.
2. *New York Times*, 14 September 1993. See Charles Krauthammer, "Israel's Enormous Risk," *Washington Post*, 3 September 1993.
3. *Forward*, 19 November 1993.
4. Professor Irwin Cotler, the lawyer for Andrei Sakharov and Anatoly Scharansky, has said: "Arafat is one of the major human rights violators of our time. He qualifies as a war criminal. You do not enter into agreements with war criminals. Your responsibility is to bring them to justice." Louis René Beres, professor of international law at Purdue University, has analyzed the Israel-PLO accord as a violation of the central precepts of international law. He spoke on "The Illegality of the Israel-PLO Agreement Under International Law" at the American Political Science Association annual meeting in September 1994.
5. The moral confusion and historical amnesia of the Rabin government have been especially evident in its muddled reactions to terror. On 13 July 1994 Rabin protested that Arafat had committed "a very grave violation of the accords" by smuggling into Gaza four PLO officials who had been involved in the Ma'alot massacre, in which 21 school children and one soldier were killed by Arab terrorists in 1974. One of these four, whom Arafat had attached to his personal entourage, had also been involved in the terror attack on Beit She'an, and another had helped to plan the massacre of the Israeli Olympic athletes in 1972. In reply to Rabin's protest, Ahmad Tibi, Arafat's advisor, said (correctly) that "The person responsible on behalf of the Palestinian people for everything that was done in the . . . conflict is Yasser Arafat, and this man shook hands with Yitzhak Rabin. . . . The people who carried out these acts now support the peace process." When terrorists presumed to be Islamic fundamentalists blew up one hundred people, mostly Jews, in Buenos Aires a few weeks later, Rabin and Peres took time out from lauding Arafat as an esteemed head of state to vow that they would "wage a war against terrorism." Apparently they believe that terrorists are not only completely wicked, but completely stupid as well.
6. An article in *National Review* (7 March 1994) by Joel Bainerman and Barry Chamish reveals that as far back as June 1991 Labor

party representatives, in clear violation of Israeli law, were already negotiating with PLO officials in order to persuade them to marshal Israeli Arabs to support Labor in the upcoming 1992 national elections. Yossi Beilin carried to Yasser Arafat's envoy Mahmud Abbas an offer from Shimon Peres to embrace, if elected, land-for-peace diplomacy, to freeze settlement activity in the administered territories, and to cancel the law against meetings between Israelis and the PLO. When the election was held on 23 June 1992, Arab voters united behind the Labor party and enabled it to become the new government of Israel. Whatever promises the Labor government may have broken to the Jewish citizens of Israel, it faithfully carried out its pledge to the PLO to reward it by supporting an "independent autonomous entity" run by Arafat.

7. In late May 1994, for example, Rabin said that the Israeli Army needed to "become a defense army again and not an occupation army against another people." He excoriated those who claimed that his peace agreement was being paid for in Jewish blood: "The blood that was spilled is because of our control of a foreign nation" (*New York Times*, 30 May 1994). A dybbuk named Peace Now seemed to have taken over the body and soul of Rabin. Meretz leader Yossi Sarid's prediction of 1992, that Rabin would serve as a "front" while his own small left-wing party would shape government policy, turned out to be true.

8. Hirsh Goodman, "Peace Indigestion," *Jerusalem Report*, 30 December 1993.

9. *New York Times*, 10 September 1993. Falling all over himself with sycophantic gratitude for this "recognition," Peres has never stopped to contemplate, as Cynthia Ozick has asked everyone to do, the indecency of that expression and its unique application. Those words "right to exist" as applied to a nation-state have never before appeared in the history of nations, ancient or modern; the phrase is purely contemporary and assigned exclusively to one country in the world: Israel. But a "right," argued Ozick, is a moral category; "existence" is not. Existence should not be subject to any test or measure of acceptance, least of all by murderous thugs like Arafat. No one has the authority to talk of a people's "right to exist." It would never occur to Shimon Peres that once such a right is raised as a thesis for discussion, the implication arises that, just as a right can be given, so can it be denied—the phrase has about it the stench of Auschwitz. See Cynthia Ozick, " 'The Right to Exist,' " *Congress Monthly*, 58 (January 1991): 7.

10. Since Arafat had personally arranged and ordered the murder of two U.S. diplomats in Khartoum in 1973, he was still officially a wanted terrorist in this country, and should, according to American

law, have been arrested as soon as he entered the U.S.; instead, he was honored on the White House lawn. American uneasiness over the implications of the Israeli embrace of the PLO for its own position against terrorism may explain why it was Warren Christopher, not Rabin, who insisted that Arafat's letter of recognition include a pledge to punish members of the PLO who might disobey the order to suspend terrorist activity. Christopher would have the task of getting the ban on the PLO lifted in Congress.

11. *Jewish Week*, 27 May–2 June 1994. See Rael Jean Isaac, "Negotiating With Oneself: Diplomacy à la Shimon Peres," *Outpost*, July–August 1994, 3.

12. In the summer of 1994, just when Rabin was boasting that he had lines of communication to the Palestinian police, a senior officer of that body—Jibril Rajub—was boasting that "We sanctify the weapons in the hands of Hamas, and will ignore them out of national responsibility" (Yigal Carmon, "Our Lost Leader," *Jerusalem Post*, 2 July 1994). No sooner had Arafat returned to Gaza and Jericho in July 1994 than he began demanding the release from prison of the leaders of Hamas, especially Sheik Ahmed Yassin. On the subject of PLO-Hamas cooperation, see Douglas J. Feith, "Land for No Peace," *Commentary*, 97 (June 1994): 33.

13. *The New Middle East* (New York: Holt, 1994), 29. In August 1994 Arafat declared, in his message to PLO officials in Arab countries, that "I will never give my hand to the annulment of one paragraph of the Palestinian National Charter" (Quoted in *Outpost*, December 1994).

14. *New York Times*, 20 May 1994. See also "The Happiest Jihad," *New Republic*, 13 June 1994.

15. *New York Times*, 26 May and 20 May 1994.

16. *New York Times*, 9 June 1994.

17. See David Bar-Illan, "Israel's New Pollyannas," *Commentary*, 96 (September 1993): 30; and *Jerusalem Post International Edition*, 5 February 1994. As of 20 October 1994 more Israelis, almost one hundred, had been killed by terrorists since the White House handshake than in any one-year period since the founding of the state in 1948, a figure nearly three times as high as in any year of the *intifada*.

18. *Jerusalem Post International Edition*, 19 February 1994.

19. *Jerusalem Post International Edition*, 4 June 1994.

20. "The Real Lessons of Camp David," *Commentary*, 96 (December 1993): 37.

21. *New York Times*, 12 February 1994.

22. *The New Middle East*, 15, 76, 36, 96, 35, 172. See Rael Jean Isaac, "Faith and Fantasy," *Commentary*, 97 (April 1994).

23. *New York Times*, 3 March 1994.

24. *New York Times*, June 13, 1994.

25. See Douglas Feith, "Land for No Peace," *Commentary*, 97 (June 1994).

26. Quoted in Moshe Kohn, "Check Your Quotes," *Jerusalem Post International Edition*, 16 October 1993.

27. See Martin Gilbert, *Exile and Return* (Philadelphia and New York: Lippincott,1978), 128–29.

28. Daniel J. Elazar, "The Peace Process and the Jewishness of the Jewish State," *Congress Monthly*, 61 (November/December 1994): 4.

29. Aharon Megged, "The Israeli Suicide Drive," *Jerusalem Post International Edition*, 2 July 1994.

30. Hillel Halkin, "Israel Against Itself," *Commentary*, 98 (November 1994): 39.

INDEX

Afrocentrism, 104–5
Allen, Woody, 15
Aloni, Shulamit, x, 34, 44, 115–16, 139; Jews blamed by, for arousing antisemitism, 117
Alsop, Stewart, 134
Alter, Robert, 192–93n; attack on Ruth Wisse by, 133–36, 138, 139n
American-Arab Anti-Discrimination Committee, xii, 52–53, 60
Amichai, Yehuda, 138
Ansky, S., 137
antisemitism, 100, 103; Arab hostility to Israel related to, 135; of Canaanites, 29–30; in Christianity, 97; cost-free nature of, 107, 112; in fascist Italy, 84–85; ignored in Holocaust curricula, 116; infectious power of, 117; among Israelis, 29–45; among Jewish converts, 26–27; of Marx, 27; multiculturalists' attraction to, 105–6; Nazi-Israeli equation in, 33–44; origins of, in Christendom, 135; and Zionist ideology, 27–29
App, Austin J., 152–53, 159
Arabs: burn Carmel forest, 138; Jewish immigration to Land of Israel opposed by, 114–15; refugees viewed by,

as political instruments, 192n; success of, in war of ideas, 180
Arafat, Yasser, 5, 45, 46, 48–49, 50, 75; descendant of Haj Amin el-Husseini, 68; disparity between English and Arabic speeches by, 94; faith in, of Peres, 177; insistence of, on White House appearance, 168; *jihad* urged by, in May 1994, 172; murder of "collaborators" urged by, 50; murder of U.S. diplomats ordered by, 197–98n; phased plan of, for Israel's destruction, 165; praises Jewish "dissenters" from Zionism, 85; and Security Council Resolutions, 54; as war criminal, 196n
Arendt, ix, 28, 70, 123, 125, 189n
Arnold, Matthew, 56–57, 132
Assad, Hafez, 83–84, 179
Auerbach, Jerold, 182
Auschwitz, convent at, 80

Baker, James, 148
Balfour Declaration (1917), 180
Ball, George, 90, 111, 136
Bar-Illan, 57–58, 170, 171–72, 198n
Bauer, Yehuda, 72
Begin, Menachem, 31
Beilin, Yossi, 169, 173, 179–80

Edward Alexander is professor of English at University of Washington, Seattle. He taught for several years at Tel Aviv University in Israel. Among his previous books are *Matthew Arnold and John Stuart Mill* (Columbia), *Arnold, Ruskin, and the Modern Temper* (Ohio State), *The Resonance of Dust* (Ohio State), *Isaac Bashevis Singer* (G. K. Hall), *The Jewish Idea and Its Enemies* (Transaction), *The Holocaust and the War of Ideas* (Transaction). He has written for many journals, including *Commentary, The Dickensian, Encounter, Congress Monthly*, and *Society*.